CW00543178

SECOND EDITION
in company

INTERMEDIATE STUDENT'S BOOK WITH CD-ROM

SECOND EDITION STUDENT'S BOOK:

▶ **15 SKILLS UNITS** focusing on everyday, functional business English language

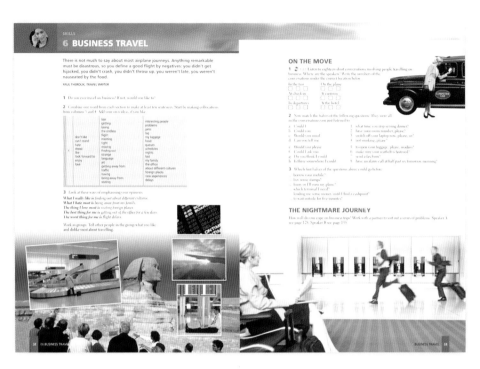

▶ **5 TOPIC DEBATES UNITS** focusing on topical business issues

▶ Phrase Bank for summary and revision

▶ **Discussion phrase bank**

I suppose what it means is …

What we should probably all be doing is …

We may also have to reconsider …

If it's true, it will totally change the way we …

▶ **15 LANGUAGE LINKS** consolidating grammar and extending vocabulary from the Skills Units

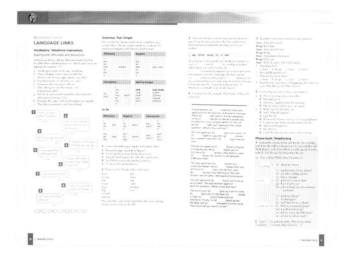

▶ **5 CASE STUDIES** reflecting real-life business scenarios

▶ **BACK-OF-BOOK MATERIAL:**

● Listening Scripts with useful phrases from the Phrase Banks in bold

● Additional material for communicative activities

SELF-STUDY CD-ROM:

● Extra listening activities
● Interactive grammar and vocabulary activities
● Interactive glossary
● Downloadable Student's Book audio
● Downloadable Student's Book Phrase Banks

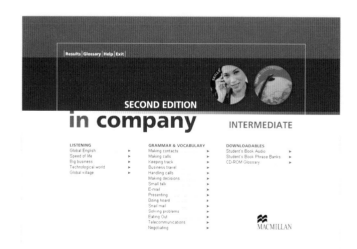

WEBSITE:

Course updates, regular e-lessons and supplementary material available at: **www.businessenglishonline.net**

CONTENTS

Unit	Communication skills	Reading and listening texts	Language links
01 Global English p6	Completing a needs analysis Doing a quiz on languages Discussing attitudes to English	**Reading** Article about English 2.0 **Listening** People talking about their attitudes to learning English	
02 Making contacts p8	Describing people Discussing appropriate conversation topics Keeping the conversation going Networking with colleagues and business contacts	**Reading** A blog about conference going **Listening** Extract from a business travel programme on conference venues **Listening** People gossiping at a conference **Listening** People socialising at a conference	**Vocabulary** Conferences **Grammar** Present Simple and Present Continuous **Phrase bank** Networking
03 Making calls p15	Receiving calls Leaving voicemails Exchanging information on the telephone	**Listening** Planning a telephone call **Listening** Voicemail messages **Listening** Telephone conversations	**Vocabulary** Telephone expressions **Grammar** Past Simple; time adverbs *for, in, during, ago, over, before* **Phrase bank** Telephoning
04 Keeping track p22	Checking & clarifying facts & figures Querying information Clearing up misunderstandings	**Listening** Extracts from meetings **Reading** Articles: the Budweiser companies **Listening** Extracts from a meeting **Listening** A briefing meeting	**Vocabulary** Business phrasal verbs **Grammar** Comparatives and superlatives **Phrase bank** Checking understanding
Case Study: High flier p28	Noting schedules and appointments Prioritising and responding to e-mails Comparing cultural styles of e-mail writing Listening to voicemails and deciding on action to be taken	**Reading** An article profiling a media entrepeneur **Listening** A briefing meeting **Reading** The boss's e-mail inbox **Listening** Business & personal voicemails	
05 What women want p30	Discussing gender and consumer spending Discussing how to make a product more appealing to women	**Listening** Business people talking about female spending power **Reading** Article about female buyer behaviour	
06 Business travel p32	Expressing likes & dislikes about travelling on business Making polite requests & enquiries Dealing with travel situations Identifying signs as British or American English Greeting visitors	**Listening** Business travel conversations **Reading** Article from *Newsweek* about people who live in two cities **Listening** Short exchanges in British & American English **Listening** Conversations at the airport **Reading** Article: travel tips	**Vocabulary** Business trips **Grammar** Polite question forms **Phrase bank** Business travel
07 Handling calls p39	Discussing your attitude to using the telephone Making polite telephone requests using *if* and *Could you … ?* Making telephone expressions with *I'll* Dealing with incoming calls	**Reading** Mini-texts: telephone statistics **Listening** Telephone conversations	**Vocabulary** Office life **Grammar** *will* **Phrase bank** Polite requests; offering assistance; making excuses to end a call
08 Making decisions p45	Doing a questionnaire on making decisions Using fixed expressions in meetings Using the language of making decisions	**Listening** Extracts from a documentary **Listening** Extract from a meeting **Reading** Article about James Bond films **Reading** Actor profiles: James Bond contenders **Listening** Interviews with James Bond contenders	**Vocabulary** Money & markets **Grammar** Conditionals (future reference) **Phrase bank** Decision-making
Case Study: Toy story p52	Discussing consumer confidence in brands Comparing cultural behaviour in meetings Scripting a short public relations video Holding a crisis meeting Presenting and fielding questions at a press conference	**Reading** Browsing a company home page **Listening** An in-flight emergency phone call **Reading** Scanning the news headlines **Reading** Press conference tips **Listening** A further phone call	
09 New world order p54	Discussing emerging economies	**Listening** Business people talking about strengths & weaknesses of emerging economies **Reading** Articles about China, Europe and America	
10 Small talk p56	Completing a questionnaire on cultural awareness Talking about experiences Engaging in small talk	**Listening** Pre-meeting conversations	**Vocabulary** Exaggeration & understatement **Grammar** Past Simple or Present Perfect **Phrase bank** Engaging in small talk
11 E-mail p62	Discussing e-mail likes & dislikes Guidelines for writing e-mail Simplifying a lengthy e-mail Exchanging e-mails	**Reading** Article about cyber-socialising **Listening** Voicemail messages	**Vocabulary** Computers **Grammar** Future forms **Phrase bank** E-mail

Unit	Communication skills	Reading and listening texts	Language links
12 **Presenting** p69	Discussing qualities of a good presentation Pausing, pacing & sentence stress Delivering a presentation Structuring a presentation Using visuals Giving a short presentation	**Listening** People conversing & giving a presentation **Listening** Toast by George Bernard Shaw to Albert Einstein **Reading** Extract from First Direct website **Listening** A presentation about a technical problem	**Vocabulary** Presentations **Grammar** Past Continuous; Past Perfect; Past Simple vs Past Continuous vs Past Perfect **Phrase bank** Presentations
Case Study: Reaching out p76	Discussing ethical investment and micro-finance Preparing a short team presentation Giving a presentation from notes using PowerPoint slides	**Reading** An internet advertisement **Reading** An e-mail from the boss **Reading** Presentation tips **Listening** Voicemail instructions **Listening** Feedback on the phone	
13 **Enter the blogosphere** p78	Discussing what you use the Internet for Presenting a response	**Listening** Web 1.0 vs Web 2.0 **Reading** Articles about technology & change **Listening** People talking about Web 2.0	
14 **Being heard** p80	Discussing attitudes to meetings Completing a questionnaire on assertiveness in meetings Interrupting a speaker Discussing meeting styles in different countries	**Listening** People talking about their attitudes to meetings **Listening** Meetings in different countries **Reading** Meeting styles in three countries	**Vocabulary** Meetings **Grammar** Modal verbs **Phrase bank** Interrupting & preventing interruption
15 **Snail mail** p87	Discussing different types of communication Correcting a formal letter Writing letters following up a sales meeting or business contact	**Listening** Someone correcting a colleague's business letter	**Vocabulary** Prepositions; prepositional phrases; preposition + noun + preposition **Grammar** Multi-verb expressions **Phrase bank** Letter-writing
16 **Solving problems** p93	Discussing solutions to problems Expressions for making suggestions Conducting problem-solving meetings	**Listening** Case studies: three problems solved **Listening** Problem-solving meetings **Reading** Articles: advice on solving problems	**Vocabulary** People & products **Grammar** Conditionals (past reference) **Phrase bank** Problem-solving; Brainstorming
Case Study: Adverse reactions p100	Discussing change in the context of mergers and takeovers Comparing cultural differences in leadership and management styles Gathering information from e-mails and appraisal interviews Holding a problem-solving meeting Drafting an e-mail outlining recommendations	**Reading** A news website **Listening** A podcast interview **Reading** An internal e-mail **Listening** Extracts from appraisal interviews	
17 **Going green** p102	Discussing social & environmental responsibility	**Listening** Business people talking about corporate social responsibility **Reading** Articles about corporate social responsibility	
18 **Eating out** p104	Describing restaurants Doing a quiz on table manners & etiquette Describing typical dishes from your country Doing business over lunch	**Listening** A conversation in a restaurant **Listening** Conversations over lunch	**Vocabulary** Food & drink **Grammar** The Passive **Phrase bank** Eating out
19 **Telecommunications** p110	Discussing teleconferencing Holding a short teleconference Dealing with e-mails and voicemail messages	**Listening** A teleconference **Reading** An e-mail exchange	**Vocabulary** Managing a project **Grammar** Reporting **Phrase bank** Teleconferencing
20 **Negotiating** p120	Sounding more diplomatic Expressions for negotiating Completing notes while listening to two negotiations Negotiating a contract	**Reading** Extract from *Getting Past No* **Listening** People's views on negotiating **Reading** Joke from *Complete Idiot's Guide to Winning Through Negotiation* **Reading** Article about football **Listening** Description of football players' transfer deals	**Vocabulary** Negotiations **Grammar** Language of diplomacy **Phrase bank** Negotiating
Case Study: Going under? p124	Discussing the pros and cons of family businesses Conducting a SWOT analysis Considering generational, cultural and gender-based issues Presenting a strategic plan to a client	**Reading** A magazine advertisement **Reading** A magazine article **Listening** An overheard conversation **Reading** An extract from a company report **Listening** Extracts from interviews with members of a family business	

Additional material p126

Listening scripts p140

1 GLOBAL ENGLISH

English is no longer 'owned' by its native speakers.

DR. JULIANE HOUSE, HAMBURG UNIVERSITY

1 Complete the following sentence. Use the words in the box if you like. Then compare with other people in the class.

'For me, learning English is ....'

> an effort   a hobby   an investment   a necessity
> a nightmare   an opportunity   a pain   a pleasure
> a problem

2 Why are you learning English? Complete the sentences below and number them in order of importance for you. Compare with a partner.

In general, I want to:

> feel   improve   learn   make   read   write

a .... fewer grammar mistakes.
b .... without using a dictionary so much.
c .... my listening skills.
d .... better, clearer English.
e .... lots of new vocabulary.
f .... more confident when I speak.

In particular, I need English for:

> doing   giving   socialising   taking   travelling   writing

g .... on business.
h .... business on the phone.
i .... e-mails, faxes and letters.
j .... with clients and colleagues.
k .... part in meetings.
l .... short presentations.

3 Are you learning English for any other reasons? Add them to the lists above. Discuss your lists with a partner.

INTERNATIONAL COMMUNICATION

1 How much do you know about English as a world language? Try the quiz on the right. Then check your answers in the article opposite.

Test your knowledge

1 How many people speak English as a first, second or third language?
a 0.5 billion
b 1 billion
c 1.5 billion
d 2 billion

2 In a recent survey, how many Europeans said everyone should speak English?
a 29%
b 49%
c 69%
d 89%

3 Which country has officially tried to ban the use of English business terms in their own language?
a France
b Germany
c Russia
d Japan

4 When is the number of English-speakers in China likely to overtake the total number of native speakers?
a by 2025
b by 2050
c by 2075
d by 2100

5 What's the current ratio of native to non-native speakers of English in the world?
a Natives outnumber non-natives 2 to 1
b They are about the same
c Non-natives outnumber natives 2 to 1
d Non-natives outnumber natives 4 to 1

6 Which is the world's fastest growing language after English?
a Spanish
b Chinese
c Hindi
d Russian

7 Over the last 15 years or so has the proportion of English websites
a risen by 30%?
b risen by 25%?
c fallen by 25%?
d fallen by 30%?

English 2.0

English is to international communication what Google is to search engines, Microsoft to software and Intel to the microchip. It is, for better or worse, the 'industry standard'. And those who don't speak at least a little risk losing business to the increasing number who do. Around a quarter of the planet currently speaks some English. That's more than one and a half billion people.

In a recent survey by Eurobarometer, 69% of Europeans said they thought everyone should speak English. More than half of EU citizens already do. For most, it's not a question of choice but of necessity, as English has rapidly become the first language of business, science and popular culture. As Professor David Crystal, author of *The Cambridge Encyclopedia of Language*, puts it, 'wave dollar bills in front of someone, and they will learn complicated spellings and grammar.'

Not everyone, however, is so tempted by the dollar bills. A few years ago, the French Ministry of Finance decided to ban English terms like *e-mail*, *Internet* and *start-up*, replacing them with French equivalents. And, even in Germany, where phrases such as *Jointventure* and *Powerpartner* are considered cool and modern, politicians have expressed concern about the growing threat of English to their national culture.

But whose English are they talking about? UK prime minister, Gordon Brown, has said: 'By 2050 the number of English-speaking Chinese is likely to exceed the number of native English speakers'. But already non-native speakers of English outnumber native speakers 4 to 1. The English they speak is certainly not the English of Shakespeare and the Queen or even of Robbie Williams and David Beckham! It's Global English, International English, what we might even call English 2.0. The grammar is a little more restricted and the vocabulary

rather more basic. But it does the job. And culture has nothing to do with it.

Some say English 2.0 can be even more effective than the original, citing the case of the South Korean airline that bought its flight simulators from a French supplier rather than a British one because they understood their English better! Indeed, English needs to evolve in this way if it is to remain the world's number one language. Spanish is growing almost as fast as it gains popularity in Asia and Africa. And, where in 1996 85% of the Internet was in English, that figure is now down to 60% and falling.

So, with increasing competition, is it still worth making the investment in learning English? The answer, for the time being at least, is emphatically yes. According to one commentator, a global market value can even be given to speaking English. Currently, it's worth $5.4 trillion, which amounts to a tenth of the world economy!

2 Discuss the following questions.

a Do you agree with the author of the article that the growth of the English language in fact presents no threat to cultural identity?

b Can you see any other languages taking over from English as the international language of business?

c Do you think that non-native speakers actually find it easier to do business with each other in English than with native speakers? Do you?

3  1.01 Listen to six business people talking about their attitudes to learning English. Take notes. Whose opinion is closest to your own?

4 Complete the following expressions. They were used by the people you just listened to.

a Learning English isn't my idea .... fun.

b I want to get .... in my career.

c English is the language .... the media.

d It's certainly not .... beautiful a language as … Italian.

e I think it's more difficult .... you get older.

f I'll always think .... Italian.

g With native English speakers, I do feel .... a disadvantage.

h That's the thing .... English – it's easy to speak a little quite quickly.

2 MAKING CONTACTS

A conference is a gathering of important people who singly can do nothing, but together decide that nothing can be done.

FRED ALLEN, US COMEDIAN

1 Your boss tells you she's sending you to a three-day international conference. Which of the following cities do you hope it's in this year?

Barcelona Budapest Buenos Aires Chicago Edinburgh Johannesburg Milan Moscow Mumbai
Munich Paris Prague Rio de Janeiro Shanghai Stockholm Sydney Tokyo Toronto Warsaw

2 Explain your preference to a partner and tell them what you'd like to do if you could add one extra day onto your trip.

3 The blog below was posted on a business travel message board. A business traveller is asking for advice. Write down two or three tips for him.

ASK ExecTravelBuddy.com

Any advice for a first time conference goer?

October 2, 2008 3:56 PM

I'm going to my first conference next month and am looking for some general tips and advice from experienced conference goers on how to get the most out of it. The conference is in Rome, which I've never been to, so I'm quite excited about going. I'm generally a bit shy in large groups, but would like to try and use the event as a networking opportunity as well as a learning experience. It's a three-day event with a reception afterwards. I'm the only person representing my company at the conference. Fortunately, I'm not giving a presentation! But my boss has told me to come back with some useful contacts. Help!

4 Swap and discuss tips with a partner.

5 Read some of the replies this posting received. Speaker A see page 126. Speaker B see page 134. Compare the tips one by one with your partner. Which advice sounds the best to you?

CONFERENCE VENUES

1 🔊 1.02 Listen to three extracts from a business travel programme. Which venues below do you think the extracts refer to?

Venue 1 = Extract ....   Venue 2 = Extract ....   Venue 3 = Extract ....

2 Listen again and match the figures to each venue. What do the figures refer to?

321	Venue ☐	2,300	Venue ☐	170–780	Venue ☐
426	Venue ☐	10–30%	Venue ☐	95	Venue ☐
27th	Venue ☐	3,000	Venue ☐	200	Venue ☐

3 What other facilities does each venue have? Complete the collocations below. They were all in the extracts you just listened to.

Venue 1		Venue 2		Venue 3	
a central	1 deluxe suites	a 24-hour	1 club	a unique	1 activities
b flight	2 location	b health	2 service	b convention	2 atmosphere
c spacious	3 connections	c car-rental	3 room service	c team-building	3 centre
d internet	4 restaurant	d express	4 pools	d banqueting	4 tournaments
e world-class	5 views	e exclusive private	5 checkout	e golf	5 space
f spectacular	6 access	f outdoor	6 beach	f exhibition	6 facilities

4 Your company agrees to send you to an international conference at one of the venues above. Which would you choose and why?

WHO'S WHO?

1 One of the main reasons for going to conferences is to meet the right people. Complete the following questions and answers using the prepositions in the box.

    at   at   by   for   in   in   on   to   with

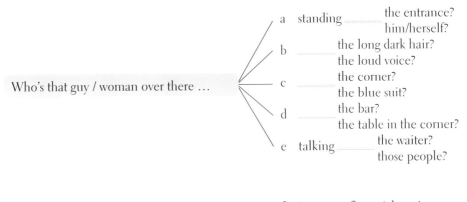

Who's that guy / woman over there …

a standing .... the entrance?
    him/herself?
b .... the long dark hair?
    the loud voice?
c .... the corner?
    the blue suit?
d .... the bar?
    the table in the corner?
e talking .... the waiter?
    those people?

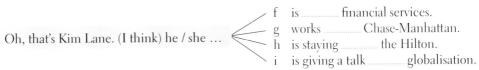

Oh, that's Kim Lane. (I think) he / she …

f is .... financial services.
g works .... Chase-Manhattan.
h is staying .... the Hilton.
i is giving a talk .... globalisation.

2 Use the model above to make new sentences with the following.

    the awful tie   the buffet   the conference organiser   the glasses   her back to us   the Hyatt
    the Italian accent   the long dress   the moustache   negotiating skills   pharmaceuticals
    the ponytail   Renault

3 🔘 **1.03–1.06** Listen to some delegates chatting at a conference reception. Decide which four people in the photo they are talking about and complete the information below.

1

Name Karl Schelling
Company ....
Position ....
Based in ....
Hotel ....
Subject of talk ....
Gossip ....

2

Name William Hall
Company ....
Position ....
Based in ....
Hotel ....
Subject of talk ....
Gossip ....

3

Name Irena Stefanowitz
Company ....
Position ....
Based in ....
Hotel ....
Subject of talk ....
Gossip ....

4

Name Margo Timmerman
Company ....
Position ....
Based in ....
Hotel ....
Subject of talk ....
Gossip ....

TABOO OR NOT TABOO?

1 Work with a partner. You meet some business people at a conference for the first time. Which of the following topics are

- interesting?
- safe?
- conversation killers?
- a bit risky?
- taboo?

books   the city you're in   clothes   your country   family   food & drink   gadgets   your health
your holiday plans   the hotel you're staying at   how work's going   jewellery   movies   music
the news   people you both know   politics   religion   sex   sport   the weather

2 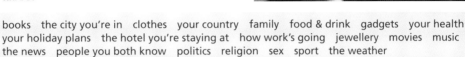 **1.07–1.11** Listen to some people socialising at a conference. What are they talking about? Do they get on with each other?

	Topics of conversation	Do the speakers get on?
a		
b		
c		
d		
e		

KEEPING THE CONVERSATION GOING

1 The expressions below were in the conversations you just listened to. Write in the first three words of each expression. Contractions (*it's, you'll, I'm,* etc.) count as one word. If necessary, listen again and check.

a .... first visit to Russia?
b .... do, by the way?
c .... you a drink?
d .... business are you in?
e .... these – they're delicious.
f .... somewhere before?
g .... me, I have to make a phone call.
h .... talking to you.
i .... your talk this morning.
j .... enjoying the conference?
k .... awful? Half a metre of snow!
l .... me a moment? I'll be right back.
m .... go and say hello to someone.
n .... many people here?
o .... you anything from the buffet?

2 Look at the expressions in 1.

a Which would be good ways of opening a conversation?
b Which would help you to keep a conversation going?
c Which could you use to politely end a conversation?

AT A CONFERENCE DRINKS PARTY

Work as a class to keep the conversation going at a conference drinks party at Disneyland, Paris. It's a warm summer evening and the place is full of delegates. The conference theme is *Web 2.0: Business in the connected economy.*

1 Invent a fantasy business card for yourself! Include the following information:
- name (you could change nationality!)
- company (you could choose a company you've always wanted to work for!)
- brief contact details (mobile phone, e-mail)

2 Complete the questions below. Think of possible answers for each and make notes in the space provided.

Q So, who / work for?

A

Q And what / do there?

A

Q Where / based?

A

Q How / business?

A

Q Can / get / drink?

A

Q Where / from originally?

A

Q first time / Paris?

A

Q How / enjoying / conference?

A

Q giving / presentation?

A

Q know many people here?

A

Q So, where / staying?

A

Q Can / get / anything / buffet?

A

3 When everyone is ready,
- mingle with the other people in the class.
- introduce yourself to as many people as possible and show interest in what they tell you.
- use the questions above to try to keep the conversation going. (Remember that you can talk about other people in the room as well as yourself.)
- exchange business cards and fix appointments with anyone you could do business with – see how many cards you can collect!

LANGUAGE LINKS

Vocabulary: Conferences

Talking shop

When business people get together they often just talk about work. This is called 'talking shop'. Write in the missing pairs of words below.

down + factory for + contract in + distributor of + job
off + workers out + product to + office
under + takeover up + plant with + supplier

a A I hear GEC are setting .... a new .... in Warsaw.

   B Warsaw? I thought it was Prague.

b A I understand you're .... talks with a local .... in Naples.

   B Yeah, that's right. In fact, we've already reached an agreement.

c A They say GM are laying .... 5,000 .... in the UK.

   B Is that right? Well, I knew they were downsizing.

d A Someone told me Sony are bringing .... a new .... in December.

   B Yes, I heard that too. Some kind of multi-media entertainment system.

e A I hear you're thinking .... leaving your .... at Hewlett-Packard.

   B Well, yes. Just between us, I'm moving to Cisco Systems.

f A I understand you're being transferred .... head .... in Stockholm.

   B Well, it's not official yet, but yes, I'm going just after Christmas.

g A They say they're .... threat from a hostile .... bid.

   B Really? It's the first I've heard of it.

h A Someone told me they're doing a deal .... a .... in Tel Aviv.

   B Well, that makes sense. They do most of their business there.

i A I hear you're bidding .... a new .... in Singapore.

   B Yeah, we are. The negotiations are going quite well, in fact.

j A Someone told me they're closing .... the Liverpool ....

   B It doesn't surprise me. From what I heard, they're trying to centralise production.

Grammar: Present Simple

About half of all spoken English is in the Present Simple. You use it to talk about actions and states which are always or generally true.

Affirmative	
I you we they	work
he she it	works

Negative	
I you we they	don't work
he she it	doesn't work

Interrogative		
do don't	I you we they	work?
does doesn't	he she it	work?

Spelling changes	
verb	he/she/it
go	goes
watch	watches
push	pushes
miss	misses
fax	faxes
try	tries

1 Correct the following using the information above.

a A Works he for the BBC?

   B No, he don't work for them anymore. He work for CNN.

b A Where work you?

   B I works for a design company in Frankfurt.

c At our firm, we doesn't work on Friday afternoons.

d On Mondays our CEO usually flys to Oslo.

2 Match sentences a–h with their functions 1–4 below.

a I live just outside Munich.

b He runs five km every day.

c Your presentation is this afternoon.

d The United States has the world's strongest economy.

e That's a good idea!

f She works Saturdays.

g I love Vienna at Christmas.

h My train leaves at 7.30.

Which sentences above mainly

1 describe habits and routines? ☐☐

2 refer to schedules and timetables? ☐☐

3 express thoughts, feelings and opinions? ☐☐

4 refer to long-term situations or facts? ☐☐

Grammar: Present Continuous

You use the Present Continuous to talk about current situations in progress and future arrangements.

- *They're staying at the Hilton.*
- *He's giving a talk on globalisation at three o'clock.*

Affirmative		Negative	
I'm		I'm not	
you're we're they're	working	you aren't we aren't they aren't	working
he's she's it's		he isn't she isn't it isn't	

Interrogative			Spelling changes	
am	I		**verb**	**-*ing* form**
are	you we they	working?	make come run drop forget lie	making coming running dropping forgetting lying
is	he she it			

3 Read the conversation.

A Alison?

B Yes. Who's calling? (a)

A It's Paco … About our appointment, we're meeting (b) on Thursday, right?

B That's right. Are you flying (c) to Heathrow?

A No. I'm working (d) in Zaragoza this month. So Gatwick's easier for me.

B Fine. Oh! The batteries are going (e) on my mobile. Can I call you back?

In the conversation above, find examples of

1 something happening right at this moment. ☐☐
2 something happening around the present time. ☐
3 a future arrangement. ☐☐

Grammar: Present Simple or Continuous?

Some verbs are not 'action' verbs, and are not usually used in the continuous form.

| be believe hear know like mean need see |
| seem think understand want |

4 Choose the best alternatives in the following conversation.

A What (a) **do you do / are you doing**?

B (b) **I'm / I'm being** an electrical engineer for Siemens.

A Really? Here in Munich?

B That's right. (c) **Do you know / Are you knowing** Munich?

A Oh, yes, great city. So, how (d) **do you enjoy / are you enjoying** the conference so far?

B Well, it's all right, (e) **I guess / I'm guessing**. (f) **Do you give / Are you giving** a talk?

A No, no. (g) **I only come / I'm only coming** to these things to get out of the office for a few days. Where (h) **do you stay / are you staying**, by the way?

B At the Avalon. (i) **I usually stay / I'm usually staying** at the Bauer Hotel in Münchenerstrasse but it was full.

A Well, if (j) **you don't do / you aren't doing** anything later, do you want to go for something to eat?

Phrase bank: Networking

Make questions and sentences by matching the beginnings and endings.

a	What do you	1	introduce you to someone. give you my card.
b	Who do you	2	enjoying the conference? getting back to your hotel?
c	Where are you	3	nice talking to you. a pleasure meeting you.
d	How are you	4	based? staying?
e	Isn't this	5	with the beard? in the dark suit?
f	Who's the guy	6	work for? know here?
g	I think he's	7	a drink? anything from the buffet?
h	Can I get you	8	a moment, I'll be right back. I have to make a phone call.
i	Let me	9	do, by the way? think of the venue?
j	If you'll excuse me	10	an amazing place? weather awful?
k	It's been	11	in logistics. giving a talk on PR.

a ☐ b ☐ c ☐ d ☐ e ☐ f ☐ g ☐ h ☐ i ☐ j ☐ k ☐

3 MAKING CALLS

Our telephone answering system has broken down. This is a human being. How can I help you?

ANONYMOUS CUSTOMER SERVICE REPRESENTATIVE

1 How comfortable are you speaking English on the phone? Work with a partner. Complete and discuss the questionnaire below using the correct form of the following verbs.

> have keep lose misunderstand shout sound try want wish

Be honest!
Can you remember a time when you ...

a totally .... what someone said on the phone?	Oh, yes ☐	No ☐
b really .... rude and unhelpful because you were busy?	Oh, yes ☐	No ☐
c constantly .... to ask the other person to repeat what they said?	Oh, yes ☐	No ☐
d just .... putting off a call because you didn't want to speak English?	Oh, yes ☐	No ☐
e actually .... at someone on the phone?	Oh, yes ☐	No ☐
f completely .... track of the conversation?	Oh, yes ☐	No ☐
g just .... you could talk to the other person face to face?	Oh, yes ☐	No ☐
h even .... pretending you were out to avoid taking a call?	Oh, yes ☐	No ☐
i really .... to kill the person on the other end of the phone?	Oh, yes ☐	No ☐

Making phone calls in a foreign language requires planning. It's especially important to know what to say right at the beginning of the call.

2 🔊 1.12 Listen to the phone call. Why does the caller get angry?

3 🔊 1.13 Listen to a better version of the same phone call and complete the following:

.... , accounts .... Marius Pot ....

4 🔊 1.14 Now listen to another phone call. Why does the caller sound so unprofessional?

5 🔊 1.15 Again, listen to a better version of the same phone call and complete the following:

.... Ramon Berenguer .... Genex Pharmaceuticals.

.... Catherine Mellor, ... ?

.... an invoice.

6 A lot of the English you need on the phone is just a small number of key words used in different combinations. Work with a partner. How many telephone expressions can you make in two minutes using one word or phrase from two or more sections below (e.g. *Can I have your name, please?*)? Write them down.

Can	I you	ask check speak to take see if help have give speak up hold on get tell leave say spell read get back to	who's me you he/she him/her your name a message someone something a moment it that	please about it again with me with you back to me I called within the hour to call me back a few details on that is there for me later today calling when he/she'll be back

7 You overhear a colleague say the following things on the phone. What questions do you think she was asked? Use some of the telephone expressions you made in 6.

a   Yes, I'd like to speak to Ifakat Karsli, please.
b   Yes, it's Ivana Medvedeva.
c   M-E-D-V-E-D-E-V-A, Medvedeva.
d   Yes. Can you just tell her Ivana called?
e   Yes, I'll tell him as soon as he gets in.
f   Of course. Your reference number is 45-81099-KM. OK?
g   Sorry, is that better?
h   Around three, I should think.
i   Can we make that two hours?
j   Certainly. Can you give me your number?
k   Sure. When can I expect to hear from you?
l   Sure. Just a minute. Where's my pen? OK, go ahead.

8 🔘 1.16 Listen and check your answers.

VOICEMAIL

1 🔘 1.17 Listen to six voicemail messages. Take notes. Which message is about

a   an order? ☐
b   some figures? ☐
c   a meeting? ☐
d   a deadline? ☐
e   a report? ☐
f   a reminder? ☐

2 Listen again and answer the questions.

Message 1 How many times did Cheryl phone yesterday?

Message 2 What's the good news about Phase One?

Message 3 What did Zoltán include in his report?

Message 4 When was the delivery?

Message 5 How late is the estimate?

Message 6 What do you think is happening at 3.00 tomorrow?

3 The messages above contain the following verbs.

a phoned, corrected, faxed

b wanted, finished, explained

c started, e-mailed, included

d talked, despatched, delivered

e called, discussed, expected

f tried, waited, booked

The '-ed' endings of regular verbs in the Past Simple can be pronounced in three different ways: /d/, /t/ or /id/. Listen to the messages again. Which verbs take the /id/ ending? Why? Put them in the third column below.

/d/	/t/	/id/

Now put the other verbs in the correct column.

4 The following messages were taken by your secretary. Work with a partner. Can you recreate the original voicemails? The first one has been done for you as an example.

Example

Svetlana (Paris)

Flight delay – late for meeting.

Start with item 2 on agenda.

Will join asap.

> Hi, it's Svetlana. Listen, my flight's been delayed and it looks like I'm going to be late for the meeting. Can you start with item two on the agenda and I'll join you as soon as I can? Thanks! See you later.

A

Seiji (Nagoya)

Negotiations going well – deadlocked on price. Authorise 14% discount on 50,000 units?

B

URGENT!

Jim (Expo in Dublin)

Lost memory stick for presentation! Pls e-mail PowerPoint slides asap!

C

Tony

Stuck in meeting at HQ. Conference arrangements progress? Pls contact speakers to confirm.

D

Kate (Seattle)

Microsoft's querying our invoice for Q3. Ask accounts to check figures + reinvoice if necessary.

E

URGENT!

Alicia

Needs Turin report – tomorrow pm latest! Call back if problems.

F

Mike

Has appointment here Fri. Meet? Beer? Ian sends his rgds.

pls = please

asap = as soon as possible

rgds = regards

HQ = headquarters

Q3 = third quarter

5 🔊 1.18 Listen to the original voicemails and compare them with your answers.

RETURNING A CALL

1 🔊 1.19–1.20 Listen to two telephone calls and answer the questions.

Call 1

1 Whose answerphone are we listening to?
2 What does the caller want?
3 Put the recorded message into the right order. The first and last parts are in the right place.

☐ Hello. This is Patterson Meats,

☐ but if you'd like to leave

☐ for calling. I'm afraid

☐ a fax, please do so

☐ your call right now,

☐ after the tone, and I'll get back

☐ Sylvia Wright's office. Thank you

☐ I'm not able to take

☐ a message or send

☐ to you as soon as I can.

Call 2

1 Who didn't come to the meeting?
   a Bill Andrews   b Stephanie Hughes   c Jonathan Powell   d Melanie Burns
2 Who does Tim already know?
   a Bill Andrews   b Stephanie Hughes   c Jonathan Powell   d Melanie Burns
3 What didn't the visitors from the UK see?
   a the processing plant   d the freezer units
   b the factory   e a presentation
   c the packing department
4 Tim was interrupted during the phone call. Complete what he said to Sylvia.
   Sorry _____ . I just _____ . Where _____ ?
5 What were the British visitors worried about?
6 Would the product they came to see be popular in your country? Would you try it?

2 Put these irregular verbs from Call 2 into the Past Simple. You have 45 seconds!

get	meet	take
do	speak	say
go	think	have
send	come	tell
be	give	

3 One of the following extracts is from the phone call. The other is incorrect. Which is incorrect and why?

a So who else did come?   b So who else came?
   Came Stephanie Hughes?   Did Stephanie Hughes come?

FINDING OUT

Work with a partner. Phone each other in order to find out some information to help you

    a   do business in a foreign city
or b   give a presentation
or c   attend a job interview

Talk to your partner before you begin and decide on the subject of your phone calls. Think of the language you will need.

Begin your phone call in this way:

Hi, ... (your partner's name). It's .... (your name) here. How are things? … And how's business?

Then use the notes below to help you ask your questions. Ask other questions if you like.

1 A business trip

Listen, I'm going to .... (city?) on business in a couple of weeks. I know you did some business there a while ago and I just wanted to ask you how it went.

a   Which airline / fly with?
b   business class?
c   Where / stay?
d   What / food like?
e   What / people like?
f   easy to work with?

g   meetings go OK?
h   language problems?
i   chance / see much / city?
j   What / do / evenings?
k   invite / their home?
l   take a present?

2 A presentation

Listen, I'm giving a presentation at .... (a meeting? a conference?) in a couple of weeks. I know you had to give a presentation a while ago and I just wanted to ask you how it went.

a   Do / talk / your own?
b   How long / take / prepare?
c   How big / audience?
d   How long / speak for?
e   nervous?
f   use PowerPoint?

g   How many / visuals?
h   tell jokes?
i   give / handouts?
j   take questions / the end?
k   any difficult ones?
l   How / deal with them?

3 A job interview

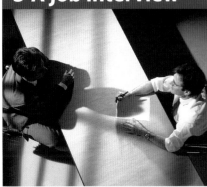

Listen, I'm going for an interview at .... (company?) in a couple of weeks. I know you had an interview with them a while ago and I just wanted to ask you how it went.

a   How long / interview / last?
b   How many interviewers?
c   How friendly?
d   say what / looking for?
e   refer / your CV?
f   How interested / qualifications?

g   trickiest question?
h   ask / personal questions?
i   have / do / a test?
j   ask them / questions?
k   What / salary / like?
l   offer you / job?

LANGUAGE LINKS

Vocabulary: Telephone expressions

Dealing with difficulties and distractions

In business, phone calls are often interrupted. Look at the difficulties and distractions a–i. Match each one to an appropriate response 1–9.

a   A colleague wants you to sign something.
b   Your colleague leaves a few seconds later.
c   There's a lot of noise right outside your office.
d   Your boss wants a word with you – now!
e   Someone else is trying to call you.
f   The caller gives you their name – it's unpronounceable!
g   You think you misunderstood the information the other person just gave you.
h   You gave the caller a lot of information very quickly.
i   The other person just won't stop talking!

1 Sorry, could you speak up a little?

2 Look, I've got someone on the other line. Can I call you back?

3 OK? Did you get all that?

4 I'll have to go, I'm afraid. Something's come up.

5 Sorry about that. Where were we?

6 Anyway, I won't keep you any longer. Speak to you soon.

7 Excuse me a moment.

8 Sorry, could you spell that for me, please?

9 Can I just check that with you?

a ☐ b ☐ c ☐ d ☐ e ☐ f ☐ g ☐ h ☐ i ☐

Grammar: Past Simple

You use the Past Simple to talk about completed, past events. Most verbs are regular, but there are about 100 important irregular verbs that are useful to learn.

Affirmative		Negative	
I you we they he she it	worked	I you we they he she it	didn't work

Interrogative			Spelling changes	
did didn't	I you we they he she it	work?	**verb** study prefer stop admit	**past simple** studied preferred stopped admitted

to be

Affirmative		Negative		Interrogative	
I he she it	was	I he she it	wasn't	was wasn't	I? he? she? it?
you we they	were	you we they	weren't	were weren't	you? we? they?

1 Correct the following using the information above.

A   Phoned Enrique about those figures?
B   No. I wait all morning, but he phoned not.
A   Typical! And I suppose he didn't the report either.
B   No. Did he went to the meeting yesterday?
A   No, but I not expected him to.

2 Write the Past Simple of the verbs below.

hurry ....   play ....
occupy ....   enjoy ....
refer ....   offer ....
confer ....   suffer ....
drop ....   develop ....
flop ....   visit ....
commit ....
transmit ....

Why don't the verbs on the right follow the same spelling changes as the verbs on the left?

3 Time adverbs help us to be more specific about the past. Using the time adverbs in the box, complete this short presentation about the development of a new product.

ago before during for in over

As you know, we first got the idea for the new product a year (a) _____ , but (b) _____ we could go to market with it, there was a lot of work to do. (c) _____ six months the product was in development at our research centre in Cambridge. We then ran tests (d) _____ a three-month period. (e) _____ that time we also conducted interviews with some of our best customers to find out what they wanted from the product. (f) _____ March we were finally ready for the launch.

4 Complete the joke using the Past Simple of the verbs in brackets.

A businessman (a) _____ (want) to interview applicants for the position of divisional manager. There (b) _____ (be) several strong candidates, so he (c) _____ (decide) to devise a simple test to select the most suitable person for the job. He (d) _____ (ask) each applicant the simple question, 'What is two and two?'

The first applicant (e) _____ (be) a journalist. He (f) _____ (light) a cigarette, (g) _____ (think) for a moment and then (h) _____ (say) 'twenty-two'.

The second applicant (i) _____ (have) a degree in engineering. He (j) _____ (take) out his calculator (k) _____ (press) a few buttons, and (l) _____ (show) the answer to be between 3.999 and 4.001.

The next applicant (m) _____ (work) as a corporate lawyer. He (n) _____ (state) that two and two (o) _____ (can) only be four, and (p) _____ (prove) it by referring to the well-known case of Gates v Monopolies Commission.

The last applicant (q) _____ (turn) out to be an accountant. The businessman again (r) _____ (put) his question, 'What is two and two?'

The accountant (s) _____ (get) up from his chair, (t) _____ (go) over to the door, (u) _____ (close) it, then (v) _____ (come) back and (w) _____ (sit) down. Finally, he (x) _____ (lean) across the desk and (y) _____ (whisper) in a low voice, 'How much do you want it to be?'

5 Read the conversation and answer the questions.

Anne Who did you tell?
Bengt Just Claire.
Anne And who told you?
Bengt Stefan.
Anne And nobody else knows?
Bengt Only you.
Anne Well, of course, I do. I told Stefan.

1 Who knew first?
   a Anne   b Bengt   c Claire   d Stefan
2 How did Bengt find out?
3 Who was the last to know?
   a Anne   b Bengt   c Claire   d Stefan
4 Read these two questions and <u>underline</u> the subject in each. *Who did you tell? Who told you?*

6 Correct the six errors in these conversations.

a **A** They're moving us to a new office.
    B Who did say so?
    A The boss. I spoke to him this morning.
    B Oh. So where said he we're moving to?
b **A** Well, I went to the interview.
    B And? What did happen?
    A I got the job!
    B What said I? I knew you'd get it. Congratulations!
c **A** I spoke to Amy at the meeting about our idea.
    B And what thought she?
    A She liked it.
    B Good. So who else did come to the meeting?

Phrase bank: Telephoning

1 Look at the phrases below and decide who probably said them: the caller or the person who received the call. Mark them C or R. If you think it could equally be both, write B. The first one has been done for you.

(a) This is [John White] from [Novartis]. C

It's I'm calling	→	(b) about an invoice.

(c) speak to Jane Green, please?
(d) ask who's calling, please?
(e) take a message?

Can I	→	(f) get back to you on that?

(g) leave it with you?
(h) call you back (in a few minutes/ an hour)?

(i) speak up, please?
(j) say that again?
(k) spell that (for me), please?

Could you	→	(l) hold on a moment, please?

(m) read that back to me?
(n) tell me when s/he'll be back?
(o) ask her to call me back?

2 'Can I ...?' is perfectly polite. Why do you think 'Could you ...?' is better than 'Can you ...?'

4 KEEPING TRACK

When the result of a meeting is to schedule more meetings it usually signals trouble.

MIKE MURPHY, BUSINESS WRITER

1 When you take part in meetings in English, it is easy to lose track of what people are saying. Who do you generally find the hardest to understand?

native speakers   other non-native speakers   people who speak too fast   people with strong accents

2 Here are six simple ways of checking what someone has just said. Write in the missing pairs of words.

catch + slow   follow + run   'm + go   missed + say   see + be   understand + explain

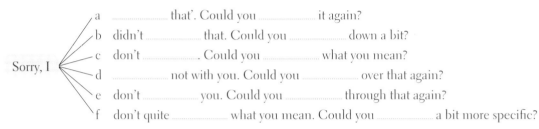

Sorry, I

a .... that'. Could you .... it again?
b didn't .... that. Could you .... down a bit?
c don't .... Could you .... what you mean?
d .... not with you. Could you .... over that again?
e don't .... you. Could you .... through that again?
f don't quite .... what you mean. Could you .... a bit more specific?

3 Which of the above do you use when you
a   didn't hear? ☐☐   b   didn't understand? ☐☐☐☐

4 Match the phrasal verbs from 2 to the meanings on the right.
a   slow down   1   mention quickly
b   go over   2   speak more slowly
c   run through   3   examine, discuss

5 Can you remember the phrases in 2 when you need them? Work with a partner. Take turns to throw dice and try to produce the exact expressions using the words below to help you.

missed – say
– again?

didn't catch
– slow – bit?

don't understand
– explain – what
you mean?

not with you – go
over – again?

don't follow you
– run through
– again?

don't quite see
– mean – bit
more specific?

SORRY?

1 In meetings where you are discussing facts and figures, saying *Sorry?* or *I don't understand* is not always enough. Sometimes you need to be more precise. Look at the following short extracts from meetings. Complete the second speaker's responses with the correct question words.

| how long   how much   what   when   where   who |

a **A** The problem is money.
    B Sorry, _____ did you say?
    A The problem is money.
    B Oh, as usual.

d **A** Ildikó Dudás spoke to me about it yesterday.
    B Sorry, _____ did you say?
    A Ildikó Dudás – from the Budapest office.
    B Oh, yes, of course.

b **A** We have to reach a decision by next week.
    B Sorry, _____ did you say?
    A Next week.
    B Oh, I see.

e **A** The company is based in Taipei.
    B Sorry, _____ did you say?
    A In Taipei.
    B Oh, really?

c **A** An upgrade will cost $3,000.
    B Sorry, _____ did you say?
    A $3,000, at least.
    B Oh, as much as that?

f **A** The whole project might take eighteen months.
    B Sorry, _____ did you say?
    A Eighteen months.
    B Oh, as long as that?

2 🔊 **1.21** Listen to the conversations in 1 and check your answers.

3 Work with a partner to practise clarifying specific points. You are going to read about two different companies, both called Budweiser. Speaker A see page 126. Speaker B see page 135.

4 Work with a partner to put this summary of the texts you read in 3 in the correct order. The first and last parts are in the right place.

1	(a)	American Budweiser is the world's bestselling
	(b)	than forty different countries. Its slogan is
	(c)	other hand, is one
	(d)	fewer resources than US Budweiser, it markets its product in more
	(e)	output than its nearest
	(f)	of the world's oldest and most
	(g)	brand of beer. The company that makes it is the biggest in
	(h)	slogan was 'Budweiser: the King of Beers'. Czech Budweiser, on the
	(i)	famous beers. With far
	(j)	competitor, Heineken. By far its most successful advertising
	(k)	the world with 50% greater
12	(l)	simply: 'Budweiser: the Beer of Kings'.

5 How many comparatives and superlatives can you find in the summary?

DIDN'T I SAY THAT?

A	So that's $13 million.
B	13 million? Isn't it 30?
A	Oh, yes, sorry. 30 million.

A	These are the figures for 2008.
B	2008? Don't you mean 2009?
A	No, I mean 2008.

A	This represents 8.6% of total sales.
B	8.6? Shouldn't that be 6.8?
A	Yes, 6.8. Didn't I say that?

1 People sometimes disagree about facts in meetings. One way of politely querying something is simply to repeat the part you think is wrong and ask a question. Look at the examples on the left.

2 Work with a partner. Take it in turns to read out the following false information. Query each other using the correct information from the box. The first one has been done for you as an example.

> 1997   Finland   Google   Korean   music   ~~the Netherlands~~   software   the Taipei 101   Tata Motors

a   The biggest Benelux country is Belgium.
Belgium? Don't you mean the Netherlands?
b   Hyundai is a well-known Japanese car manufacturer.
c   China regained control of Hong Kong in 1998.
d   Microsoft is the world's leading computer hardware manufacturer.
e   Jaguar cars are owned by Ford.
f   America has more mobile phones per household than any other country.
g   MTV is the biggest news channel in the world.
h   Yahoo is the most popular search engine in the world.
i   The tallest skyscraper in the world is the Petronas Towers.

3 Write down a few false business facts of your own. Read them out to the rest of the class. Can they correct you?

4 🔘 **1.22** Listen to an extract from a meeting and tick the sentences which are correct.
a   The meeting is being held to discuss last month's sales figures.
b   Overall, sales are up by 2.6%.
c   The best results are in Denmark and Norway.
d   30,000 units have been sold in Scandinavia.
e   Last month was June.
f   John Munroe is head of Northern Europe.
g   Munroe is in Scotland at the moment.

5 Listen again and correct the mistakes in 4.

6 The following expressions are used to query information you are less sure about. They were all in the conversation you just listened to. Complete them.

> mistake   right   sound   sure

a   Are you _____ ?
b   There must be some _____ .
c   That can't be _____ .
d   That doesn't _____ right to me.

7 How good is your business general knowledge? <u>Underline</u> the correct information below.

World business records

a **The number of Cokes consumed in the world per day exceeds**
1.3 million / 130 million / 1.3 billion

b **The biggest company in the world in terms of revenue is**
Wal-Mart / Exxon Mobil / Royal Dutch Shell

c **The world's bestselling model of car is**
the VW Golf / the Toyota Corolla / the Fiat Brava

d **The world's oldest airline is**
KLM / British Airways / Singapore Airlines

e **The world's bestselling business paper is**
The Wall Street Journal / The Financial Times / The Yomiuri Shimbun

f **According to the *Financial Times*, the world's most valuable luxury brand is**
Louis Vuitton / Chanel / Cartier

g **The world's most popular toy is**
Barbie / Lego / Rubik's Cube

h **The single invention with the highest global turnover is**
the personal computer / the electric light bulb / the automobile

i **The world's biggest exporter of computer software is**
the USA / Ireland / India

j **The world's number one PC manufacturer is**
IBM / Dell / Hewlett-Packard

k **The world's richest country in GDP per head is**
the USA / Luxembourg / Switzerland

l **According to *Fortune* magazine, the world's most admired company is**
Proctor & Gamble / Disney / General Electric

Answers on page 126

Now work with a partner to practise querying information. Take it in turns to read out your answers to the quiz. Query anything you think is wrong.

8 Sometimes what people say in meetings conflicts with what they said earlier:

A Eight out of ten members of staff liked the proposal. So, 90% is a good result.

B **Wait a minute.** 90%? **I thought you said** eight out of ten …

A Oh, yeah. Sorry, 80%, of course.

9 Work in pairs to practise pointing out discrepancies. Speaker A see page 126. Speaker B see page 135.

THE BRIEFING MEETING

🔘 1.23 A mergers and acquisitions specialist has been transferred to the Tokyo office of his bank to work as part of a project team during a takeover bid. He is attending his first briefing meeting, but things don't go quite as he expected. Listen and complete his notes.

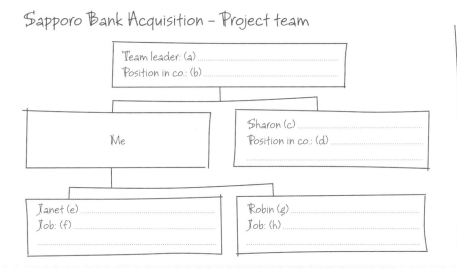

Sapporo Bank Acquisition – Project team

Team leader: (a) ....
Position in co.: (b) ....

Me

Sharon (c) ....
Position in co.: (d) ....

Janet (e) ....
Job: (f) ....

Robin (g) ....
Job: (h) ....

- I'll be based at the (i) .... office.

- My main responsibility will be (j) ....

- First project meeting scheduled for (k) ....

- First round of negotiations begin on (l) ....

LANGUAGE LINKS

Vocabulary: Business phrasal verbs

Complete each dialogue using one of the five words in the box. Then match each phrasal verb in the dialogue to a verb similar in meaning.

| down off on out up |

a   The project meeting

A	OK, that's item two. Let's move		to item three: new projects.
B	Now, just hold		a minute, Sylvia.
A	Kim, I'm counting		you to get us the Zurich contract.
B	But this is not the time to be taking		more work.

continue = ...   accept = ...   rely = ...   wait = ...

b   The troubleshooting meeting

A	Right. Have you managed to sort		the problem with our computers?
B	To be honest, we haven't really found		exactly what the problem is yet.
A	Well, can I just point		that it's now affecting everyone on the first floor?
B	Yes, I know. We're carrying		tests on the system now. Give us a couple of hours.

say = ...   discover = ...   do = ...   solve = ...

c   The union negotiation

A	The question is, will you agree to call		the strike?
B	Not if you're still planning to lay		a quarter of the workforce, no.
A	I'm afraid that's a decision we can't put		any longer.
B	Then, I'm sorry, we shall have to break		these negotiations.

fire = ...   end = ...   cancel = ...   postpone = ...

d   The marketing meeting

A	We really must fix		a meeting to discuss our pricing strategy.
B	Our prices are fine. We're trying to build		market share, Otto. Profits can wait.
A	Yes, but our overheads have gone		nearly 20% over the last eighteen months.
B	I know, but that's no reason to put		prices. We'll just lose customers.

rise = ...   raise = ...   arrange = ...   develop = ...

e   The budget meeting

A	I'm afraid they've turned		our application for a bigger budget.
B	That's because group turnover's gone		again. So where are we supposed to make cuts?
A	We could start by cutting		the amount of time we waste in these meetings!
B	Now, calm		everybody. We need to be practical.

reduce = ...   relax = ...   reject = ...   decrease = ...

Grammar: Comparatives and superlatives

Type	adjective	comparative	superlative
1	cheap	cheap**er**	**the** cheap**est**
2	safe	safe**r**	**the** safe**st**
3	big	big**ger**	**the** big**gest**
4	early	earl**ier**	**the** earl**iest**
5	important	**more** important	**the most** important
6	good	**better**	**the best**

1 Classify the adjectives below as type 1–6.

clever ☐   high ☐   sad ☐
hot ☐   global ☐   thin ☐
dirty ☐   bad ☐   fat ☐
helpful ☐   wealthy ☐   late ☐
hard ☐   easy ☐   effective ☐
heavy ☐   rich ☐   reliable ☐

What generalisations can you make about one-syllable, two-syllable and three-syllable adjectives?

2 Use your own personal experiences to complete the following sentences. If necessary, use a dictionary to help you choose the right adjectives.

a The job I've got now is a lot .... than my previous one. On the other hand, it's not quite as
....

b I found .... to be a fairly .... city, but I think .... is even ....

c To be honest, I don't really like .... music. I prefer something a bit ....

d I'll never forget the view from .... It's even .... than the one from ....

e I find .... food fairly .... , but it's not quite as .... as people think.

f I think the .... building I've ever seen must be .... Either that or .... , which was just as .... , but in a different way.

g The people in .... are some of the .... I've ever met – apart from the .... , who are even ....

h I drive a .... these days. In terms of .... , it's the .... car I've ever had, but it's not as .... as the .... I used to have.

3 Complete the following humorous article using the comparative and superlative expressions in the box.

a – g	by far the lowest compared with even worse little safer a lot more much better world's highest
h – n	10% longer as famous as half as many a little more one of the best significantly happier twice as likely

Phrase bank: Checking understanding

Look at the phrases and expressions phrases below. Which do you use when you:

... didn't understand?   ... understood differently?
... didn't hear?

a
Sorry, I → missed that. / didn't catch that.

Could you just → say it again? / go over that again?

b
Sorry, I → 'm not (quite) with you. / don't (quite) follow you. / don't (quite) see what you mean.

Could you just → explain what you mean? / be (a bit) more specific? / say (a bit) more about that?

c
Isn't it / Don't you mean / Shouldn't that be / I thought you said   12%?

What's the effect of using the words in brackets ()?

How to live forever: 8 golden rules

Rule 1 Don't live in Iceland. With long dark winters, sub-zero temperatures and active volcanos, it has the (a) .... suicide rate. Move to Palm Beach, Florida, where you have a (b) .... chance of living to be over a 100 – like the rest of the residents.

Rule 2 Don't go to Johannesburg. It's the murder capital of the world. Statistically, it's (c) .... dangerous than São Paolo or New York. Milan's a (d) .... but try not to breathe. The pollution's (e) .... than in Mexico City.

Rule 3 Don't get sick in Equatorial Guinea. There's only one doctor to every 70,000 patients and no anaesthetic. If you have to be ill, be ill in Kuwait. It has (f) .... death rate in the world. Only 3.1 people per thousand die annually, (g) .... 11.2 in Britain.

Rule 4 If you're a man, think of becoming a woman. On average, women live (h) .... than men. If you're a woman, stay single. Crime figures show women are (i) .... to be killed by their partner than anyone else.

Rule 5 Smoke one cigarette a day. It won't do you much harm and, according to some doctors, it's (j) .... ways of avoiding senility in old age.

Rule 6 Drink red wine – in moderation. (k) .... red wine drinkers suffer from heart conditions as white wine and beer drinkers. Drinking all three is not an option!

Rule 7 Become a 'chocoholic'. Chocolate isn't good for you, but it releases chemicals in the brain that make you (l) .... And it's a medical fact that happiness prolongs life.

Rule 8 Die young and famous – like Elvis, James Dean and John Lennon. People will keep believing you're still alive. Even if you can't be (m) .... Marilyn Monroe or Kurt Cobain, you can be (n) .... careful than they were. No sex, no drugs, no rock 'n' roll. You won't actually live longer. It will just seem like it!

HIGH FLIER

1 Read the magazine extract. What kind of employer do you think Shavi Kumar is? Do you agree with his views on getting rid of the laptop, the mobile and escaping the office?

Is Shavi Kumar, owner of the Cobrax Entertainment Group, the youngest internet billionaire in India or just the most eccentric? In an exclusive interview with *Cool Million* magazine, Kumar, the 27-year-old, Cambridge-educated, extreme sport-loving serial entrepreneur from Hyderabad, claimed that the secret of his success is regularly skipping work and 'going off on one of my adventures'. 'I get my best ideas scuba-diving in Mauritius or paragliding in the hills near Mumbai, never in the boardroom' says Kumar, who has bought and sold 21 companies since his 17th birthday. 'Or sometimes meditating on a mountain-top in Nepal is just what I need. But, wherever I go, I always make sure I leave my laptop and mobile behind.' So how does he run his media empire from the beach and the ski-slope? 'I don't' he smiles. 'I leave all that to my team back at the office. I believe in employing people who can run my business as well as I can if they have to.' But isn't he ever shocked at some of the decisions they've made without him when he returns? 'Sometimes' he confesses. 'Actually, last time I came back they'd lost me thirteen million dollars on a deal that went wrong. But that's life! If I'd never taken any chances, now where would I be?' And as he climbs into his bronze Aston Martin DBS to race to his next appointment, you have to admit, he has a point!

2 🔊 1.24 You work at the Cobrax Entertainment Group international headquarters in Mumbai. At 8.45am on Friday April 14th Shavi Kumar calls you all into his office to talk you through his schedule for the next two weeks. Listen and complete the personal organiser below.

	a.m.	p.m.
MON 17		
TUE 18		
WED 19		
THU 20		
FRI 21		

	a.m.	p.m.
MON 24		
TUE 25		
WED 26		
THU 27		
FRI 28		

3 Work in small teams. By 6 p.m. on the Friday afternoon, you find Shavi's e-mail full as usual. Check through some of his e-mails and prioritise them according to how important and / or urgent they are. Decide if and how you are going to reply to each. If you've time, draft a few replies.

✉↑ | ✉↓ | ✏

From: Candace Law, senior account handler (RippleEffect.co.uk)
Subject: Internet advertising

Dear Mr Kumar
After our last phone call, I was wondering if you'd thought any more about meeting to discuss your internet advertising needs. As you know, at RippleEffect, we specialise in using social networks to promote brand awareness online. In fact, our creative team has already come up with some preliminary ideas I'd like to share with you. When might be a convenient time to set up a videoconference?

Priority: .... Action: ....

✉↑ | ✉↓ | ✏

From: David R. Miller, director, legal dept. (Cobrax USA)
Subject: Viacom contract

Shavi
I hate to spoil the celebrations, but I've been going through the contract we're about to sign with Viacom and there are one or two points your team totally missed when they were negotiating the deal which could cost us a lot of money. And I mean a lot. We could be talking millions! What were your people thinking of? We clearly need to talk. Call me over the weekend, OK?

Priority: .... Action: ....

From: Hanna Fischer, estate management director (Cobrax Europe)
Subject: Do we have the go-ahead?

Dear Mr Kumar
Sorry to bother you at such a busy time, but we are still waiting for you to approve the sale of our old film studios in Berlin. I know you were hoping to finalise the purchase of the Baumann Studio before making a final decision, but the current offer from Film Forum is really very reasonable and I don't think I can put them off much longer. I've promised them a firm answer on Monday. What shall I say?

Priority: .... Action: ....

From: Munidar Singh, chief accountant (Cobrax International)
Subject: Smart move!

Shavi
You're a genius! How did you find out that the lead singer with The Purple Vedas is the favourite nephew of the Business Loans Director at the Bank of India? No wonder you scheduled a meeting to sign the band the week after we ask the bank to lend us 20 billion rupees. Give us the cash, uncle Anil, and junior gets to be a star! You'd better take very good care of these talented young musicians!

Priority: .... Action: ....

From: Danny Armstrong, CEO (Cobrax Gaming Division, USA)
Subject: A meeting with Nintendo

Shavi
Look, I know you're tied up with Sony Pictures right now, but I've finally managed to get a meeting with the guys from Nintendo at their head office in Kyoto. It was like getting an appointment with god! As you know, outside India, the computer games industry is now even bigger than movies and, frankly, I think it's the real future of this company. Can you fly out and join me in Japan the week after next?

Priority: .... Action: ....

From: Ajay Gupta, features editor, Mumbai Nights magazine
Subject: Affairs of the heart

Dear Mr Kumar
You might like to know that *Mumbai Nights* is planning to run an exclusive interview in its next edition with the actress Monica Masina, in which she promises to tell the inside story of your three-year relationship. In view of your recent engagement to Ms Sashi Ambani, I thought you might prefer not to see this interview published. If you'd like to contact me directly, the usual arrangement will be satisfactory.

Priority: .... Action: ....

From: Dr Ipsita Kamat, director (The Punarjanm Foundation)
Subject: A special request

Dear Mr Kumar
Allow me to introduce myself. I represent the charity Punarjanm. We work to promote involvement in the arts amongst disadvantaged, young people. Having heard that you are going to be in Delhi next week, I wanted to ask whether you might find a small space in your schedule to open our annual exhibition at 7 p.m. on Apr 19th. Now, we obviously wouldn't expect a speech at such short notice.

Priority: .... Action: ....

From: Sashi Ambani
Subject: Lunch

Hi Shavi
You've obviously disappeared again. Thanks for letting me know! Just remember that we're having lunch on Mon 24th. No excuses this time! I'm bringing some friends I'd like you to meet.
Oh, I got a phone call this morning from some guy at *Mumbai Nights* magazine. Said he might want to interview me 'to get my side of the story'. What story? Do you have any idea what he's talking about?

Priority: .... Action: ....

4   Do you notice any differences in the writing style of the e-mails? Think about formality, purpose, cultural background.

5   🔊 1.25 The following Monday you decide to check Shavi's voicemail. Take notes on the messages and discuss with your group what action, if any, you're going to take. How does this new information affect your previous arrangements?

Voicemail 1	Priority:	Action: ....
Voicemail 2	Priority:	Action: ....
Voicemail 3	Priority:	Action: ....
Voicemail 4	Priority:	Action: ....
Voicemail 5	Priority:	Action: ....
Voicemail 6	Priority:	Action: ....
Voicemail 7	Priority:	Action: ....
Voicemail 8	Priority:	Action: ....

6   Shavi unexpectedly phones in to the office while you're out, so you miss his call. He sends an e-mail instead. Turn to page 127 to read it and see if you've made the right decisions while he's been away!

7   Write a short e-mail to Shavi explaining the arrangements and decisions you've made in his absence.

5 WHAT WOMEN WANT

The future is female.

IAN PEARSON, BRITISH TELECOM FUTUROLOGIST

1 What importance does your company give to marketing specifically to women? Does it make sense to target women differently in all businesses or only in obvious things like fashion and cosmetics?

2 Do you know who your real customers are? Try the following quiz on gender and consumer spending. Answer each question with 'men' or 'women'.

Gender spenders

Who has 10% more credit cards?

Who opens 89% of new bank accounts?

Who makes 85% of car-buying decisions?

Who makes 92% of family holiday choices?

Who makes three-quarters of all house-purchase decisions?

Who makes more online purchases?

Who buys 66% of all PCs?

Who makes 85% of all consumer purchases?

3 Check your answers to the quiz on page 126. Are you especially surprised by any of the statistics?

4 🔊 1.26 Listen to business people from different industries talking about the importance of female spending power and answer the questions.

a What does the Swedish executive say about the difference between his male and female clients? Have you found the same thing? What's his name for this kind of marketing?

b What does the Chinese executive say about Confucian tradition? Are you the head of your household or do you share that role?

c What points does the Spanish executive make about families in northern Europe compared with his native Spain? What's the situation in your country?

d The American executive mentions two 'schools of thought'. Which one do you belong to? What advice does she give about marketing to women?

5 Work in small groups. Discuss what strategies (if any) the companies below use to attract female customers. What *could* they be doing to sell more to women?

> Apple   Ikea   Manchester United   McDonald's
> Starbucks   Virgin Airlines   Yamaha Motorcycles

6 With a partner discuss whether you think the following statements are true. Then read the article opposite and find out.

a On average, women earn about 25% less than men.

b Men shop around more before buying.

c Women take more notice of adverts than men do.

d In the last 30 years women's pay has increased 100 times more than men's.

e A third of married women make more money than their partners.

f When buying electronic goods women are not put off by technical details.

g Sometimes 'feminising' a product can be as simple as just changing the colour.

I AM WOMAN, **HEAR ME SHOP**

Rising female consumer power is changing the way companies design, make and market products. It's not **free-spending** teens or men aged 25–50. It's women. Thanks to their **purchasing power** and **decision-making authority**, working women have **emerged as a potent force in the marketplace**.

Women earn less money – 78 cents for every dollar a man gets. But they make more than 80% of buying decisions in all homes. And women shop differently from the way men do, **research more extensively** and are less likely to be influenced by ads. 'Today's woman is the chief purchasing agent of the family and marketers have to recognize that,' says Michael Silverstein, principal at Boston Consulting Group.

Smart companies already have. Product manufacturers are paying more attention to style and form and marketers are **shifting away from** TV ads in favor of promotional efforts women trust: reviews in women's magazines and spots on TV shows like *Oprah* and *Extreme Makeover: Home Edition*.

Women's decision-making authority has grown in part because more households **are headed** by women. Their buying power has grown, too. In the past three decades, men's income has barely moved – up just 0.6% – while women's has **soared** 63%. Some 30% of working women **out-earn** their husbands. The Employment Policy Foundation says the number of women earning $100,000 or more has **tripled** in the last 10 years.

That's why it was good news for Dell when Oprah's Favorite Things Shopping List included two of its products. In the two weeks after the episode, sales of Dell's plasma TVs **spiked**, accounting for 70% of its units sold.

Retailers have had to change their approach to the women's market as well. To give female shoppers the kind of information they're looking for, Best Buy is retraining its floor sales staff to talk to women in practical terms, not in **geekspeak**.

Marketers **warn** that retailers and manufacturers assume that marketing to women is as easy as changing the color of a product to pink. 'If you're serious about reaching the female consumer', says Silverstein 'you have to care about her and get to know what she desires.'

www.businessweek.com

7 Briefly discuss some of the implications of the article. Some of the phrases on the right may help you.

8 With a partner try to guess the meanings of the words and expressions in bold from their context.

9 Work in small groups. Choose *one* of the products or services below and decide

- what modifications you would make to appeal more to women
- what name you would give to your product or service
- how you would promote the product in order to gain maximum impact on female customers

banking services   beer   DIY products   laptops
MP3 player accessories   sportswear

> **Discussion phrase bank**
> I suppose what it means is …
> What we should probably all be doing is …
> We may also have to reconsider …
> If it's true, it will totally change the way we …

10 Present your ideas to the rest of your class and/or teacher. Who gets the 'What Women Want Award'?

11 Turn to page 127 to see how six real companies responded to the same challenges you faced in 9.

6 BUSINESS TRAVEL

There is not much to say about most airplane journeys. Anything remarkable must be disastrous, so you define a good flight by negatives: you didn't get hijacked, you didn't crash, you didn't throw up, you weren't late, you weren't nauseated by the food.

PAUL THEROUX, TRAVEL WRITER

1 Do you ever travel on business? If not, would you like to?

2 Combine one word from each section to make at least ten sentences. Start by making collocations from columns 3 and 4. Add your own ideas, if you like.

		late	interesting people
		getting	problems
		losing	jams
		the endless	lag
	don't like	flight	my luggage
	can't stand	meeting	food
	hate	tight	queues
	dread	missing	schedules
I	like	finding out	nights
	look forward to	strange	lost
	enjoy	language	my family
	love	jet	the office
		getting away from	about different cultures
		traffic	foreign places
		having	new experiences
		being away from	delays
		visiting	

3 Look at these ways of emphasising your opinions.

What I really like is finding out about different cultures.
What I hate most is being away from my family.
The thing I love most is visiting foreign places.
The best thing for me is getting out of the office for a few days.
The worst thing for me is flight delays.

Work in groups. Tell other people in the group what you like and dislike most about travelling.

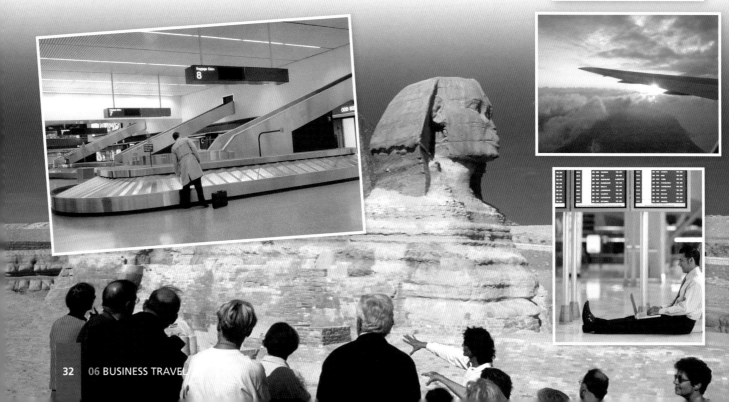

ON THE MOVE

1 🎧 1.27 Listen to eighteen short conversations involving people travelling on business. Where are the speakers? Write the numbers of the conversations under the correct location below.

In the taxi

☐ ☐ ☐

On the plane

☐ ☐ ☐

At check-in

☐ ☐ ☐

At customs

☐ ☐ ☐

In departures

☐ ☐ ☐

At the hotel

☐ ☐ ☐

2 Now match the halves of the following questions. They were all in the conversations you just listened to.

a Could I
b Could you
c Would you mind
d Can you tell me

e Would you please
f Could I ask you
g Do you think I could
h Is there somewhere I could

1 what time you stop serving dinner?
2 have your room number, please?
3 switch off your laptop now, please, sir?
4 not smoking, please?

5 to open your luggage, please, madam?
6 make sure your seatbelt is fastened?
7 send a fax from?
8 have an alarm call at half past six tomorrow morning?

3 Which first halves of the questions above could go before

… borrow your mobile?
… buy some stamps?
… hurry or I'll miss my plane?
… which terminal I need?
… lending me some money until I find a cashpoint?
… to wait outside for five minutes?

THE NIGHTMARE JOURNEY

How well do you cope on business trips? Work with a partner to sort out a series of problems. Speaker A see page 128. Speaker B see page 135.

TRANSATLANTIC CROSSING

1 If your company asked you to relocate to Britain or the States, which would you choose?

2 Look at the article below. What do you think the title means? Read the first paragraph to find out.

3 Now read the article and think about the questions on the right. Then discuss them with a partner.

The NY-Lon *life*

Ron Kastner is a classic New Yorker: first off the plane, first out of the airport. Carrying a single small bag, he walks straight through immigration and customs. He doesn't look like he's spent six hours in the air (business class will do that to you). He owns an apartment in the East Village in Manhattan, but tonight London is home: a flat in Belgravia, London's **wealthiest neighbourhood**. Kastner is a resident of a place called NY-Lon, a single city inconveniently separated by an ocean. He flies between the two cities up to five times a month. David Eastman lives there too. A Londoner who is a VP at Agency.com in New York, he travels the JFK–Heathrow route so often he's **on a first-name basis** with the Virgin Atlantic business class cabin crew.

As different as New York and London are, a growing number of people are living, working and playing in the two cities as if they were one. The cities **are drawn together by** a shared language and culture, but mostly by money – more of which **flows** through Wall Street and the City each day than all the rest of the world's financial centres combined. The **boom** in financial services attracted advertising agencies, accounting firms and management consultancies to both cities. Then came hotel and restaurant businesses, architecture and design, **real estate** and construction, air travel, tourism and other service industries.

Trevor Beattie, the London-based creative director of ad agency TBWA says 'New York and London are both so **trendy** and so modern now in terms of fashion, art, photography, music.' 'We dream about each other's cities,' says Joel Kissin, a New Zealander who after 25 years in London bought a **penthouse** on New York's Fifth Avenue. 'If you're in New York your dream is London, and if you're in London your dream is New York.'

Newsweek Magazine

a Is business class really that much better than economy?
b Would you like Ron Kastner's life?
c Do you have a favourite airline?
d Do New York and London share a culture? Or even a language?
e What other financial centres could eventually overtake London and New York?
f What are the other boom industries these days?
g Which two cities would you like to have homes in?

4 Try to guess the meanings of the words and expressions in **bold** from their context.

WHERE IN THE WORLD?

1 Where would a business traveller see the following? Half of them are in New York and half in London. Write NY or L next to each.

a   Walk/Don't walk ....
b   Freeway 2m ....
c   City center ....
d   Rest rooms ....
e   Underground ....
f   Lift out of order ....
g   Gas station ....
h   Motorway services 15m ....
i   Roundabout ahead ....

j   Open Mon thru Fri ....
k   Parking lot ....
l   Taxis: queue here ....
m   Car park full ....
n   Chemists ....
o   Truck stop ....
p   Colour copies 10p ....
q   Subway ....
r   Trolleys ....

2 ⊙ **1.28** Listen to the recording. Where do the conversations take place? Write the numbers in the boxes.

London ☐ ☐ ☐ ☐   New York ☐ ☐ ☐ ☐

IN ARRIVALS

1 ⊙ **1.29–1.32** Listen to four conversations in which people meet at the airport and answer the questions.

	Conversation 1	Conversation 2	Conversation 3	Conversation 4
Have the speakers met before?				
What topics do they discuss?				
What plans do they make?				

2 Complete the following by putting one word in each box. All the expressions were in the conversations you just listened to.

You	(a)	be waiting for me.	... if that's	(f)	with you.
You		be tired after your long flight.	I hope that's		
You		be Alan Hayes.	He	(g)	his apologies.
(b)		me take those for you.	Susan		her love.
		me help you with your bags.	Martin		his regards.
We	(c)	you into the Savoy.	Luckily, I managed to	(h)	some sleep on the plane.
We		a table for 1.30.	I thought we could		some lunch.
So,		are things?	Now, let's see if we can		a taxi.
So,	(d)	is married life?	I was expecting to		Mr Hill.
So,		is business?	Thanks for coming to	(i)	me.
So,		was your flight?	I'd like you to		Graham Banks.
I	(e)	upgraded.	Pleased to		you.
I've		a taxi waiting outside.			

3 The red-eye is a long-haul night flight. Work with a partner to practise meeting a colleague off the red-eye in New York. Speaker A see page 128. Speaker B see page 136.

TRAVEL TIPS

1 Bruce Tulgan is the CEO of Rainmaker Thinking Inc., the author of *Winning the Talent Wars* and an experienced business traveller. Complete his travel tips using the pairs of words in the box.

> business + pleasure   children + passengers   connections + flights   evening + destination
> magazines + newspapers   movies + view   receipts + cards   thing + problem
> travellers + lines   water + bags   work + plane

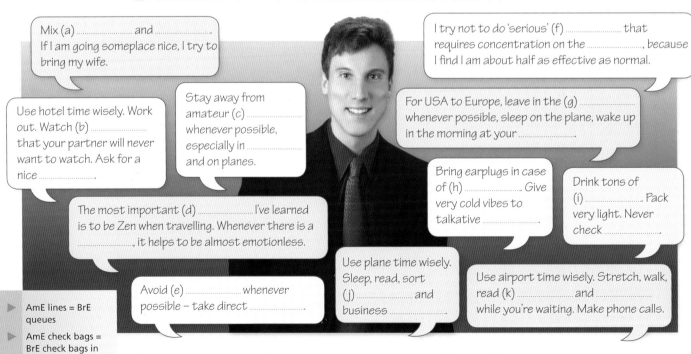

Mix (a) .... and .... If I am going someplace nice, I try to bring my wife.

Use hotel time wisely. Work out. Watch (b) .... that your partner will never want to watch. Ask for a nice ....

Stay away from amateur (c) .... whenever possible, especially in .... and on planes.

The most important (d) .... I've learned is to be Zen when travelling. Whenever there is a ...., it helps to be almost emotionless.

Avoid (e) .... whenever possible – take direct ....

Use plane time wisely. Sleep, read, sort (j) .... and business ....

I try not to do 'serious' (f) .... that requires concentration on the ...., because I find I am about half as effective as normal.

For USA to Europe, leave in the (g) .... whenever possible, sleep on the plane, wake up in the morning at your ....

Bring earplugs in case of (h) .... Give very cold vibes to talkative ....

Drink tons of (i) .... Pack very light. Never check ....

Use airport time wisely. Stretch, walk, read (k) .... and .... while you're waiting. Make phone calls.

▶ AmE lines = BrE queues

▶ AmE check bags = BrE check bags in

2 Discuss Tulgan's travel tips with a partner. Do you share his attitudes?

LANGUAGE LINKS

Vocabulary: Business trips

Think about the business trips you've been on in the past. The events below are listed in the order they usually happen. Complete them using the words in the box.

the airport check-in destination flight lounge movie plane shopping sleep	arrivals bags control customs hotel a meal night traffic your things

a   confirm your ....
b   take a taxi to ....
c   queue at ....
d   do some ....
e   wait in the departure ....
f   board the ....
g   watch the in-flight ....
h   try to get some ....
i   arrive at your ....

j   go through passport ....
k   collect your ....
l   go through ....
m   be met in ....
n   get stuck in the ....
o   check into your ....
p   unpack ....
q   go out for ....
r   get an early ....

Grammar: Polite question forms

When you make enquiries and requests, polite question forms and indirect questions are often more appropriate than imperatives and direct questions.

Imperative / direct question	Polite question form / indirect question
Where's the nearest taxi rank? (enquiry)	***Could you tell me** where the nearest taxi rank is?*
Why is the flight delayed? (enquiry)	***Do you think you could tell me** why the flight is delayed?*
Can I open the window? (request)	***Could I** open the window?* ***Do you mind if I** open the window?* ***Would you mind if I** opened the window?*
Help me with my bags! (request)	***Could you** help me with my bags?* ***Would you** help me with my bags?* ***Would you mind** helping me with my bags?*

1   You've just got a new boss. Your old boss was rude and a nightmare to work for. Fortunately, your new boss is much nicer. Look at some of the things your old boss used to say to you below and change them into what your new boss would probably say using a polite question form. Think carefully about word order and grammar.

a   Coffee!
    Could you ....
b   Remember to use the spell check in future!
    Would you please ....
c   I want a word with you in private!
    Could I ....
d   Where do I plug this mobile in?
    Is there somewhere ....
e   Check these figures again!
    Would you mind ....
f   How does this damn computer work?
    Could you tell ....
g   What's the phone code for Greece?
    Do you happen ....
h   You'll have to work overtime this evening.
    Do you think I could ask ....

2 When you're rushing around on business, it's easy to sound more aggressive than you mean to. Use polite question forms or indirect questions to make these enquiries and requests sound more polite.

a   I want a window seat.
b   Help me with my bags!
c   Where's a cashpoint?
d   Change this twenty-pound note!
e   Don't drive so fast!

f   Lend me your mobile!
g   I need to recharge my laptop somewhere.
h   You'll have to give me three separate receipts.
i   What time is it?
j   How far is it to the airport?

Phrase bank: Business travel

Complete the following expressions using the words and phrases in the box.

> Can you   Could I   Could you tell me   How   OK, I'll   Let me
> We've booked   What time do   You must be

In arrivals

(a)	→	waiting for me.
		Ms Suzuki.
		tired after your long flight.

(b)	→	are things?
		is business?
		was your flight?

(c)	→	take those for you.
		help you with your bags.
		see if I can get us a taxi.

(d)	→	you into the Hyatt.
		a table for 8.30.
		you onto a later return flight.

In the taxi

(e)	→	drop you off at your hotel first.
		pick you up at eight, shall I?
		just pay the driver.

(f)	→	change a fifty?
		drop me on the corner of New Street?
		give me a receipt, please?

At the hotel

(g)	→	change some money, please?
		have an alarm call at seven?
		have breakfast sent to my room?

(h)	→	you start serving breakfast?
		you stop serving dinner?
		I need to be out of my room?

(i)	→	how I get wifi in my room?
		how I can get a line out?
		if there's a bank near here?

7 HANDLING CALLS

The reason computers can do more work than people is that computers never have to answer the phone.

ANONYMOUS

1 Work in groups and discuss the questions.

a What percentage of your time at work do you spend on the phone?

b How many of the calls you make and receive are essential?

c Can you not answer the phone? When you answer, is it:
- out of curiosity – it might be some good news for a change?
- with a sigh of relief – it must be less boring than whatever you're doing?
- because you're so indispensable, no one else is capable of dealing with it?
- force of habit – the phone rings, you pick it up?
- because if you don't, no one else will?
- for fear of what might happen to you if you don't?

2 Read the statistics below. What points are they making about phone calls at work?

Time-management consultancy Priority Management found that 55% of all calls received by executives are less important than the work they interrupt and 21% are a complete waste of time. To test this theory, the Northwestern Mutual Life Assurance Company decided to block all incoming calls for just one hour a week and productivity rose by an amazing 23%.

According to an article in the Associated Press, an increasing number of the world's 2.5 million Blackberry owners are so used to incessant calls they report feeling 'phantom vibrations' even when they don't have their smartphones on them. Compulsive texting has also given them a medical condition known as 'Blackberry thumb'.

According to a survey by marketing and media consultancy BBDO, 15% of cell phone users are so addicted to their mobiles they are even prepared to interrupt love-making to answer them! 'People can't bear to miss a call' says Christine Hannis, head of communications for BBDO Europe. 'Everybody thinks the next call could be something really exciting.'

3 Use the pairs of words in the box to complete the sentences.

> busy + ring   disturbed + hold   expecting + pick up   important + leave
> out + divert   possible + answer   real + unplug

a   If I'm _____ , I just let the phone _____ .
b   If I don't want to be _____ , I tell my secretary to _____ all my calls.
c   If _____ , I try to _____ the phone before the fourth ring.
d   If I'm _____ a call from the boss, I _____ the phone immediately.
e   If I'm in the middle of something _____ , I let them _____ a voicemail.
f   If I'm having a _____ crisis, I _____ the damn thing!
g   If I'm going to be _____ of the office, I _____ my calls.

4 How many of the statements in 3 are true for you? Compare with a partner.

ASKING POLITELY

1 Use the words and phrases in the box to make seven useful expressions which start with *if*.

> can   got a minute   got time   not too busy
> not too much trouble   possible   would

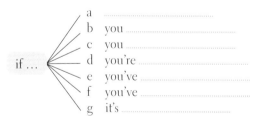

if …
a   _____
b   you _____
c   you _____
d   you're _____
e   you've _____
f   you've _____
g   it's _____

2 Divide the text into twelve things someone might phone to ask you to do. All the requests start with Could you …?

Could you … ?   emailmemyflightdetailsletmehaveacopyofthe
reportgetontooursuppliergetbacktomewithinthe
hourtakeaquicklookattheproposalarrangefor
somebodytomeetthematthestationsetupameeting
withtheheadsofdepartmentsendtheiraccounts
departmentareminderfixmeanappointmentbook
theconferenceroomforthreefaxthefiguresthrough
tomeorganiseatouroftheplantforsomevisitors

3 Work with a partner. Make and answer polite telephone requests using the language from 1 and 2 above. Speaker A see page 128. Speaker B see page 136.

UNEXPECTED PHONE CALLS

1 1.33–1.36 Listen to four telephone calls and match them to their description.

Call 1   a The caller is kept waiting.
Call 2   b A business contact calls to ask a favour.
Call 3   c A sales executive calls with a quote.
Call 4   d There is a communication breakdown.

2 Listen again and answer the questions.

Call 1
a What's the misunderstanding?
b How does the man receiving the call deal with the problem?
c Do you ever have difficulties answering calls in English?

Call 2
a How does the person receiving the call avoid another call?
b Do you think he is really in a meeting?
c Do you ever pretend you're busy just to get someone off the phone?

Call 3
a How would you describe the telephone manner of the person receiving the call?
b What is the caller calling about?
c Have you ever been treated unprofessionally on the phone?

Call 4
a Where did the speakers meet?
b What does the caller want?
c Have you ever received a phone call from someone you have met but can't remember?

3 All the expressions below were in the telephone conversations you just listened to. Can you remember the first three words of each expression? *It's* and *I'm* count as one word.

Call 1
a .... me through to Yves Dupont?
b .... don't understand.
c .... more slowly, please?

Call 2
a .... those prices you wanted.
b .... can't talk right now.
c .... you back – say, in an hour?

Call 3
a .... do for you?
b .... when he'll be back?
c .... speaking to?

Call 4
a .... bother you.
b .... who's calling?
c .... me a contact number?

4 Use the phrases in the box to make nine responses to the statements on the left. All the responses were in the telephone conversations you just listened to.

> back to you tomorrow   back later   to hear from you then
> if I can reach him on his cellphone   someone who speaks better English
> something out   that right away   what I can do   to you later

a   I need to be on the next flight to Oslo.
b   I keep calling Mr Kirk at his office and getting no answer.
c   I'm afraid Angela's not here at the moment.
d   Could you fax me a map of the city centre?
e   I've got to go, I'm afraid. I've got a meeting.
f   I should be able to give you an answer by this afternoon.
g   I need somebody to come and have a look at my PC.
h   I'm sorry, I don't speak German.
i   I need those figures within the next 24 hours.

OK, I'll …

see ....
see ....
call ....
do ....
speak ....
wait ....
sort ....
get ....
get ....

5 Work in pairs to deal with incoming phone calls. Speaker A see page 129. Speaker B see page 136.

6 a   Complete the diagram below with the names of four to six people who typically phone you at work to ask you to do things. Write down what they usually ask you to do. Include private calls if you like.

b   Categorise each call: urgent (must be done now), important (but can wait), social (just keeping in touch), a nuisance (time-wasting).

c   Swap diagrams with a partner and practise phoning each other. What excuses can you give to avoid doing what they ask? Or what can you offer to do to get them off the phone?

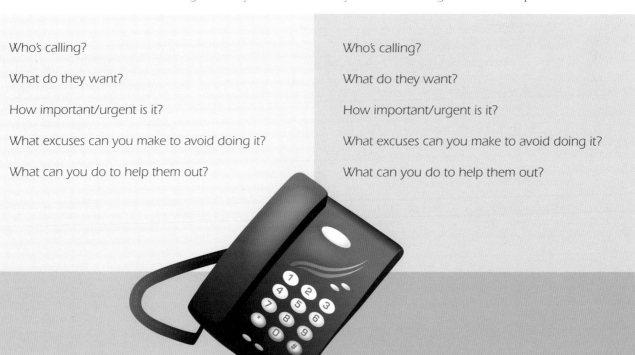

Who's calling?

What do they want?

How important/urgent is it?

What excuses can you make to avoid doing it?

What can you do to help them out?

Who's calling?

What do they want?

How important/urgent is it?

What excuses can you make to avoid doing it?

What can you do to help them out?

Who's calling?

What do they want?

How important/urgent is it?

What excuses can you make to avoid doing it?

What can you do to help them out?

Who's calling?

What do they want?

How important/urgent is it?

What excuses can you make to avoid doing it?

What can you do to help them out?

LANGUAGE LINKS

Vocabulary: Office life

Complete the poem about a day at the office using the verbs on the right. Use the rhyme to help you.

To do today

First, there's a report to [1].................	check
Then I'll [2]................. those figures through.	get
Flight details.	do
[3]................. e-mails.	fax
Don't worry, I'll [4]................. back to you.	
A memo now to [5].................	update
Nasty jobs to [6].................	circulate
Travel miles.	running
[7]................. files.	delegate
Can't stop now! I'm [8]................. late.	
[9]................. my calls till half past ten.	cleared
Should have [10]................. my desk by then.	grab
[11]................. a copy.	hold
[12]................. a coffee.	cancel
[13]................. English class again!	print
Messages to [14]................. to.	meet
One moment, please, I'll [15]................. you through.	arrange
[16]................. at three.	listen
[17]................. PC!	put
[18]................. another interview.	crash
[19]................. up clients at the station.	give
[20]................. a formal presentation.	make
[21]................. a list	break
Of deadlines [22].................	missed
[23]................. off the negotiation!	pick
[24]................. supplier in Milan –	postpone
[25]................. an appointment if you [26].................	get
[27]................. that phone!	contact
Must [28].................	fix
The teleconference with Japan.	can
[29]................. work at half past eight.	phone
Must [30]................. home – I may be late.	hit
[31]................. the car.	celebrate
[32]................. the bar.	finish
Damn it – why not [33]................. ?	leave
So, you [34]................. the presentation!	draft
[35]................. up the negotiation!	hand
[36]................. better?	screwed
[37]................. a letter.	blew
Now [38]................. in your resignation!	feeling

Is your office anything like this?

Grammar: *will*

Will is a modal verb (like *can*, *must* and *should*).

Affirmative			Negative		
I you he she it we they	will ('ll)	work	I you he she it we they	will not (won't)	work

Interrogative		
will won't	I you he she it we they	work?

1 Correct the following sentences using the information above.

a   Do you will help me?

b   Stop making personal calls or I'll to charge you for them.

c   I expect the company will to do well.

d   I don't will accept anything less than 2%.

e   Don't worry, he wills phone you back within the hour.

f   I'll to take that call, if you like.

g   I'll sending the figures right away.

2 Match the corrected sentences in 1 to their functions below.

1   a prediction about the future ☐
2   a spontaneous decision/reaction ☐
3   an offer ☐
4   a request ☐
5   a promise ☐
6   a refusal ☐
7   a threat ☐

3 Match the following to make five short conversations.

a **A** I really need that report today.
b **A** My plane gets in at seven.
c **A** I'm just off to a meeting.
d **A** Eva's off sick today.
e **A** She wants to see you – now!
   B I'll have to speak to her, I'm afraid.
   B I'll be right there.
   B I'll finish it this morning.
   B I'll phone you later, then.
   B I'll come and meet you at the airport.
   A Good. I'll tell her you're on your way.
   A Fine, I'll just give you my mobile number.
   A OK, I'll see if I can reach her at home.
   A Great. I'll see you there, then.
   A OK, I'll look forward to seeing it.

You can often qualify sentences containing *will* with *if*.

* *I'll try to get you onto an earlier flight if I can.*
* *If you've got time, I'll show you round the factory.*
* *I'll send you a copy of our brochure if you like.*
* *If you prefer, I'll meet you at the station.*

4 Complete the conversation using the pairs of words in the box.

> busy + later   desk + look   give + right   leave + OK
> make + know   nothing + away   try + time   wait + details

József knocks on his boss's door and goes in. Tom is working hard at the computer and doesn't look up.

József Oh, sorry. If you're (a) _____ , I'll come back _____ .

Tom No, no, come in, József. If you (b) _____ me two minutes, I'll be _____ with you. … I'll just save what I'm doing. … Now, what can I do for you?

József Well, I just need you to check and sign these documents for me.

Tom Sure. If you leave them on my (c) _____ , I'll have a _____ at them this afternoon.

József Fine. I'll just put them here, then.

Tom By the way, it's not urgent, but did you call Budapest about next week's meeting?

József Er, no. I'll (d) _____ to do it before lunch if I have _____ .

Tom OK.

József And I'll get someone to (e) _____ the travel arrangements if you let me _____ how many people are coming.

Tom Oh, right. I think it's four. If you (f) _____ a second, I'll give you the _____ . … Yeah, here we are. They're sending their unit manager and three sales executives.

József OK, I'll see to it.

Tom Good. And I'll (g) _____ it to you to sort out the conference room, if that's _____ . We'll need the usual AV equipment and refreshments.

József Of course. Well, if there's (h) _____ else, I'll get on with it right _____ .

Tom Thanks, József.

Phrase bank: Polite requests

Look at the following requests. Which refer to people, which to events and which to documents or figures? Tick the boxes.

Polite requests			P	E	D
		(a) get on to	☐	☐	☐
		(b) take a quick look at	☐	☐	☐
		(c) let me have a copy of	☐	☐	☐
you can		(d) organise	☐	☐	☐
you're not		(e) set up a meeting with	☐	☐	☐
If too busy	could you	(f) fax through	☐	☐	☐
you've got a minute		(g) check the arrangements for	☐	☐	☐
		(h) get back to	☐	☐	☐
		(i) send them	☐	☐	☐

Offering assistance

Complete the following offers of assistance with the verbs in the box. You'll need some more than once.

> call   do   get   see   sort   speak

		(a) _____ what I can do.	
		(b) _____ on to it straightaway.	
		(c) _____ if I can reach her on her mobile.	
		(d) _____ something out.	
don't worry.		(e) _____ back to you later.	
OK, no problem. I'll		(f) _____ you back with the figures.	
leave it with me.		(g) _____ to the people in marketing about it.	
		(h) _____ what I can, all right?	
		(i) _____ on to accounts.	
		(j) _____ someone to deal with it.	

Ending a call

Complete the expressions below using the words in the box.

> catch   have   get   got   keep   speak

a I'll _____ to go, I'm afraid.
b Well, I won't _____ you. I'm sure you're very busy.
c OK, I'll let you _____ on. _____ to you later.
d Look, I've _____ a meeting. _____ you later, OK?

8 MAKING DECISIONS

Nothing is more difficult, and therefore more precious, than to be able to decide.

NAPOLEON BONAPARTE

1 Are you good at making quick decisions or are you a more methodical thinker? Answer yes, no or it depends to the following in under 90 seconds.

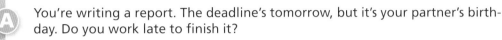

How decisive are you?

A You're writing a report. The deadline's tomorrow, but it's your partner's birthday. Do you work late to finish it?

B You're with a major client who wants to stay out clubbing all night. You don't want to. Do you politely say good night?

C You're shopping for a suit, but the only one you like costs twice what you want to pay. Do you buy it anyway?

D A friend in banking gives you an investment tip. You could make or lose a lot of money. Do you take the risk?

E You're beating your boss at golf and he's a really bad loser. You could drop a shot or two. Do you?

F A good friend is starting her own business. She asks you if she can borrow $10,000. You can afford it. Do you lend it to her?

G You're offered twice your current salary to take a boring job in a beautiful city. Do you take it?

For an analysis of your answers see page 129.

2 What kind of decisions do you have to make at work? What's the hardest decision you've ever had to make?

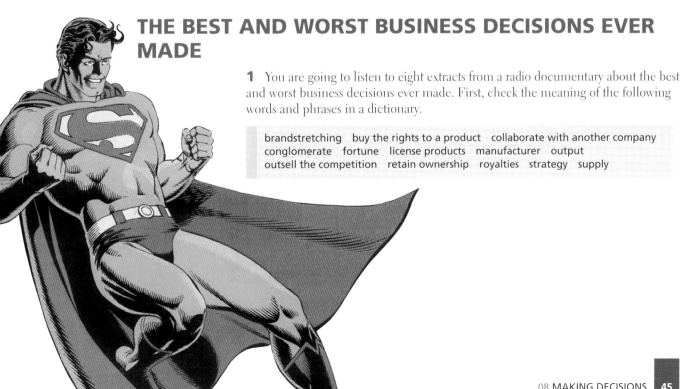

THE BEST AND WORST BUSINESS DECISIONS EVER MADE

1 You are going to listen to eight extracts from a radio documentary about the best and worst business decisions ever made. First, check the meaning of the following words and phrases in a dictionary.

> brandstretching   buy the rights to a product   collaborate with another company
> conglomerate   fortune   license products   manufacturer   output
> outsell the competition   retain ownership   royalties   strategy   supply

2 🔘 **1.37** Listen and write down the name of the company or product referred to.

a .... c .... e .... g ....

b .... d .... f .... h ....

3 Listen again. What do these figures refer to?

a $1
   1 bn

b 9%
   50%

c 1991
   21,000

d 1955
   $35,000

e 1961
   2 secs

f 1938
   $130

g 1977
   $100bn

h 1m kg
   70%

4 What are the best and the worst decisions you've ever made at work?

THE DECISION-MAKING PROCESS

1 Put the following stages in the decision-making process into the most likely order.

- consider the options   ☐
- define your objectives   ☐
- collect information   ☐

- monitor the effects   ☐
- implement your decision   ☐
- choose the best course of action   ☐

2 Look at the agenda for a decision-making meeting on the left. Decide which two statements below were made at each stage in the meeting.

a **We're here to decide** whether to go ahead with the project.
b **One option would be** to do detailed market research.
c **The most important thing is**: can we make this profitable?
d **The advantage of** doing market research is we reduce risk.
e **Have a look at** these figures.
f **Above all, we must** be sure there's a market for our service.
g **What we've agreed, then, is to** start marketing this service now.
h **Another alternative is to** offer the service on a trial basis.
i **On the other hand**, market research takes time.
j **Our aim is to** find out if there's a good chance of success.
k **As you can see**, client feedback is very positive.
l **So, that's it – we're going ahead** with the project.

AGENDA

1 Objectives   ☐ ☐
2 Priorities   ☐ ☐
3 Data analysis   ☐ ☐
4 Alternatives   ☐ ☐
5 Pros & cons   ☐ ☐
6 Final decision ☐ ☐

THE LANGUAGE OF MEETINGS

1 The following expressions are useful in meetings, but some letters are missing from the final words. When you have completed them, the letters down the middle spell out a good piece of advice for the chairperson!

a   OK, let's get down to …
b   Can I just stop you there for a …
c   I totally …
d   Perhaps I didn't make myself …
e   What do you …

f   With respect, you don't quite seem to …
g   I agree with you up to a …

h   If I could just finish what I was …
i   OK, let's move …
j   I'm afraid that's completely out of the …
k   Perhaps we can come back to this …

l   Maybe we should take a short …
m   Does anyone have any …
n   Can I just come in …
o   Sorry, I don't quite see what you …
p   I think that's as far as we can go …
q   We'll have to break off here, I'm …

2 🔊 **1.38** Listen to an extract from a meeting about a company relocating to the UK and tick the expressions in 1 as you hear them. Which one is not used?

3 Which expressions in 1 are used to:

1	open a meeting ☐	8	disagree ☐
2	ask for an opinion ☐	9	half-agree ☐
3	interrupt ☐ ☐	10	explain ☐ ☐
4	prevent interruption ☐	11	delay ☐
5	get some fresh air ☐	12	ask for ideas ☐
6	speed things up ☐	13	reject a proposal ☐
7	ask for clarification ☐	14	close a meeting ☐ ☐

4 Some managers are facing a cash flow crisis. Match the halves of the statements in the conversation below.

a   I just don't see how we can go on
b   No, I think we'll be OK,
c   Maybe, but unless we do,
d   In my opinion, we'd save a lot of money,
e   Look, we're in a hi-tech industry. If we cut wages,
f   No, wait. If we gave them a stake in the company,
g   No, no, no. How is that going to work,
h   OK. Look, if we can't reach agreement on this,

1   I suggest we break off here.
2   they might stay on. Or how about profit share?
3   our people will simply go and work for the competition.
4   if we keep overspending like this.
5   if we aren't making any profit?
6   we're going to be in serious financial trouble.
7   if we just reduced wages. Our wages bills are enormous!
8   providing we get this Russian contract.

THE DECISION-MAKING MEETING

1 One of the toughest businesses is the film business, with millions of dollars made or lost on a single decision: who to cast as the star. First, work with a partner to match up and check the meaning of the collocations below in a dictionary. Then read the article.

a	current	brand	d	combined	earnings	g	commercial	news
b	profit	turnover	e	key	awareness	h	front-page	series
c	bestselling	margins	f	brand	factor	i	film	success

NOBODY
does it better

The James Bond movies are the longest-running, highest grossing film series in history. Current turnover stands at over $6 billion. In fact, the combined earnings of the *Star Wars* and *Star Trek* series and the most successful single film ever, *Gone with the Wind*, still fall $750 million short of Bond at the box office. It is said that half the population of the world has seen a James Bond movie.

Bond is also the most profitable film series ever. The special effects may cost much more these days, but the films still enjoy 30% profit margins, not including merchandising. Even Stephen Spielberg's blockbusters *ET*, *Jurassic Park* and the *Indiana Jones* series can't compete.

Bond appeals to men and women, adults and children alike. *From Russia with Love* was one of President Kennedy's top ten favourite books. But James Bond is no longer just a Hollywood hero; he's a bestselling brand.

Although the actor playing Bond has changed several times over the last forty years, and although there are no more Ian Fleming novels on which to base the films, the series goes on and on.

The film business is risky – seven out of ten movies lose money. But brand awareness of Bond is so strong that even people who don't like the films instantly recognise the Bond music, fast cars and glamorous women. They know that James takes his vodka martini 'shaken not stirred'.

And then there is Bond himself – certainly the key factor in 007's commercial success. With so much money at stake, the choice of a new Bond always makes front-page news. Not everyone agreed in 1962 with the decision to choose a virtually unknown Sean Connery as the first James Bond, and Connery was only paid £7,000 for *Dr No*, but it was perhaps one of the best recruitment decisions ever made. And the rest, as they say, is history.

2 According to the article, what are the main reasons for the success of the Bond films? Tick the correct answers.

the special effects	☐	the actors playing Bond	☐
the sex and violence	☐	the novels the films are based on	☐
the 007 brand name	☐	the Bond character	☐

3 Now work in small groups to decide who's going to be the next Bond! First, make a list of the qualities you think an ideal Bond actor should have. Then look at the actor profiles on the next page and read the agenda of the casting meeting. You may find the expressions on pages 46 and 47 useful in your decision-making meeting.

CASTING MEETING

1 Appoint a chairperson

2 Review actor profiles

3 Discuss alternatives

4 🔘 **1.39** Listen to interview extracts

5 Make final decision

name and age
Peter Aston-Sharpe 43

nationality
English

marital status
divorced

height and build
1.83m slim

physical pursuits
scuba-diving, pilot's licence

experience
Leading actor for the last 8 years with the Royal Shakespeare Company, Stratford. Has also done a lot of TV work, playing mostly romantic leads in costume dramas. Has starred in two fairly low-budget, but successful, British films.

achievements
Won an Oscar nomination for his part in *Shadows*, a psychological thriller.

usual fee
Doesn't earn much in the theatre, but was paid $750,000 for his last TV series.

comments
Some say he can be moody and difficult to work with. Ex-wife says 'he's just the sort of male chauvinist pig you need to play Bond.'

name and age
Sam Landon 39

nationality
American

marital status
single

height and build
1.90m muscular

physical pursuits
body-building, kick-boxing

experience
Discovered by Hollywood while working as a cocktail waiter in LA. Has starred in several high-action blockbusters, although his last film, a comedy, lost money. Best-known for his cop movie character, Detective Eddie Stone, in the late 90s.

achievements
Surprise winner of an Oscar for Best Supporting Actor for his role as a disabled war veteran.

usual fee
A run of box-office hits behind him, he is now firmly established as a $20 million-a-film actor.

comments
Seems easy-going, with none of the ego problems big stars usually have. Has calmed down a lot since his early 'hell-raising' days.

name and age
Jon McCabe 31

nationality
Scottish

marital status
single

height and build
1.83m athletic

physical pursuits
shooting, climbing, hang-gliding

experience
Ex-European light-heavyweight boxing champion turned male model. Very little acting, but his recent supporting role in a London gangster movie won praise on both sides of the Atlantic. Soon to star in the new Jaguar commercials.

achievements
Voted 'World's Sexiest Man' two years running by *She* magazine.

usual fee
As a model, he earns $15,000 a day, but is prepared to do his first Bond film for just $200,000.

comments
A charismatic and intelligent man, who knows what he wants and usually gets it. His failure to win a world boxing title is something he still refuses to talk about.

name and age
Charles Fox 35

nationality
English

marital status
married

height and build
1.88m muscular

physical pursuits
canoeing, passion for motorbikes

experience
Big British star who has never quite lived up to his potential. Lost out to Val Kilmer for the lead in *The Saint*, but made a successful comedy with Julia Roberts last year. 'Britain's favourite sex symbol.'

achievements
Won a television award for his role in a long-running hospital drama.

usual fee
Makes $3–5 million per film.

comments
Apparently desperate to get the Bond part. He wanted it last time it was on offer, but was unable to break his contract with another studio. According to his agent, 'Charles is obsessed with Bond.'

4 If you are unable to reach a decision, see page 130 for Plan B.

LANGUAGE LINKS

Vocabulary: Money and markets

1 All the verbs and adjectives in the box can be used to talk about bigger or smaller increases and decreases in prices. Fit them into the diagram.

> ~~cut~~ falling freeze hike plunging raise rising slash soaring stable

	Verbs		Adjectives	
+	a		f	
↑	b		g	
0	c	prices	h	prices
↓	d cut		i	
−	e		j	

2 Put the two sets of adjectives below in order of scale from the smallest to biggest.

> huge   modest   reasonable   record

	The company made a	a	....	profit.
+		b	....	
↕		c	....	
−		d	....	

> crippling   heavy   moderate   slight

	The company suffered	e	....	losses.
+		f	....	
↕		g	....	
−		h	....	

3 Make collocations containing the word 'market' by writing the following words before or after it.

> ~~break into~~   be forced out of   challenger   competitive declining   dominate   enter   flood   forces   growing leadership   mass   niche   ~~research~~   saturation   share supply

break into (the)   *research*

market

4 Complete the following sentences using some of the collocations you made in 3.

a Market .... occurs when the demand for a product is satisfied but you continue to .... that market.

b Even a very small or .... market can be profitable if you totally .... it.

c Pepsi has always been the No 2, the market .... threatening Coke's global market ....

d The PC market has been so fiercely .... that many European firms have .... it altogether.

Grammar: Conditionals (future reference)

You can connect two related ideas in one sentence using *if*. Look at the dialogue below.

A **If *we take on another project***, we'll need more staff.
B But we'll need a bigger office **if *we employ more people***.
C No, not **if *we hire teleworkers***, we won't.

The sentences above are examples of conditionals. The *if*-clause (underlined) introduces a possibility (e.g. *we take on another project*). The main clause shows what the speaker thinks the result of that possibility will be (e.g. *we'll need more staff*).

The *if*-clause can come at the beginning or end of a sentence. When it comes at the end, there is no comma (,) after the main clause.

1 Match the sentence halves in the following extracts from a meeting about a product that is still in development.

Extract 1

A Look, Jean, the product is still in development. If we rush the launch through,

B I realise that. But if I gave you another six weeks,

A Well, we might be able to

B Ian, you know if I give you more people,

A Well, if you can't give me any more staff,

B You realise we may lose our technological lead

A Yes, but I'd prefer to be second onto the market

B Hm. You wouldn't say that

a could we have it ready for the Seoul Trade Fair?

b if it means we make a superior product.

c if we don't get this product out before our competitors?

d we won't have time to run the final tests.

e if we had more people working on the project.

f there's no way we're going to be ready. I'm sorry.

g if you had to deal with the marketing department!

h I'll have to take them off other projects. And I can't do that.

Extract 2

A Well, if we're going to meet our deadline without extra staff,
B OK, fair enough. And if I get you that bigger budget,
A I promise. But if we spent more,
B We'll let Finance worry about that. If we can solve this problem with a bit of overtime,
A Excellent. Because we're missing the publicity event of the year
B You're telling me! If we didn't have a stand at the Fair,
A OK. That's decided then. I'll get us to the launch stage on time
B Great. Now, if you're not rushing off home,

a it would be a disaster.
b if we're not at Seoul.
c can you promise me we'll be ready on schedule?
d I'll buy you that drink I owe you!
e I'll do what I can to get you the budget for that.
f wouldn't that affect our profit margins?
g I'm going to need a bigger budget, Jean, so I can pay my people overtime.
h if you get head office to OK a budget increase.

2 Look again at the extracts in 1. Which of the grammatical structures below come in the *if*-clause, which in the main clause and which in both?

> *can* + infinitive   *could* + infinitive   *going to* + infinitive   *may* + infinitive   *might* + infinitive
> Past Simple   Present Continuous   Present Simple   *will* + infinitive   *would* + infinitive

if-clause	main clause

As well as *if*, we can use other words to connect two related ideas in a conditional sentence.

- **Unless** *we reach a decision by this afternoon, it may be too late. (= If we don't reach a decision …)*
- *The product will be ready in time* **provided/providing (that), as/so long as** *everyone does overtime. (= … if, but only if, everyone does overtime.)*
- **Suppose/Supposing** *the tourist industry is affected, what'll we do then? (= What if the tourist industry …)*

3 Rephrase the sentences below using the word(s) in brackets.

a If they offer you a promotion, what will you do? (supposing)
b We'll go ahead with the new design, but only if the market research is positive. (provided that)
c We'll lose the contract if we don't lower the price. (unless)
d You can go to the conference, but only if you give a talk. (as long as)

Phrase bank: Decision-making

Match each of the six stages of a decision-making meeting to two things you might say.

a Define your objectives

b Set priorities

c Analyse data

d Present alternatives

e Weigh up pros and cons

f Make final decision

1 **The most important thing is**: will there be synergy?
2 **As you can see**, they do have exactly the expertise we need.
3 **So, that's it**: we've decided to go ahead with a full alliance.
4 **One option would be to** work with them on just this project.
5 **We're here to** decide whether to proceed with this alliance.
6 **The main advantage of** an alliance is reduced costs.
7 **Have a look at** this feasibility study.
8 **What we've agreed, then, is to** accept their proposal.
9 **Our aim is to** reach a final decision by the end of this meeting.
10 **Another alternative is to** form a more strategic alliance.
11 **On the other hand**, this would be a very serious step to take.
12 **Above all**, we must be sure our two cultures are compatible.

a ☐ ☐   b ☐ ☐   c ☐ ☐   d ☐ ☐   e ☐ ☐   f ☐ ☐

TOY STORY

1 Business writer Watts Wacker famously said: 'A brand is a promise'. What do you think he meant? Think of some well-known brands. What 'promises' are they making?

2 There are many ways customers can lose confidence in a company. Which of the following customer concerns about a product do you think could most seriously affect a business? Discuss with a partner.

The product is found to be…

> defective   overpriced   unreliable   unsafe
> unethically produced   environmentally unfriendly

3 Look at the homepage at the Thompson Toys corporate website. What kind of image is the company presenting? What message is it trying to communicate about its brand and its values?

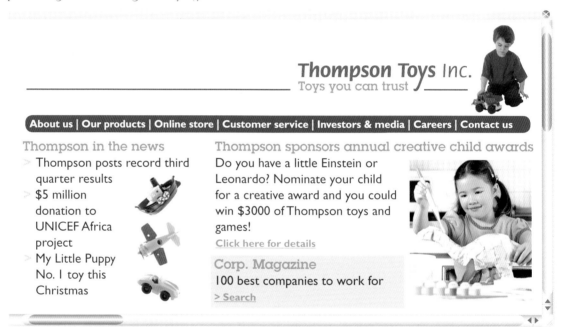

4 🔊 2.01 Fiona Sheridan, vice-president of Asian Operations for Thompson, is flying to a meeting in Shanghai when she receives an unexpected phone call from the safety lab in Shenzhen. Listen to the call and answer the questions.

a   What customer complaints has the company received over the last few weeks?
b   What are the results of the tests lab director, Michael Fu, has been running?
c   How many toys may be affected?
d   What is Fiona planning to do as soon as she touches down in Shanghai?

5 Two days later, Simon Anderson, head of public relations, flies out from head office in Philadelphia to join Fiona for a second meeting with the Chinese plant owner in Hangzhou. Look at the cross-cultural comparison of North American and Chinese behaviour in meetings. With a partner, try to predict some of the communication problems they may face.

Prime objective:	Business	USA		China		Relationship
Directness:	Direct	USA			China	Indirect
Formality:	Informal		USA		China	Formal
Commitment:	Contractual	USA		China		Personal

6 🔊 2.02 Now listen to an extract from the meeting in Hangzhou. How would you describe the atmosphere?

7 What's the probable cause of the problems? Whose fault do you think it is?

8 Do you agree with Fiona's decision? Do you think relations will be damaged with the Chinese?

9 Read the headlines that filled the international press in the weeks after Fiona Sheridan ordered the product recall. How has the situation worsened?

Toxic scare: 1.5m toys removed from shelves

My Little Poisonous Puppy?

Inquiry into safety standards at Thompson's Chinese factories

Thompson toys in crisis in run-up to Christmas

Concerned parents boycott Thompson Toys throughout USA

Who's to blame? | **Thompson share price falls by 39%**

TOYING WITH OUR CHILDREN'S HEALTH: ANOTHER PRODUCT RECALL AT THOMPSON TOYS

10 🔊 2.03 Listen to Fiona Sheridan phoning Thompson's CEO, Daniel Cleveland, about the last headline above. What's the latest news? Take notes.

Thompson CEO Daniel J Cleveland

- ....-million unit product recall announced this ....
- Defective magnets possibly due to ....
- Similar problem in .... led to .... million products being withdrawn from sale.
- Chinese manufacturers accusing Thompson of over .... and damaging their ....
- Questions being raised about .... conditions in Asian plants and Thompson's .... margins. Possible global .... on the sale of Thompson Toys pending investigations.

11 Work in small teams. You are Thompson's PR department and have been instructed by your boss, Simon Anderson, to write a one-minute personal statement from the CEO to be video-filmed and posted on the customer service page of Thompson's website. The CEO's message should sound apologetic, but confident, and reassure parents that the company has withdrawn all unsafe products from sale and is thoroughly investigating the cause of the problems.

12 As the situation worsens, your PR team decides to hold an international press conference in New York to reinforce its message that the company has everything under control and that customers have no cause for alarm. Work together to predict the kind of questions you may be asked by members of the press and how you will answer them.

Press conference tips

- maintain a friendly atmosphere – smile and use the questioner's name
- create rapport with the questioner – you're a parent too, share their concerns etc.
- try to sound apologetic but confident
- be totally clear in your explanations
- do not speculate about anything you cannot answer
- do not react to hostile questions in a hostile way
- try to rephrase negative questions in a more positive way
- don't get angry if you have to repeat yourself
- make sure you say what you came to say, regardless of the questions you're asked
- thank your audience for attending at the end

> **Useful phrases**
>
> **Welcome question**
> I'm glad you raised that point.
> I'm happy to answer that one.
>
> **Defer answer**
> Can we get back to you on that?
> I'm afraid we don't have the answer to that yet.
>
> **Decline to answer**
> We're not in a position to comment on that.
> Sorry, I'm not prepared to answer that at the moment.

13 🔊 2.04 Listen to the questions from the press one by one and decide which member of your team will deal with them. Don't be too surprised if you get a few questions you weren't expecting! The phrases on the right may help you to answer confidently and diplomatically.

9 NEW WORLD ORDER

When I was growing up, my parents used to say to me 'Finish your dinner – people in China are starving.' I, by contrast, find myself wanting to say to my daughters: 'Finish your homework – people in China and India are starving for your jobs.'

THOMAS FRIEDMAN, NEW YORK TIMES COLUMNIST AND AUTHOR OF *THE WORLD IS FLAT*

1 Do you think the developed economies, like the USA, Japan and Germany, see emerging economies, like China and India, more as a threat or as an opportunity? Are we seeing a global power shift?

2 Complete the following newspaper headlines using the pairs of words in the box.

boom + prices   deficit + day   drain + workers   explosion + threat   imports + markets
outsourcing + jobs   rate + figures   resources + recovery   shortage + sector   surplus + per cent

A US trade .... with China grows by $1 billion a ....

B Skills .... in Chinese business ....

C Natural .... drive .... in Brazil

D Chinese trade .... up 500 ....

E CHEAP ASIAN .... FLOOD WESTERN ....

F Population .... poses global ....

G China's economic growth hits double ....

H Russian economic .... as gas .... soar

I .... killing .... say US steel unions

J BRAIN .... AS EDUCATED .... LEAVE INDIA

3 With a partner choose some of the headlines in 2 and discuss their short- and long-term implications.

4 ♫ 2.05–2.08 Listen to business people from the so-called BRIC emerging economies of Brazil, Russia, India and China talking about some of the strengths and weaknesses of their economies and take notes.

	Speaker 1: Brazil	Speaker 2: Russia	Speaker 3: India	Speaker 4: China
Strengths				
Weaknesses				

5 Compare notes. Which of the BRICs would be the best to (a) outsource to, (b) trade with, (c) relocate to?

6 Work in groups of three. Each of you should read one of the articles below and think of a title for it.

1

Wang Zhongjun is **loaded**. He wears Prada shoes, Versace jackets, and a Piaget watch. He smokes Cohiba cigars from Cuba. He drives a white Mercedes-Benz SL600, a silver BMW Z8, and a red Ferrari 360. His art collection includes hundreds of sculptures and paintings. Value: $30 million or so. Home sweet home is a 22,000 square-foot mansion north of Beijing with antique British and French furniture, a billiard room with bar, and an indoor pool. 'Entrepreneurs in China today feel much safer than before,' says Wang, a 45-year-old movie producer. 'We are more accepted by the media, government, and society today.'

That's for sure. Even though Deng Xiaoping declared that getting rich is **glorious** nearly three decades ago, just a few years back China's millionaires **were running scared**. Now China is embracing them. More than 300,000 Chinese have a net worth over $1 million, excluding property, according to Merrill Lynch & Co. And mainland millionaires control some $530 billion in assets.

www.businessweek.com

2

These days we all talk about the rise of Asia and the challenge to America, but **it may well turn out** that the most important trend of the next decade will be the economic decline of Europe.

It's often noted that the European Union has a combined gross domestic product approximately the same as that of the United States. But the EU has 170 million more people. **If present trends continue**, in 20 years the average US citizen will be twice as rich as the average Frenchman or German.

In March 2000, EU heads of state agreed to make the European Union 'the most competitive and **dynamic knowledge-driven economy** by 2010'. Today this looks like a joke.

Talk to top-level scientists about the future of scientific research and they will rarely even mention Europe. In the biomedical sciences Europe **is not on the map**. The chief executive of a large pharmaceutical company told me that in 10 years, the three most important countries for his industry will be the United States, China and India.

Washington Post

3

America is still standing. Despite the emergence of India and China, **the dot-com bust** and **the war on terror**, the United States remains **the economic powerhouse of the world**. Why? Because of innovation. Why? Because innovation creates temporary monopolies which **allow you to print money**. Why are Americans so innovative and, as a result, so **affluent**?

The answer is **straightforward**. America's success lies in its ability to attract the greatest talent. The brightest minds from China, India, Russia, Brazil and elsewhere **flock** to the US. Why? Because the US is an *idea*, not a country. Anyone can become an American. It takes two or three generations to become German, Spanish, Swedish or French. If you can't attract the best people, how are you going to become the world's most innovative place?

Funky Business Forever
by Jonas Ridderstråle and Kjell Nordström

7 Summarise the article you read and explain your choice of title to the others in your group.

8 Briefly discuss the issues. Some of the phrases on the right may help you.

9 With a partner try to guess the meanings of the words and expressions **in bold** from their context.

10 Prepare to talk for a minute or two about how competition from emerging markets has affected or may affect your industry in the future.

So far … Up until now … Over the last / next few years … At the moment … Looking further ahead …

> **Discussion phrase bank**
> I basically agree with the point about …
> I totally disagree with the point about …
> I seriously question the point about …
> I think the most significant thing is …

10 SMALL TALK

A friendship founded on business is better than a business founded on friendship.

JOHN D ROCKEFELLER, AMERICAN INDUSTRIALIST

1 What exactly is small talk? How important do you think it is in business?

2 How culturally aware are you? Try a cultural sensitivity test. Speaker A see page 130. Speaker B see page 137.

GETTING DOWN TO BUSINESS

1 In *When Cultures Collide* cross-cultural consultant Richard D Lewis talks about the role of small talk in international business. The diagram below shows how long it takes different nationalities to get down to business. Try to complete the chart with the names of the countries in the box.

> Finland   France   Germany   Japan   Spain & Italy   UK   USA

a .... ⟶
Formal introduction. Sit down. Begin.

b .... ⟶
Formal introduction. Cup of coffee. Sit down. Begin.

c .... ⟶
Informal introduction. Cup of coffee. Joke. Begin.

d .... ⟶
Formal introduction. Cup of tea and biscuits. 10 mins small talk (weather, sport). Casual beginning.

e .... ⟶
Formal introduction. 15 mins small talk (politics, scandal). Begin.

f .... ⟶
Formal introduction. Formal seating. Green tea. 15–20 mins small talk (pleasantries). Signal from superior. Begin.

g .... ⟶
20–30 mins small talk (football, family) while others arrive. Begin when everyone's there.

| Mins | 0 | 5 | 10 | 15 | 20 | 25 | 30 |

2 🔊 **2.09–2.15** Listen to extracts from seven meetings. Check your answers in 1 by matching each extract to the correct country.

3 Listen again and answer the questions. There is one question for each extract.
a Where exactly is Tom Pearson asked to sit?
b How long is Dr Alan Winter going to spend in Berlin?
c What was Miss Sterling's father's job?
d What kind of snack is served at the meeting?
e Why was Catherine in Finland before?
f In the joke, what score do both the man and the woman get in the test?
g What commonly happens in their meetings these days?

4 Place your own nationality on the chart, if it's not there already. If it is there, do you agree with where it's placed?

5 Look at these excerpts from the conversations you just listened to and <u>underline</u> the best grammatical choice. Then listen again and check.
a **A Did you try / Have you tried** green tea before, Mr Pearson?
   B Er, yes I **did / have**. I **had / have had** it last time I **was / have been** here. I like it very much.
b **A** I'd like to introduce you all to Dr Alan Winter, who **came / has come** over from the Atlanta office to spend a few days at our research centre. Welcome to Berlin, Dr Winter.
   B Thank you very much, Wolfgang. It **was / has been** kind of you to invite me.
c **A** … And then Juventus **scored / has scored** the winner. It **was / has been** an incredible goal! **Did you see / Have you seen** the Lazio game last night, Miss Sterling?
   B Yes, I **did / have**. **Wasn't it / Hasn't it** been a great match? One of the best I **ever saw / have ever seen**.
d **A** Rain **stopped / has stopped** play again yesterday, I see.
   B Sorry?
   A The cricket. They **cancelled / have cancelled** the match.
   B Oh, they **didn't / haven't**! Well, we certainly **didn't see / haven't seen** much cricket this summer.
e **A** I think this is your first time in Finland, isn't it Catherine? Or **were you / have you been** here before?
   B Actually, I **came / have come** here on holiday once, but that **was / has been** a long time ago.
f **A** That's a terrible joke, Marty.
   B No, you see, he **copied / has copied** her test, right?
   A Marty, we **heard / 've heard** the joke before. It's ancient. OK, everybody, time to work.
   B I **thought / have thought** it **was / has been** funny.
g **A** What I do worry about is what's going on between our vice-president and our head of finance.
   B They're having an affair?
   A **Didn't you hear / Haven't you heard**? I **thought / have thought** everybody **knew / has known**.
   B God, no! No one ever tells me anything.

TALKING ABOUT EXPERIENCES

1 A good way to socialise in English is to talk a little about some of the experiences you've had. You're going to play *The Experiences Game*. Prepare by thinking about what you could put in the gaps on the board. Some of the verbs and adjectives in the boxes below may be useful, but you'll need to change their grammatical form.

> be eat go happen hate have hear know like love meet read see spend stay

> amazing attractive beautiful boring brilliant delicious disgusting dull entertaining exciting
> fabulous fascinating frightening funny great hard intelligent interesting lousy luxurious
> marvellous nasty nice relaxing strange stressful stupid terrible ugly violent wonderful

2 Play the game with a partner. Move around the board talking about your experiences.

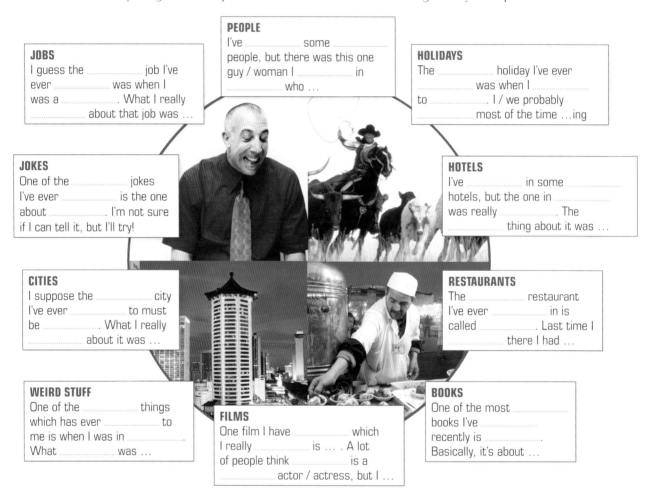

JOBS
I guess the .... job I've ever .... was when I was a .... What I really .... about that job was …

PEOPLE
I've .... some .... people, but there was this one guy / woman I .... in .... who …

HOLIDAYS
The .... holiday I've ever .... was when I .... to .... I / we probably .... most of the time …ing

JOKES
One of the .... jokes I've ever .... is the one about .... I'm not sure if I can tell it, but I'll try!

HOTELS
I've .... in some .... hotels, but the one in .... was really .... The .... thing about it was …

CITIES
I suppose the .... city I've ever .... to must be .... What I really .... about it was …

RESTAURANTS
The .... restaurant I've ever .... in is called .... Last time I .... there I had …

WEIRD STUFF
One of the .... things which has ever .... to me is when I was in .... What .... was …

FILMS
One film I have .... which I really .... is … . A lot of people think .... is a .... actor / actress, but I …

BOOKS
One of the most .... books I've .... recently is .... Basically, it's about …

3 In conversation we often want to describe our experiences. What do the following adjectives describe? Choose nouns from the box.

> ~~city~~ clothes economy movie people weather

> book car holiday hotel job news

a   sophisticated/cosmopolitan/industrial ....city..........
b   marvellous/changeable/miserable ....
c   strong/weak/depressed ....
d   smart/designer/casual ....
e   friendly/hard-working/enterprising ....
f   exciting/classic/unforgettable ....

g   great/shocking/latest ....
h   secure/challenging/well-paid ....
i   economical/luxury/flashy ....
j   relaxing/beach/sightseeing ....
k   comfortable/poor/luxurious ....
l   dull/brilliant/well-written ....

AT A CONFERENCE DINNER

Work with a partner to practise small talk at a conference dinner.

You are sitting next to each other at a conference dinner in a city you both know well, and have just sat through an incredibly long and boring opening speech. You have not been introduced.

First decide
- where the conference is being held
- what the conference theme is
- why you are there (to give a presentation, to network, to do deals?).

Then look at the conversation notes below and prepare what you are going to say.

Speaker A
Start the conversation:
'I think that must be the longest opening speech I've ever heard! I'm .... (name), by the way. I don't think we've met.'

Speaker B
'Pleased to meet you. I'm .... (name).'
Continue the conversation by asking about one or more of the following:
- what your partner thought of the conference (fun? dull?)
- talks your partner's been to (any interesting ones?)
- the dinner you've just eaten (local dishes, wine)

Speaker A
Continue the conversation by asking about one or more of the following:
- your partner's company (location, main activities)
- your partner's job (how long he/she's had it)
- where your partner's staying (service, comfort, convenience)

Speaker B
Continue the conversation by talking about one or more of the following:
- the city (architecture, people, prices, local economy)
- the weather (typical for the time of year?)
- shopping (the best places you've found to buy presents)

Speaker A
Continue the conversation by talking about one or more of the following:
- sightseeing (a place of interest you've visited)
- the nightlife (a restaurant, bar or club you've been to)
- a recent item of news (politics, sport, scandal)

Speaker B
Break off the conversation:
'Oh, wait a minute, it looks like the next speaker is going to begin. Let's hope this one's better than the last.'

LANGUAGE LINKS

Vocabulary: Exaggeration and understatement

Are you the sort of person who tends to exaggerate or are you a master of understatement?

Exaggeration
A *I hear it was a fairly dirty hotel.*
B *Yeah, **it was absolutely filthy**!*
Understatement
A *I hear it was a fairly dirty hotel.*
B *Well, **it wasn't exactly the cleanest** I've ever stayed in.*

1 Respond to the following statements using the words in the box to exaggerate.

> boiling enormous fascinating freezing
> gorgeous tiny

a A I suppose Helsinki was pretty cold.
   B _____
b A Thailand is an interesting country.
   B _____
c A So, he's got a big house in the country?
   B _____
d A It's actually a very small place.
   B _____
e A She's quite a beautiful woman.
   B _____
f A Of course, Turkey's hot in summer.
   B _____

2 Now do the same to understate.

a A It's a dull book, isn't it?
   B (interesting / read) _____
b A So it was quite an ordinary meal?
   B (amazing / had) _____
c A Well, that was a boring party!
   B (exciting / been to) _____
d A It's been a stressful week.
   B (relaxing / had) _____
e A It was a pathetic joke.
   B (funny / heard) _____
f A Isn't Chicago dangerous?
   B (safe place / been to) _____

Grammar: Past Simple or Present Perfect

The Present Perfect is a present tense. You use it to talk about

- things that start in the past and continue up to the present.
  We haven't seen much cricket this summer.
- people's experiences, no *matter* when they happened.
  I've tried green tea before.
- things that have an obvious connection to the present.
  Dr Winter has come over from the Atlanta office. (= he's here now)

Affirmative/negative			Interrogative		
I you we they	have haven't	worked	have haven't	I you we they	worked?
he she it	has hasn't		has hasn't	he she it	

1 Read the three sentences below.

*The Thomke family **came** to America from Switzerland forty years **ago** and **started** a business. (a)*
*Since the 1980s they **have been** extremely successful. (b)*
*In fact, **for** the last five years they **have been** the market leader in their field. (c)*

a Which of the sentences above refers to
   a point in time? ☐ a period of time? ☐ both? ☐
b Which two pieces of information are basically **history**? Which tense is used?
c Which two pieces of information are most relevant to the family's **current success**? Which tense is used?

2 Look at the following time expressions and decide which are used before *ago*, after *for* and after *since*. Fill in the table. Some expressions can be used more than once.

> the 1990s 2001 Christmas a couple of days
> the day before yesterday half past four last month
> a long time the oil crisis over an hour Thursday
> a week years

ago	for	since

3 Using the rules you've worked out so far, try the following quiz about the people who said these sentences. Write yes, no or maybe.

a *I lived in Lisbon.*
   Does he live there now? ....

b *I lived in Helsinki for six months.*
   Does she live there now? ....

c *I've lived in Toronto.*
   Does he live there now? ....

d *I've lived in Taipei for three years.*
   Does she live there now? ....

e *I've been in all morning and she hasn't phoned.*
   Is he in now? .... Is it still morning? ....

f *I was in all morning and he didn't phone.*
   Is she in now? .... Is it still morning? ....

4 Complete the conversation using the items in brackets in either the Past Simple or Present Perfect.

Tibor, a sales manager, is planning to send his staff on a team-building survival course.

Tibor Right now (a) .... you all .... (get) my e-mail yesterday about the training course?

Fydor Er, yes … (b) .... (be) it a joke?

Tibor I certainly (c) .... (not mean) it to be a joke, Fydor. No, I (d) .... (notice) recently that we need to work as a team more. Last year's interpersonal skills course obviously (e) .... (not be) as successful as I (f) .... (hope), and so I (g) .... (now decide) to send you all on a management survival course.

Fydor At the Death or Glory Training Camp.

Tibor That's right. (h) .... you .... (hear) of it?

Fydor No.

Eva Erm, you (i) .... (say) in your e-mail, Tibor, that you won't be coming on the course with us yourself. Is that right?

Tibor Er, unfortunately, yes. Obviously, I (j) .... (want) to join you, but I'm going to be much too busy, I'm afraid. For one thing, I still (k) .... (not do) the quarterly sales figures.

Ivan Tibor, why (l) .... (not tell) us about this at the departmental meeting last week?

Tibor Well, I (m) .... (not make up) my mind until today. But I, er, (n) .... (think) it would bring us all together.

Fydor It (o) .... (already bring) us together. None of us wants to go!

Tibor Now, look, Fydor, don't be so negative. Wait until you (p) .... (have) a chance to think about it. I (q) .... even .... (not show) you the course brochure yet. Anyway, what do the rest of you think?

Eva I think it's the most ridiculous thing you (r) .... (ever ask) us to do. And, god knows, the interpersonal skills training (s) .... (be) bad enough. I am not being dumped on a freezing hillside by some sadistic ex-commando, stripped to my underwear and told to find my way back to civilisation with a fruit knife, a chocolate bar and a ball of string!

Phrase bank: Engaging in small talk

Listed below are some questions which might keep the conversation going at a business event. Complete them using the correct form of the verbs in the box. You'll need to use some of them more than once.

> be   have   make   come   go   give   see   read   meet
> stay   find   enjoy   try   hear

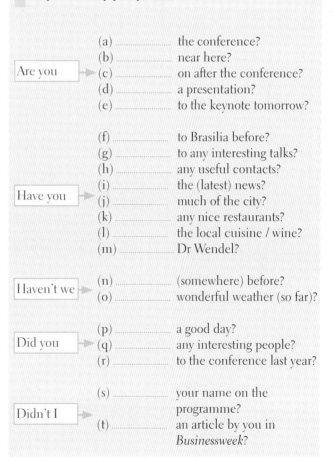

(a)	the conference?
(b)	near here?
Are you → (c)	on after the conference?
(d)	a presentation?
(e)	to the keynote tomorrow?
(f)	to Brasilia before?
(g)	to any interesting talks?
(h)	any useful contacts?
(i)	the (latest) news?
Have you → (j)	much of the city?
(k)	any nice restaurants?
(l)	the local cuisine / wine?
(m)	Dr Wendel?
Haven't we → (n)	(somewhere) before?
(o)	wonderful weather (so far)?
(p)	a good day?
Did you → (q)	any interesting people?
(r)	to the conference last year?
(s)	your name on the programme?
Didn't I → (t)	an article by you in *Businessweek*?

When you write a letter, you take some care over your words. Why is ti that when we send an e-mail we jutst wirte down anyold nonselnce? and press send and thetn hoep for the best ½.

LUCY KELLAWAY, *FINANCIAL TIMES*

1 When do you e-mail rather than pick up the phone? Discuss with a partner.

2 Read the article below and discuss the questions on the right with a partner.

How text addicts cost offices billions of dollars in lost profits

You're sitting at your desk, deep in concentration, when suddenly you hear that familiar 'ping' from your computer. An e-mail has landed. With one hour to go to the deadline for the report you are working on, you try to ignore the temptation to check who it's from. But minutes later there's a second 'ping' and it's too much to resist. Before you know it, you are having a full-blown cyber-chat with your friend, fifteen minutes have passed, and your weekend plans may be intact but your report certainly isn't.

If this sounds all too familiar, then there is a good chance you are a text addict – someone who cannot resist messaging, e-mailing and texting, even if it disrupts and dominates your day and cuts hours from your working week.

It is a phenomenon which, according to some experts, is costing businesses all over the world billions of dollars in lost productivity and errors caused by distracted workers. A recent survey by Hewlett Packard claimed 43% of office workers spent more time socialising online with friends than they did working – an average of four hours a day!

According to workplace psychologist Dr David Lewis, people are spending longer hours in the office and having less face-to-face contact with their friends, so they are compensating by cyber-socializing in work time. But they are also more likely to check work e-mails during their leisure time.

'You have a situation where 80 per cent of our time is spent managing just 20 per cent of our workload, by that I mean e-mails,' says businessman Stephen Barnes. 'They are a big problem for business. They take over. It is not unusual for people to have 2,000 e-mails in their inboxes. Imagine having 2,000 things in your in-tray on your desk!'

www.monstersandcritics.com

a How often do you check your e-mail in a day? Do you set aside a particular time to check it?

b Who's the bigger text addict: you or your partner?

c Do you believe these statistics? Do you think computer company employees might be worse cyber-chatters than most?

d Are you working longer hours than you used to? Do you ever bring work home with you? Would you say you had a good life-work balance?

e Do you know how many old e-mails you have sitting in your inbox right now? Are you in control of your e-mail or is it in control of you?

3 You're going to listen to some business people being interviewed about what they love and hate about e-mail. First divide the following phrases into love and hate. Label them L or H.

> I'm a big fan of ...   I'm not crazy about ...   I'm not keen on ...   It drives me nuts.
> It's really cool.   That really bugs me.   The really neat thing is ...
> What I can't stand is ...   What really annoys me is ...

4 Working with a partner, see if you can predict what the interviewees will say. Make notes below according to how likely you think they are to mention it.

	What I love about e-mail	What I hate about e-mail
Sure to mention ...		
Might mention ...		

5 🔘 2.16 Now listen and tick off the likes and dislikes. Make a note of any you missed.

6 What's your own special 'pet hate'? Tell the rest of the class what really bugs you about it.

WRITING E-MAIL

1 How important is the ability to write in business? Read this extract from the book *E-Writing*. Do you agree?

The importance of writing stands to reason. Your boss, co-workers or customers don't follow you around on the job. They don't see how you handle people or projects day to day. They simply see the *results* of your work – database notes, e-mail, reports, proposals. Clear writing reflects clear thinking. Your writing becomes your face on the page or screen. Not only must your writing be clear, correct, complete and concise, but it also has to connect. Your entire relationship with co-workers or customers may rest solely on your e-mail exchanges. In a world of emotional disconnection, people long to be treated as special, important individuals.

2 With a partner, think of short, simple ways in which you can 'connect' with the people you e-mail.

3 There are no universally accepted rules for writing e-mail, but here are some useful guidelines. Match each rule (a–h) to the reason why it is useful.

a   Create a subject line with impact.
b   Write short sentences.
c   Keep paragraphs short.
d   Don't always trust your spell check.
e   Put your signature on the message.
f   Proofread the message before sending it.
g   Use headings, bullets and numbering.
h   Add one personal touch to your message

It saves people scrolling down to see if there's more text. ☐
These will guide the reader and make the message easier to grasp. ☐
It can't tell the difference between *your* and *you're*, or *theirs* and *there's*! ☐
It is more likely that someone will read your e-mail. ☐
On one level, *all* business is personal. ☐
There's less chance the reader will miss anything. ☐
It creates a more professional image if there are no silly errors. ☐
You don't need complex grammar or punctuation. ☐

4 People you know well may send you e-mails with certain grammar words missing. What three types of grammar word are missing in these examples?

~~It's a~~ great idea.
~~I'm~~ presenting it to ~~the~~ board today.
~~I'll~~ speak to you later.

Now put the missing words back into the e-mail below.

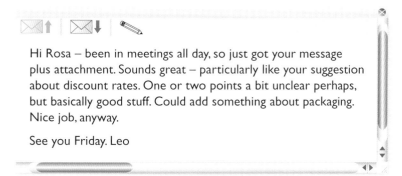

Hi Rosa – been in meetings all day, so just got your message plus attachment. Sounds great – particularly like your suggestion about discount rates. One or two points a bit unclear perhaps, but basically good stuff. Could add something about packaging. Nice job, anyway.

See you Friday. Leo

5 E-mails generally contain fewer fixed expressions and are less formal than business letters. Rewrite the following extracts from business letters as e-mails using the expressions in the boxes.

> Bad news: ...   Cheers.   Could you do me a favour and ...?   Good news: from ...
> Got your message on ...   Hi ...   Shall I ...?   Sorry about ...   Sorry, but I can't make ...

A

Dear Louisa,

Thank you for your letter of September 12th. **Unfortunately, I shall be unable to attend** the meeting on the 21st. **I would appreciate it if you could** send me a copy of the minutes.

Best wishes,

Tom Hunt

B

I'm delighted to tell you that as of Jan 2 we are offering substantial discounts on all orders over €1,000. **If you wish, I would be happy to** send you further details and a copy of our new catalogue.

C

I regret to inform you that the board turned down your proposal. **I would like to apologise for** not getting back to you sooner on this, but I've been in Montreal all week.

> About ...   Are we still OK for ...?   Following ...   If you have any questions, let me know.
> I'm sending you ... as an attachment.   Please ...   See you ...   Speak to you soon.   Thanks.

D

I am writing to confirm our appointment on May 3rd. My flight gets in about 11am. **With regard to** my presentation on the 4th, could you make the necessary arrangements? **I enclose** a list of the equipment I'll need.

I look forward to meeting you next week.

Charlotte De Vere

E

Further to our telephone conversation this morning, **I'd be grateful if you could** send me a full description of the problem and I'll pass it on to our technical department.

Thank you for taking the time to do this. If I can be of any further assistance, please do contact me again.

I look forward to hearing from you.

6 Rearrange the information in the e-mail below and rewrite it to make it clearer. Give it paragraphs and a suitable subject line.

Subject: [   ]

Otto

How are you doing? Got the joke you sent me – very funny. I've e-mailed you those statistics you wanted, by the way. Hope they come in useful for your presentation. Spoke to Cheryl in accounts the other day. She sends her regards. On the subject of accounts, did you send your quarterlies in? I don't seem to have them. Let me know how the presentation goes. And don't forget those figures.

7 Make the message below simpler and clearer by deleting as many unnecessary words as possible without changing the meaning.

Subject: [   ]

Dear Mr Nordqvist,

On behalf of myself and my colleague, Karen Sharpe, may I take this opportunity to thank you and your team once again for your kind hospitality during our brief stay in Malmö. Karen and I both felt that the two-hour meeting we had with you at your headquarters last week was, without doubt, a great success, and we very much look forward to discussing our ideas with you in much more detail than we were able to in that extremely short but highly productive meeting.

I am sure you will be pleased to know that I passed on your valuable comments to our Managing Director, Diane Lee, and she assures me that she will certainly be in contact with you over the next couple of weeks or so. In the meantime, let me just say that it was a very great pleasure meeting you, your managers and enthusiastic staff and exploring the possibilities of some kind of a joint venture between us in the not too distant future.

With my very best wishes,

Sam White, Senior Product Manager, Thermoflex (UK)

8 Having edited the e-mail in 7 down to a more manageable size, add one or two personal touches at appropriate points in the message. You know that Niels Nordqvist has just been promoted to vice-president (finance) and that his wife has just had their first child.

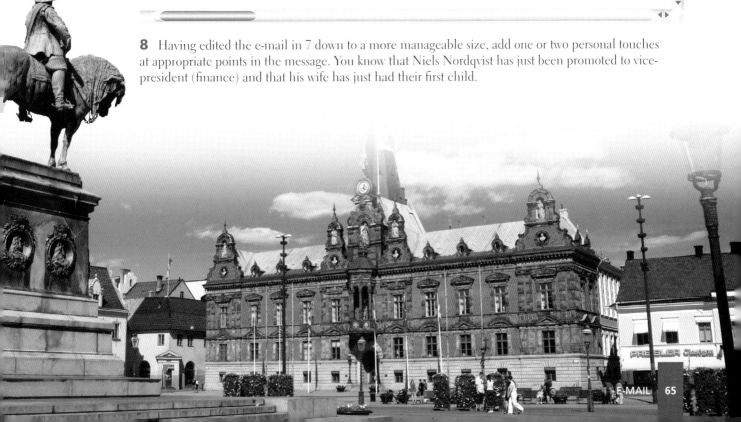

CHANGING ARRANGEMENTS

1 2.17–2.19 Sarah is organising a business trip to Japan for herself and her colleague Peter. She has left three voicemail messages for Koichi, her contact in Nagoya. Listen and answer the questions.

Message 1
a When will Sarah and Peter arrive in Nagoya?
b Why are they going to be two days late?

Message 2
a Why can't Sarah and Peter stay at the Radisson?
b What does Sarah ask Koichi to do?

Message 3
a How long will the presentation be?
b What software and hardware do they need?

2 Complete the extracts from the messages in 1.

a Peter and I .... arrive in Nagoya on Monday …

b That .... possible now, I'm afraid …

c So, we .... get there by Wednesday …

d Peter and I .... stay at the Radisson …

e … I .... e-mail you about this yesterday.

f We .... to keep the presentation itself quite short …

g … we .... use PowerPoint …

h … we .... need a projector and screen …

3 Which of the above

1 are predictions?
2 refer to current plans or intentions?
3 refer to past plans or intentions?

4 Write the e-mail that Koichi might write in response to Sarah's messages.

YOU'VE GOT MAIL

Work in groups of three or four to exchange e-mails.

1 Write a short e-mail message (no more than 60 words) to each member of your group, starting with one of the introductory expressions on the left. Make sure the information in your e-mail is connected to your own job or experience. Include your e-mail address, that of the person you are e-mailing and a suitable subject line.

2 After five minutes place your message in the 'inbox' at the front of the class and take out any messages addressed to you.

3 Write a reply to each message you receive directly below the original message. Invent any information you have to.

4 After another five minutes, put your replies back in the 'inbox' and take out any addressed to you.

5 Repeat the above procedure until you have dealt with at least five different topics.

6 In your group, compare the sequences of e-mails you have produced.

> **Useful phrases**
>
> Change of plan. I was going to …, but …
>
> Have you heard …?
>
> Don't want to be a pain, but …
>
> I was thinking of …
>
> I want to go on a training course to …
>
> I've just heard …
>
> I'm giving a presentation about …
>
> A few of us are planning to …

LANGUAGE LINKS

Vocabulary: Computers

1 Combine the words in the box into at least ten computer terms. Some are written as two words and some as one.

> ad banner base board data desk disk
> engine hard help home key menu
> page search sheet site spread top web

2 Match each verb on the left with the item on the right that it collocates most strongly with.

a	surf	a program
b	enter	files off the Net
c	run	on an icon
d	download	data into a computer
e	click	a computer
f	transmit	the Internet
g	crash	a virus
h	install	the trash
i	burn	an attachment
j	send	the Web
k	empty	text
l	browse	to a better model
m	upgrade	CDs
n	cut and paste	software

3 Complete the song about computers using the verbs on the right. Use the rhyme and rhythm to help you. Have you experienced similar problems?

My PC is Giving Me Problems
(to the tune of *My Bonnie Lies Over the Ocean*, traditional)

My PC is giving me problems.
My PC is giving me hell.
It says it's got Intel inside it.
But its Intel inside is not well.

Chorus
*Bring back, bring back, oh bring back my
typewriter, please, oh please.
Bring back, bring back, oh bring back my
typewriter, please.*

It ¹................ on me three times this morning.	virus
And wouldn't connect to the ².................	Net
It ³................ my trash without warning.	crashed
It's some kind of ⁴................, I bet.	emptied
I ⁵................ head office a memo	attachment
And sent an ⁶................ in Word,	error
But HQ's computers are Apple	occurred
And that's when an ⁷................ ⁸.................	e-mailed
I ⁹................ on an icon to ¹⁰.................	program
A ¹¹................ that iMacs can read	files
But lost half the ¹²................ on my hard disk	download
So somehow I must have miskeyed.	clicked

Now my spreadsheet has lost all its ¹³.................	upgrade
And sadly no ¹⁴................ were made.	helpline
I phoned up the ¹⁵................ at Compaq.	data
They told me I need to ¹⁶.................	backups
They finally sent a ¹⁷................,	type
Who debugged my ¹⁸................ with ease,	printer
But something's gone wrong with my ¹⁹................,	technician
'Cause when I ²⁰................'d's it prints 'c's.	desktop
I guess I'm ²¹................ illiterate –	keyboard
I don't know my ²²................ from my RAM.	spam
My ²³................ skills are a disaster	computer
And my e-mail has filled up with ²⁴.................	ROM
I think I should ²⁵................ down my PC.	Resources
Admit that I'm going ²⁶.................	retrain
Arrange to see Human ²⁷.................	shut
And tell them I want to ²⁸................!	insane

Grammar: Future forms

In English there are many ways of talking about the future. The differences between them have less to do with time than with the speaker's attitude to the future event. Study the following examples, all of which refer to the same point in time: next Sunday.

- *I'm forty on Sunday. (1)*
- *I fly home on Sunday. (2)*
- *I'll let you know on Sunday. (3)*
- *You won't have a problem getting a taxi on Sunday. (4)*
- *I'm going to a wedding on Sunday. (5)*
- *No! I'm not working on Sunday! (6)*
- *It's going to snow on Sunday. (7)*
- *I'm going to have a good rest on Sunday. (8)*

The form we choose can depend on such things as:

- whether we are talking about a fact or an opinion
- how sure we are
- whether we have already made plans or arrangements
- how determined we are
- whether we want the thing to happen

1 Match sentences 1–8 above to their main function.

a a fixed arrangement
b a scheduled or timetabled event
c an informed prediction
d an offer or promise
e a plan, intention or decision
f an indisputable fact
g a refusal
h an opinion about the future

In practice, the difference in meaning between certain future forms is often very small.

2 Match sentences 1–8 above to those below which are similar in structure and function.

a   My plane leaves at five.
b   I'm going to go on a diet.
c   It's going to be a difficult meeting.
d   It's Christmas in three weeks.
e   I'll get back to you within the hour.
f   We're getting a new car on Friday.
g   There'll be a lot of traffic on the roads.
h   I'm not giving someone like him the job.

3 Look at the following structures for expressing intention. Put them in order of certainty.

> aiming to   going to   hoping to   intending to   planning to

more certain → I am/was a ....
b ....
I am/was ← c ....
d ....
less certain ↓ I am/was e ....

4 <u>Underline</u> the most appropriate verb forms in the conversation below.

It's 8pm. Cleo is just leaving work, when she sees the light on in Eric's office.

Cleo Hello, Eric. Are you still here?

Eric Hi, Cleo. Yeah, I'm just checking everything for my talk tomorrow.

Cleo Oh yes, (a) **you'll give / you're giving** your presentation to the board. Are you nervous?

Eric Not yet. But (b) **I will be / I am** if I don't get this PowerPoint thing to work properly.

Cleo Oh, I use PowerPoint a lot. (c) **I'll help / I'm going to help** you if you like.

Eric Thanks, but I think I've had enough for tonight. The presentation (d) **isn't being / isn't** till 11, so (e) **I'll still have / I'm still having** a couple of hours tomorrow morning to get things ready.

Cleo Well, some of us (f) **will go / are going** out for a Chinese meal and then maybe to that new club if you want to join us.

Eric Hm, sounds like (g) **you're having / you're going to have** a pretty late night. I think (h) **I'll give / I'm giving** it a miss this time.

Cleo Well, (i) **we go / we're going** for a drink first. Why don't you come? (j) **It'll take / It's going to take** your mind off tomorrow.

Eric Well, maybe you're right. Look, (k) **I'm just checking / I'm just going to check** this thing one last time and (l) **I'm / I'll be** right with you.

Cleo OK. See you there.

Phrase bank: E-mail

Match the following informal e-mail expressions and acronyms to their functions.

a   Hi.
b   Got your message, thanks.
c   Sorry, but I can't make it.
d   Could you do me a favour?
e   Are we still OK for Fri?
f   About the conference, …
g   Good / Bad news.
h   See attachment.

1   Cancelling a meeting
2   Introducing a topic
3   Requesting information / action
4   Giving positive / negative information
5   Greeting
6   Referring to an extra document
7   Confirming a meeting
8   Replying to an e-mail

a ☐ b ☐ c ☐ d ☐ e ☐ f ☐ g ☐ h ☐

i   asap
j   Following our phone call, …
k   I'll chase it up.
l   BTW.
m   Fri's fine by me.
n   Let me know how it goes.
o   I'll be in touch.
p   Cheers.

9   Adding an extra point
10 Offering to contact someone again
11 Saying goodbye
12 Confirming an appointment
13 Showing interest
14 Referring to an earlier conversation
15 Offering to look into something
16 Requesting / offering urgent action

i ☐ j ☐ k ☐ l ☐ m ☐ n ☐ o ☐ p ☐

▶ asap = as soon as possible
▶ BTW = by the way

12 PRESENTING

Talk low, talk slow and don't say too much.

JOHN WAYNE, HOLLYWOOD FILM STAR

1 Think of successful talks you've been to in the past. What made them so successful? Complete the following list of elements that make a good presentation using the words in the boxes.

a – e	appearance contact humour knowledge talk
f – j	attitude language preparation visuals voice

To be a good presenter you need …
a   a well-structured ....
b   thorough subject ....
c   a smart and professional ....
d   a good sense of ....
e   good eye ....

f   an enthusiastic ....
g   a strong ....
h   a creative use of ....
i   expressive body ....
j   careful ....

2 With a partner, discuss the elements in 1 and number them in order of importance. Use the phrases below in your discussion.

What you need most of all is …   You don't need …, as long as …
Another important thing is …   … can make a real difference
I think … is pretty important too   It helps if …, but it's not essential

3 Add your own ideas to the list in 1.

DELIVERY

1 Read the text below. Is it good advice?

> **Did you know ...** that almost thirty million business presentations are given every day? And yet, in surveys, most managers say they are more afraid of public speaking than anything else – even death! To overcome nerves, a lot of presentation trainers advise you to 'just be yourself'.

2 2.20 Listen to three people speaking. Concentrate on the way they sound. Do you think they are having a conversation or giving a presentation? Write C or P next to each extract.

1 ☐   4 ☐
2 ☐   5 ☐
3 ☐   6 ☐

3 Discuss with a partner. How is speaking to an audience – even a small one – different from speaking to a group of friends? Think about the following:

- how clearly you speak
- how quickly you speak
- how often you pause
- how emphatic you are

4 2.21 Look at this famous toast to Albert Einstein by writer, George Bernard Shaw. The extract is unpunctuated. Mark (|) where you think the speaker paused. Then listen and check.

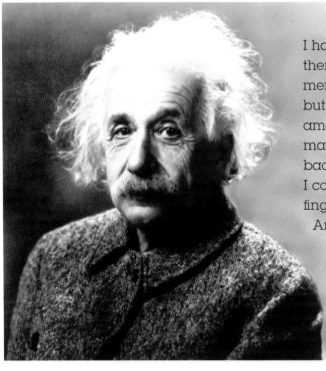

I have said that great men are a mixed lot but there are orders of great men there are great men who are great men amongst all men but there are also great men who are great amongst great men and that is the sort of great man whom you have amongst you tonight I go back 2,500 years and how many of them can I count in that period I can count them on the fingers of my two hands Pythagoras Ptolemy Aristotle Copernicus Kepler Galileo Newton Einstein and I still have two fingers left vacant my lords ladies and gentlemen are you ready for the toast health and length of days to the greatest of our contemporaries Einstein.

5 a Listen again and <u>underline</u> the stressed words.
   b Is there a connection between what we stress and where we pause?
   c What's the effect of pausing
     less often?
     more often?

A TEAM PRESENTATION

1 Look at the following information from First Direct. You are going to use this information to practise delivering a presentation. Mark the pauses and stressed words. With a partner, first 'present' the information clearly and professionally. Then 'present' the information enthusiastically and dramatically. Which sounds better?

Presenter 1

When you join First Direct you experience something unbelievable. A bank designed around you, which doesn't expect you to fit round it.

Presenter 2

A bank which recruits people who like to talk. A bank which gives its people all the information they need to enable them to help you. A bank which believes in sorting your money out for you without you having to ask.

Presenter 1

Funny kind of bank? Unbelievable? Even a little magical? Yes, but also efficient, safe and secure.

Presenter 2

You can, naturally, choose when, where and how to deal with your money. We're open 24 hours a day. Our people are ready to talk to you, whenever you call.

Presenter 1

And wherever you might be in the world, you can bank online. Receive information online. Buy online. We can even send banking messages to your mobile phone.

Presenter 2

Join First Direct and feel good about your bank; it's your money after all.

2 In the extract above find examples of

a   repetition
b   rhetorical questions
c   grouping points in threes
d   pairs of contrasting points

3 Match the items in 2 to why they are effective.

1   you invite your audience to try to anticipate your answer ☐
2   you create a satisfying sense of completeness ☐
3   you make sure your audience doesn't miss your main points ☐
4   you emphasise what you're saying by using the power of opposites ☐

STRUCTURING A PRESENTATION

1 The following expressions help you to give a clear structure to a presentation. Complete them using the correct preposition.

> about   back   for   of   off   on   to   up

a   To start ...., then, ...
b   To move .... to my next point, ...
c   To go .... to what I was saying, ...
d   To turn now .... a different matter, ...
e   To say a bit more .... that, ...
f   To give you an example .... what I mean, ...
g   To digress .... a moment, ...
h   To sum ...., then, ...

2 Which of the expressions above are used to

1   return to an important point? ☐
2   repeat the main points? ☐
3   talk about something unconnected? ☐
4   begin the presentation? ☐
5   expand a point? ☐ ☐
6   change the subject? ☐ ☐

USING VISUALS

1 You can draw attention to your visuals by using the phrases below. Complete them using the words in the box.

give   have   mean   point   see   show

a .... a look at this.
b As you can ...., ...
c I'd like to .... out ...

d The figures clearly ....
e To .... you the background to this.
f So, what does this .... in terms of...

2 Which parts of the graph on the right do the following verbs refer to?

rise ☐   level off ☐   fluctuate ☐   peak ☐
recover ☐   bottom out ☐   fall ☐

A TECHNICAL PROBLEM

1 🎧 2.22–2.24 Listen to a stock trading company manager describe how his team solved a problem with the company's website.

Part A

1 <u>Underline</u> the two things the manager does to open his presentation.
   a ask a question
   b tell a joke
   c tell a story
   d quote some figures
2 What's the significance of the following facts and figures?
   a 9
   b 250,000
   c 3
   d 60,000

Part B

3 What three problems was the company having with its website?
4 Having improved the website, what are E-Stock's two current objectives?

Part C

5 Which graph on the right does the speaker refer to?
6 What three things does the manager do to close his presentation?
   a he sums up his talk
   b he quotes a well-known person
   c he refers people to his report
   d he invites questions

2 Read the following sentences from the presentation in 1.

a When we first **went** online, we **were getting** over 250,000 hits a day.
b The problem **was** not the service we **were offering**, but the website itself.
c A fault we **hadn't noticed** in the programming **caused** 1,500 people to invest in a company that didn't even exist.
d The next thing **was** internet advertising, winning back the customer confidence we**'d lost**.

In which of the sentences above do the verbs in **bold** refer to things

happening at the same time? ☐ ☐
happening one after the other? ☐ ☐

GIVING A SHORT PRESENTATION

Choose one of the situations below and prepare a short presentation.

Situation 1

You have been given the job of introducing a celebrity guest speaker who has come to give a motivational speech to your company. You can choose anyone you like from the worlds of business, sport, entertainment, media, science or politics.

Use some of the frameworks below to help you prepare, but change whatever you need to. Try to use contrasts, repetition, rhetorical questions and groups of three in your speech. You should aim to speak for about two minutes. Your guest speaker is making a surprise appearance, so don't announce who it is until the end of your introduction. See if people can guess who it is!

It was ... who said ... . Our guest this evening is a perfect example of that.

How do you describe someone who ..., who ... and who ...?

He/She showed the first signs of ... at the age of ... .

And at the age of ..., he/she had already ... and was beginning to ... .

Highlights of his/her career include ..., ... and ... . When asked ... , he/she said ... .

Not only is our guest ..., he/she is also ... . A good example of that is when ... .

Truly, in the world of ... no-one has done more to ..., to ... and to ...

Ladies and gentlemen, please give a warm welcome to ...

Situation 2

You have been chosen to present the Business World award for most innovative product of the last quarter-century. You can choose any product you like from household to electrical goods, cars to clothes and machines to medicines.

Use some of the frameworks below to help you prepare, but change whatever you need to. Try to use contrasts, repetition, rhetorical questions and groups of three in your speech. You should aim to speak for about two minutes. Nobody at the awards ceremony knows who the winner is, so don't announce who it is until the end of your introduction. See if people can guess what it is!

Once every ... years or so a product comes along which totally changes the way we ... .

... is/was such a product. Not only is/was it ..., it is/was also ... and ... .

How do you begin to describe something which literally revolutionised the ... industry?

When I tell you that it sold over ... million units, you will not be surprised.

... once said that this product was the most ... .

I could also tell you that it is/was... and that ... . But that would fail to do it justice.

The ... is quite simply the best ... ever invented.

Ladies and gentlemen, the winner of the award for most innovative product is ...

12 PRESENTING

LANGUAGE LINKS

Vocabulary: Presentations

Communication skills

Complete the collocations by writing the nouns in the right-hand boxes. They are all things you might do in a presentation.

figures	a graph	an issue	jokes	a point	questions

make stress		describe refer to	
quote compare		tell crack	
address raise		field deal with	

Trends and change

Read the following news headlines and mark each of the verbs and nouns of change according to what it describes: ↘, ↗, ↑, ↓, →, ∨, ∿, ∧, ∨. The first three have been done for you as examples.

a **Housing slump [↓] as interest rates climb [↗] to 7%.**

b **Oil prices reach new peak [∧] as fear of terrorism increases [ ].**

c **Asian stocks recover [ ] after sudden fall [ ] to monthly low [ ].**

d **As China rises [ ], pollution soars [ ] to all-time high [ ].**

e **Spanish market stabilises [ ] after two-month slide [ ].**

f **Wild fluctuations [ ] in the price of paper destabilise [ ] the publishing industry.**

g **Stocks rebound [ ] after substantial losses [ ] in early trading.**

h **Steady decline [ ] in white-collar jobs in the West caused by outsourcing boom [ ].**

Grammar: Past continuous

Affirmative / Negative			Interrogative		
I he she it	was / wasn't	working	was wasn't	I you we they	working?
you we they	were / weren't		were weren't	he she it	

---

1 Match the examples of the Past Continuous below to what they describe.

*I met my wife while I **was working** as a teacher in Barcelona. (1)*

*He **was studying** to be a doctor when he dropped out of university and decided to go into business instead. (2)*

*We **were going** to Vienna for a training weekend, but it was cancelled. (3)*

*You **were** always **working** late when you had that job in the City. (4)*

a a past action which was interrupted or not completed ☐

b the background to a more important event ☐

c repeated actions in the past ☐

d previous plans ☐

2 Correct the following conversation. Three of the verbs in the Past Continuous should be in the Past Simple and vice versa.

Inge Ah, Peter. I was wondering if I could have a word with you?

Peter Hello, Inge. Er, sure. I just went out for lunch, but, er, what was it about?

Inge Well, I was seeing Dieter the other day and he told me you're leaving.

Peter Oh, well, yeah, that's right. Actually, I was deciding a month ago, but I didn't think anybody was knowing about it yet.

Inge Oh, yes. The whole department talked about it when I came in this morning. They still talked about it when I left.

The Past Continuous can suggest a continuing feeling or attitude, so you can use it when you want to put gentle pressure on someone to do something.

- *I **was wondering** if you could help me. (And I still am. So will you help me?)*
- *I **was looking** for something cheaper. (And I still am. So have you got anything cheaper?)*
- *We **were hoping** for a bigger discount. (And we still are. So how about a bigger discount?)*

Past Perfect

Affirmative / Negative			Interrogative		
I you he she it we they	had / hadn't	worked	had hadn't	I you he she it we they	worked?

- *By the time I arrived at the party everyone **had left**. (1)*
- *I was halfway to the airport before I realised **I'd forgotten** my passport. (2)*

3 Look at the examples on page 74.

a What happened first: my arrival or everyone's else's departure?

b Put the events in chronological order: getting halfway to the airport, forgetting your passport, realising your mistake.

The Past Perfect is often used to look back from a time in the past to an earlier time.

Past Simple, Past Continuous or Past Perfect?

4 Complete the following anecdote by <u>underlining</u> the most appropriate verb forms. Read the whole sentence before you make your choice.

'Apparently, there was this guy working for a financial services company in the City. Anyway, it (a) **was being / had been** a really tough year, so he (b) **decided / was deciding** to take a nice long holiday. He (c) **just cleared / was just clearing** his desk, when he (d) **suddenly remembered / had suddenly remembered** what (e) **was happening / had happened** the last time he (f) **was / was being** off work. He (g) **was coming / had come** back to an inbox containing hundreds of e-mails. So this time he (h) **came up / had come up** with a bright idea to prevent it happening again.

What he (i) **did / was doing** was this: he (j) **set / had set** his computer to automatically send a message to anyone e-mailing him, telling them that he (k) **was / had been** in the Caribbean for two weeks and not to e-mail him again till he (l) **got back / was getting back**. Then, just as he (m) **was leaving / had left** the office, he (n) **thought / was thinking** he would e-mail his best friend and tell him all about his holiday plans.

Unfortunately, his best friend, who (o) **was going / had gone** on holiday the day before, (p) **was setting up / had set up** his computer in exactly the same way. So the two PCs (q) **proceeded / were proceeding** to e-mail each other every few seconds for the whole fortnight, while these two guys (r) **were enjoying / had enjoyed** themselves on holiday, totally unaware. I (s) **heard / had heard** that so many messages (t) **were finally building up / had finally built** up on the company's server that it (u) **crashed / was crashing**, costing the firm millions! True story. Austin in accounts told me.'

Phrase bank: The language of presentations

The following expressions are all useful in presentations, but some letters are missing from the final words. When you have completed them, the letters down the middle should make a good piece of advice for a presenter.

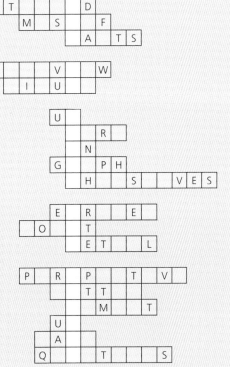

a Can everybody hear me …
b Right, let's get …
c Let me introduce …
d I've divided my presentation into three main …

e Just to give you a brief …
f I'll be saying more about this in a …

g I'm sure the implications of this are clear to all of …
h There's an important point to be made …
i OK, let's move …
j I'd like you to look at this …
k As you can see, the figures speak for …

l To go back to what I was saying …
m Are there any questions you'd like to ask at this …
n I'd like to look at this in more …

o Let's just put this into some kind of …
p Perhaps I should expand on that a …
q To digress for a …
s So, to sum …
t That brings me to the end of my …
u Thank you. I'm sure you have many …

1 Do you agree that investment is a better answer to the world's problems than charity?

2 Should investment in the developing world be left to organisations like the World Bank and the International Monetary Fund or can individuals make a difference too? How can the private investor be sure their money is going to the right people?

3 Read the advertisement for Equitus.com. Would you be interested in finding out more about the company?

Equitus.com

Microfinance, an idea pioneered by Nobel prize-winner and Grameen Bank founder Mohammed Yunus, is based on a brilliantly simple principle – the world's poor do want your money, but they don't want your charity. Lend them the money they need and watch them build their businesses with your help and climb out of poverty. At Equitus we don't donate. We connect private investors via the Internet with small businesses in the developing world. And with a 97% repayment rate many investment banks would envy, being good is very good for business!

> If anybody tells me today that poor people are not creditworthy, I can scream at the top of my voice! I can say this is a big lie. The truth is, they are very much creditworthy.

4 You've just joined the marketing department at Equitus. You and a couple of new recruits like yourself were due to support your boss, who was going to give a presentation about your organisation at the Social Entrepreneurship Conference in Madrid. But there's been a slight change of plan. Read the following e-mail and attachments from your boss, Angel Zafón.

To: a.berman@equitus.com, j.senna@equitus.com, k.lammermeier@equitus.com
From: a.zafón
Subject: Your presentation
Attach: PPT Slides, Presentation Tips 1, Presentation Tips 2

Hi team

Unfortunately, I've been called to an important meeting in Belize, so I won't be able to make it to the conference in Madrid as planned. But I'm sure you'll do a great job without me!

I've attached some PowerPoint slides for the presentation along with some brief notes on what to say about each. I suggest you look at the last slide first, as this explains how our business works. You've only got a very short slot on the programme, so make sure you leave plenty of time to talk about this. The other slides are really just to set the scene and put what we do into context. Bear in mind you'll be presenting to a multinational audience. I've attached some tips about this.

Try to find some time before you fly out to Spain to get together and practise the presentation. I think it would be nice if you could each present one or two of the visuals and hand over to each other during your talk. As our business is about connecting people across the world, I think this would work well.

Let me know if you need anything else. Good luck!

Angel

Presentation tips 1

Different cultures have different ideas about what makes a good presentation. Here are a few guidelines to help you prepare. You can't be all things to all people, but do your best!

Americans: strong visuals, slogans
Britons: stories, humour (but not jokes!)
Spaniards: warmth, good eye contact
French: innovation, eloquence
Italians: style, pace, aesthetics
Germans: technology, data, expertise

Brazilians: enthusiasm, extroversion
Chinese: humility, words of wisdom
Indians: descriptive language, trust
Russians: emotion, the little-known truth
Poles: logic, the personal touch
Arabs: energy, respect, know-how

Presentation tips 2

Some presentation techniques work well in all cultures. Here are a few important ones. Make sure you:

1 **Show your enthusiasm**

   This really is the golden rule. If it matters to you, it will matter to them. One way to do this is to use a lot of positive adjectives like 'amazing', 'incredible', 'exciting', 'fantastic', 'revolutionary'. Don't overdo it, but try to be upbeat throughout your talk.

2 **Clearly signpost your talk**

   Be crystal clear. Lead your audience through your talk by using phrases like 'We're going to talk about A, B and C', 'OK, we've looked at A and B. Now let's take a look at C', 'Oh, and before we finish, a word about D'.

3 **Start and finish strongly**

   Have a good beginning, a good ending and keep them close together! One good way to start is with a bold statement: 'Today, we're going to talk about changing the world'. Or ask the audience a question ('How many of you have wondered …?'). Or quote an amazing statistic ('Did you know that …?'). End with something positive, a call for action or return to your opening remark.

4 **Keep your visuals simple and … visual!**

   If you don't want to compete with your visuals, make sure they only tell HALF the story. This allows you to tell the audience the other half. It means you don't need lots of figures. It also means your audience is listening!

5 **Contextualise figures**

   Big numbers often mean nothing by themselves. Make sure you put them into context: 'This year we've sold five million units – that's roughly one every six seconds!'

6 **State the problem; then present the solution**

   Bad news first to build up audience involvement. Then the good news – send them away happier than when they arrived.

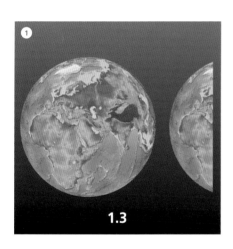

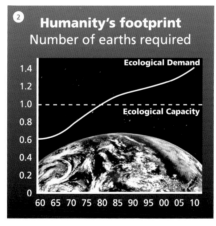

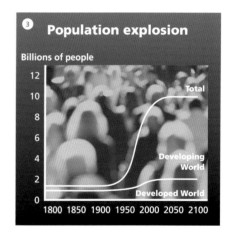

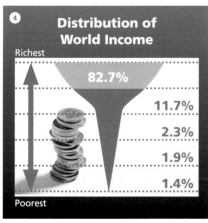

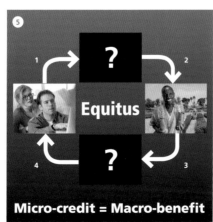

5 🔊 2.25 Your boss forgot to attach the notes for each PowerPoint slide. He calls you at your hotel. Listen and take notes.

6 Work in small groups. Share your notes, decide who is going to present each slide and prepare to give a three- to four-minute presentation.

7 Give your presentation.

8 🔊 2.26 Your boss calls you from Belize to ask you how the talk went. Listen and answer his questions.

13 ENTER THE BLOGOSPHERE

If I can operate Google, I can find anything. And with wireless, it means I will be able to find anything, anywhere, anytime. Which is why I say that Google, combined with Wi-Fi, is a little bit like God.

ALAN COHEN, VICE-PRESIDENT OF WI-FI PROVIDER AIRESPACE

1 What impact has the Internet had on your own life? Are you a technophile or a technophobe?

2 What do you use the Internet for? Match and discuss the following.

a	googling for	podcasts	e	writing	purchases
b	exchanging	chatrooms	f	downloading	online
c	listening to	e-mails	g	studying	music
d	socialising in	information	h	making	blogs

3 How familiar are you with the following websites? Do you use them or ones like them? Compare experiences with the rest of your class.

www.wikipedia.org
www.youtube.com
www.digg.com
www.secondlife.com
www.facebook.com
www.myspace.com

www.linkedin.com
www.blogger.com
http://del.ici.ous
www.technorati.com
www.flickr.com
www.ebay.com

4 🔘 2.27 The generation that has grown up with the Internet is sometimes called the Net Gen. Listen to a member of the Net Gen explaining the difference between Web 1.0 (old Internet) and Web 2.0 (new Internet) and complete the chart. If you're Net Gen yourself, see if you can complete it before you listen.

Web 1.0	**Web 2.0**	**Discussion phrase bank**
dial-up charges	a ba................ co................	I think the biggest effect has been …
wired	b wi................	
companies	c co................	We're seeing a major change in the way …
websites	d bl................	
reading	e wr................	We're now in a position to …
information	f co................	Increasingly, what's happening is …
owning	g sh................	The danger now is …

5 How do you think the Internet has changed the way we do business? With a partner, discuss the issues below. Some of the phrases in the Discussion phrase bank may help you.

communicating with customers
creating publicity
protecting your intellectual capital

6 Now read the texts opposite and compare your ideas.

Change is good

Technology has changed everything. Traditional **media channels** are no longer the only means through which large audiences can be reached. CEOs, like JetBlue's David Neeleman, post videos directly to YouTube. General Motors executives communicate directly to customers and other **stakeholders** through blogs.

These days it seems as if every company, organization, and individual – a billion-dollar multinational, a local government, or a person with a passion – is navigating the new communications landscape and experimenting with blogs, video, and **custom publishing**. In this regard, we are all in it together. We are all content producers.

Viacom sues YouTube over copyright

Entertainment giant Viacom, home to cable television networks such as MTV and Comedy Central, has taken its **battle** with Google's YouTube to court, **suing** the video website over what it calls **copyright violations**.

Viacom, which is asking for $1 billion **in damages**, **alleges** that YouTube does little or nothing to prevent users from posting copyrighted videos on its site, largely because such popular videos help **drive viewers** to the ads that appear on YouTube.

Google said yesterday that YouTube is operating within the law. YouTube, which allows anyone to post video to the Web for viewing by a global audience, includes both amateur videos and **clips** produced by professionals, such as Viacom. Last month, Viacom agreed to license much of its content to Joost, a YouTube rival.

Interactive viral campaigns ask consumers to spread the word

During the early days of Internet advertising, **sceptics** often argued that Web ads would never sell goods effectively.

As more Americans become comfortable with the Web, though, major marketers are increasingly asking agencies to produce elaborate, interactive online campaigns.

One of these is the developing field of viral advertising, in which companies try to create messages so **compelling**, funny or **suggestive** that consumers share them with friends, often through e-mail or cellphone text messages. The goal is the **exponential spread** of ads that are **endorsed** by consumers' own friends.

7 With a partner try to guess the meanings of the words and expressions in bold from their context.

8 ◗ 2.28 Listen to some business people talking about the influence of Web 2.0 technologies on their industries and number their opinions in the order you hear them.

a   being in direct contact with your consumers is key ☐
b   inter-company collaboration is the answer ☐
c   social networking sites are taking over from search engines ☐
d   sharing copyright material is not stealing ☐
e   most of what's on the Net has no commercial interest at all ☐
f   viral ads have killed conventional ads ☐

9 Work with a partner. Choose one of the speakers in 7 and produce a 90-second response to the comments they made. Present it to the rest of your class. Some of the phrases on the right may help you.

> **Discussion phrase bank**
>
> I'd like to respond to the guy/ woman who said that ...
>
> The first thing I'd like to say is ...
>
> I take his/her point about ...
>
> And I definitely go along with what he/she said about ...
>
> But I'm afraid I can't agree with the point about ...
>
> If you ask me, ...

14 BEING HEARD

Why is there no conflict at this meeting?

MICHAEL EISNER, HEAD OF DISNEY

1 Work with a partner. Complete and discuss the statements below.

> chat criticise discuss exchange find make waste

Meetings are …
a an ideal opportunity to _____ points of view.
b the best place to _____ key decisions.
c a safe environment in which to _____ important issues.
d a rare chance to _____ with people from other departments.
e the only way to _____ out what's really going on.
f an open invitation to _____ each other.
g the perfect excuse to _____ an entire morning!

Which is closest to the kind of meetings you have?

2 🔘 2.29 Listen to ten business people from different countries complaining about meetings. Match each extract with the correct topic below.

a there's no fixed agenda ☐
b meetings are boring ☐
c preparation is lacking ☐
d only the boss's opinions count ☐
e it's all about status ☐
f the follow-up is never clear ☐
g the venues are inappropriate ☐
h meetings go on too long ☐
i no decisions are made ☐
j interruption is a problem ☐

3 Read the statements in 2 again. Do you agree or disagree with them?

4 How assertive are you in meetings? What if the meeting is held in English?

5 Complete the questionnaire using the words below. Then discuss each point.

conflict   conversation   people   room   rubbish   silences   time   things

Questionnaire ···

a	You shouldn't interrupt too much – it just creates _____ .	agree	disagree
b	If someone's talking _____ , I'm afraid you just have to stop them.	agree	disagree
c	You should always try to avoid embarrassing _____ in meetings.	agree	disagree
d	You must always think before you speak – take your _____ .	agree	disagree
e	You can't expect everybody to see _____ your way all the time.	agree	disagree
f	You mustn't let other _____ push you around.	agree	disagree
g	You don't have to wait until the _____ stops before you speak.	agree	disagree
h	If people refuse to listen, you can just walk out of the _____ .	agree	disagree

For comments on your answers see page 131.

6 Each sentence in 5 contains a modal verb. Match each modal verb to its meaning below.

1 it's a good idea   ☐   4 it's not necessary   ☐
2 it's a bad idea   ☐   5 it's acceptable   ☐
3 it's necessary   ☐ ☐   6 it's not acceptable   ☐ ☐

CULTURAL DIFFERENCES

1 In *Riding the Waves of Culture*, communications expert Fons Trompenaars shows how different cultures have different discussion styles. The diagram below illustrates his results. The lines represent the two speakers and the spaces represent the silences. When lines and spaces overlap, this shows that people are speaking at the same time.

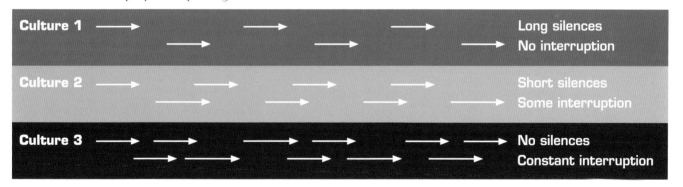

2 Work with a partner. On the diagram above, where would you typically place

a Asians?   d Middle Easterners?   g Africans?
b Northern Europeans?   e North Americans?   h Australasians?
c Southern Europeans?   f Latin Americans?   i your own nationality?

3 2.30–2.32 Listen to extracts from three business meetings. Which of the cultural types are they?

Extract 1 _____
Extract 2 _____
Extract 3 _____

INTERRUPTION STRATEGIES

1 What do you think is the most effective way to do the following? Tick your answers.

Interrupt in meetings		Prevent interruption	
I raise my hand.	☐	I gesture that I haven't finished.	☐
I cough.	☐	I raise my VOICE!	☐
I say *Errrrrm* …	☐	I avoid eye contact with the other person.	☐
I say the speaker's name.	☐	I just keep talking!	☐
I just start speaking!	☐	I glare at the person interrupting.	☐

2 Rearrange the words to make complete expressions. They were all in the conversations you just listened to.

a   a just minute ....

b   me let finish ....

c   no me out hear ....

d   on hang second a ....

e   again to sorry interrupt ....

f   could if finish I just … ....

g   here can just I in come? ....

h   just I something say can? ....

i   what I finish could just saying was I? ....

3 Label the expressions in 2 'interrupting' or 'preventing interruption'. Which two can be both?

HANG ON A MINUTE!

1 Work with a partner. You are going to practise interrupting and preventing interruption. Speaker A see page 130. Speaker B see page 137.

2 Try the activity again, this time without the time limit. The reader should try to deal with each question, before moving on.

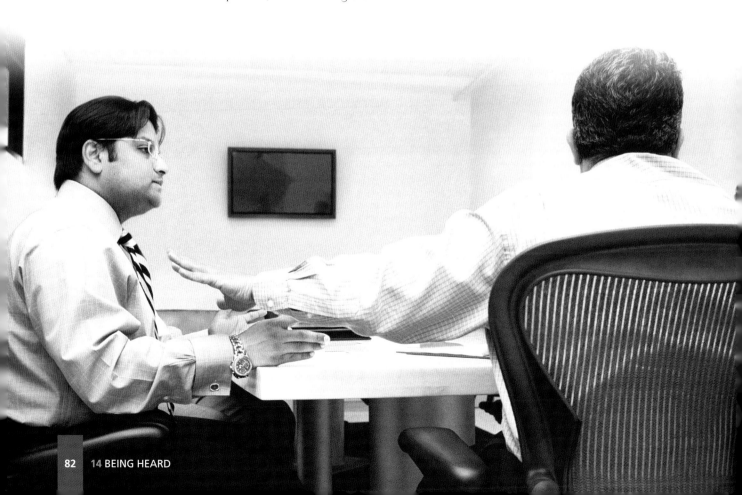

MEETING ACROSS CULTURE

1 Work in three groups. Choose one of the following three scenarios describing a British salesman's experience in different countries. Read the text and do the vocabulary exercises in your group. Then look at question 2.

Saudi Arabia

Brilliant white walls, luxurious carpets and the soft hum of air conditioning. A British salesman sits a little uncomfortably in the office of a Saudi manager. An hour passes in little more than small talk – recent news, horse-racing, the Royal Family. The salesman casually compliments his host on his taste in art and, after several futile attempts to refuse, ends up accepting a valuable-looking vase as a gift.

When the meeting finally gets underway there are almost constant interruptions and it is difficult to stick to any kind of agenda. People drift into the office unannounced, talk loudly and excitedly and leave. Several subjects seem to be under discussion at once. It is sometimes difficult to be heard above the noise. The salesman smiles uncertainly as he accepts a third cup of hot sweet tea.

Five days later a second meeting is in progress. This time the questions are more direct. A senior Arab manager is present on this occasion, but says very little. The arrival of yet another visitor holds up the conversation by a further 40 minutes. The salesman tries hard to hide his frustration.

Meeting three. Terms are negotiated in a lively haggling session. The salesman finds the Saudis more easily persuaded by rhetoric than hard facts. They clearly want to do business. The question is whether they want to do business with him. Their initial demands seem unrealistic, but slowly they begin to make concessions. As the Arabs say, 'When God made time, he made plenty of it!'

a   Match the following to make collocations from the text.
   stick to   the conversation
   hold up   concessions
   negotiate   an agenda
   make   terms

b   Find the words or phrases which mean:
   start (para 2)
   be happening (para 3)
   argument about a price (para 4)
   impressive speech (para 4)

Germany

Rain beats against the mirror-glass windows of a Frankfurt office block. The British salesman's appointment was fixed for 9.30. At 9.29 he's shaking the hand of his prospective client and stepping into the spot-lit orderliness of the German's office. Technical diagrams and flowcharts cover the magnetic whiteboard. A secretary brings machine coffee in styrofoam cups and it's straight to business.

The salesman starts to set up his PowerPoint presentation, but there's a problem loading the disc and he ends up borrowing the German's top-of-the-range Fujitsu. He tries to make a joke of the problem – rather unsuccessfully. When he finally gets going, objections seem to be raised to nearly everything in his proposal. 'Are you sure this is a more efficient system?' 'Do you have figures to back that up?' 'Ah, we tried that before and it didn't work.'

Sixty minutes have been allocated to the meeting. An electronic alarm on the German's watch marks the hour. Shortly afterwards there's a call from reception to say the salesman's taxi has just arrived. He is accompanied to the lift staggering under the weight of six technical manuals, a 200-page printout of production quotas and a promotional video.

Over the next eighteen months the Germans have an endless supply of questions. Dozens of e-mails are exchanged and diagrams faxed before any agreement is reached. After the deal goes through, the salesman is surprised to be invited to dinner at the German manager's family home. But he never gets to meet 'the big boss'.

c   Match the following to make collocations from the text.

raise   agreement
allocate   objections
exchange   time
reach   e-mails

d   Find the words or phrases which mean:
get something ready (para 2)
start (para 2)
support a fact (para 2)
be completed (para 4)

Brazil

São Paolo. 2am. A jet-lagged British salesman and his better-dressed Brazilian client wait outside the elegant restaurant in which they've hardly talked business all night. Their car is driven right up to the door. This is a good part of town, but you don't want to be walking to the parking lot in a smart suit and expensive watch. The Brazilian suggests a nightclub, but tomorrow's meeting is scheduled for 9am, and maybe the salesman's already had one caipirinha* too many.

By 9.35 the following morning the meeting's about to begin. The salesman is introduced to everyone round the table in turn. A large number of them seem to be related. The conversation ranges from football to families to traffic problems and back to football. The atmosphere's relaxed, but the salesman's barely started his technical presentation before someone cuts in. Soon everybody's joining in the discussion with wildly creative ideas of their own. If this is a negotiation, it's hard to see how the Brazilians are working as a team.

The salesman is surprised to find his hosts so enthusiastic about his product. Did he really win them over that easily – or will there be problems later on? The meeting has overrun. He decides to press them for a decision. All eyes turn to the boss. 'We needn't worry about the contractual details at this stage,' says the senior Brazilian manager, smiling, his hand on the Briton's shoulder. 'I'm sure we can work something out. Let's think about the future.'

*a Brazilian drink made from sugar cane alcohol, crushed limes, ice and sugar

e   Match the following to make collocations from the text.
talk   a decision
schedule   a team
work as   business
press for   a meeting

f   Find the words or phrases which mean:
interrupt (para 2)
persuade (para 3)
continue for too long (para 3)
find a solution (para 3)

2   Form new groups with people who read different case studies. Discuss the different attitudes to:

delegation   hierarchy   interruption   power
relationship-building   technical matters   time

In which of the three countries would you feel most at home?

LANGUAGE LINKS

Vocabulary: Meetings

Complete the collocations by writing the nouns and noun phrases in the right-hand boxes. They are all things you might do before, during or after a meeting.

an action plan	the agenda	agreement	comments
a decision	details	ideas	an opinion	a point

set stick to	(a)	reach be in	(e)
brainstorm exchange	(b)	make invite	(f)
hold express	(c)	draw up implement	(g)
raise clarify	(d)	go into sort out	(h)
		come to reconsider	(i)

Comments & opinions

In meetings, certain expressions help you to introduce your comments and indicate your opinions more clearly. Look at the following five extracts from meetings. Replace the phrases in **bold** with ones in the box which have a similar meaning.

As a matter of fact	Clearly	Essentially	Frankly
If you ask me	Incidentally	In short	In theory
Luckily	On the other hand	Overall	Strangely enough

A **Personally,** / (a) .... I think this whole project has been a waste of time.

B **To be honest,** / (b) .... I tend to agree with you.

A **However,** / (c) .... we've put too much money into it to cancel it now.

A **By the way,** / (d) .... did you get in touch with our agent in Warsaw?

B **Actually,** / (e) .... she phoned me. I'll talk to you about it later.

A **Obviously,** / (f) .... we don't want to have a strike on our hands.

B **Fortunately,** / (g) .... we may not have to. I spoke to the union rep this morning.

A **In general,** / (h) .... did people like the idea of open-plan offices?

B **Funnily enough,** / (i) .... they didn't. We may have to rethink our proposal.

A **To sum up,** / (j) .... by year-end we should be nearing the break-even point.

B **Basically,** / (k) .... then, we're going to make a net loss?

A **Technically,** / (l) .... yes. But that's because we're channelling so much money back into the business.

Grammar: Modal verbs

can	could	may	might	shall	should	will	would	must

You don't add an *s* in the 3rd person singular.

Modal verbs are followed by the infinitive without *to*. (NB After *ought*, use *to* + infinitive: *She ought to go.*)

Couldn't he attend the meeting?

You don't use *do* or *does* to make questions.

You don't use *do* or *does* to make negatives.

You use modal verbs to express many different functions. (See 1.)

be able to	be allowed to	have to

Be able to, have to and *be allowed to* are often used in place of modal verbs. You use these verbs to express concepts that are not possible with modal verbs.

- **Will** you **be able to** finish the report tomorrow? (~~will you can~~ is not possible)
- I **had to** attend a meeting last night. (*must* has no past form)

1 Modal verbs say as much about the speaker's attitude as about the factual content of the sentence. Match the modal verbs in bold to their main function.

A They **should** be here by now. (a)
B I'**ll** phone and check. (b)
A No, wait a minute, that **must** be them. (c)

A **Could** I leave early tomorrow, do you think? (d)
B Well, I **might** need you to check the monthly figures. (e)
A But I **have to** pick up the kids from school. (f)

expressing obligation
expressing certainty
asking for permission
expressing possibility
expressing probability
taking the initiative

Now do the same with these:

A You **mustn't** load that software onto your company PC! (g)
B But I **can't** do this job without it. (h)
A Well, you **ought to** speak to IT, then. (i)

giving advice
saying something isn't necessary
expressing inability
making a request

A I'm getting a drink from the machine. **Can** I get you anything? (j) prohibiting something
B Oh, thanks. **Could** you get me a Coke or something? (k) making an offer
A Sure. What's this? You **don't have to** give me the money! (l)

2 Try to complete the following modal verbs quiz in less than five minutes.

I	*You mustn't do that.* Will there be trouble if you do it?
2	*You don't have to do that.* Will there be trouble if you do it?
3	Put these sentences into the past: a *I can't talk to you now.* b *I hope we'll meet again.* c *I must fly to Geneva.*
4	What's the opposite of *That can't be right?*
5	What does *She should be here at nine* mean? a She's supposed to be here at nine. b I expect she'll be here at nine. c Either.
6	*I could do it* refers to a the past. b the present. c the future. d it depends.
7	*They needn't have done it.* Did they do it?
8	*They didn't need to do it.* Did they do it?
9	Are these two sentences possible? a *I could swim by the age of two.* b *I was able to swim by the age of two.*
10	Are these two sentences possible? a *I took the exam three times and finally I could pass.* b *I took the exam three times and finally I was able to pass.*

Phrase bank: Interrupting and preventing interruption

1 Add the expressions below to the diagram according to whether they are ways of interrupting, preventing interruption or both.

> Can I just come in here?   Could I just finish what I was saying?
> Erm,…   Hang on a minute.
> Hold on a second. Can I just say something?
> If I could just finish…   Just a moment.   Let me finish.
> No, hear me out.   Sorry to interrupt (again).   Wait a minute.

Interrupting   Preventing interruption

Just a moment

2 Which of these statements means you want Juan to stop speaking? Which means you want someone else to stop speaking, so Juan can say something?

a Thanks, Juan.   b Thanks. Juan?

How does your voice go up and down when saying these two expressions? Which sounds like this ↘↗? And which sounds like this ↗↘?

3 Put the following conversation in order. The first one has been done for you.

a Yes, what is it?   ☐
b You were saying…   ☐
c Can I come back to those later?   ☐
d Can you give us the figures for that? ☐
e Where was I?   ☐
f Can I stop you there?   ☐ 1
g OK, sorry. Go on.   ☐

15 SNAIL MAIL

Writing without thinking is like shooting without aiming.

ARNOLD GLASOW

1 According to management guru Henry Mintzberg, even in the age of the electronic office most of us still spend a third of our time doing routine paperwork. What kind of documents cross your desk in a typical day?

2 Different managers are talking about the paperwork they have to do. Complete what they say below by writing in the documents they are referring to.

> contracts   copies   diagrams   figures   forms   invoices   letters   mail   memos
> post-it   questionnaires   receipts   record   report   trade journals

a   The first thing I do when I get into the office is get myself a coffee and check the morning
....

b   Whenever I have important .... to write, I usually draft them several times before finally sending them.

c   One thing I can't stand is filling in .... – they never give you enough space to write your answers!

d   I try to read as many .... as possible – just to keep up with what's going on.

e   I work in the legal department, so that means a lot of drafting and drawing up of
....

f   I work for a design firm, so I often find myself faxing .... of plans and
....

g   I have to keep a .... of all my expenses, so I always ask for .... – I have a pile by the end of the month!

h   I try to settle .... as quickly as possible, but I query them immediately if the
.... don't add up.

i   I used to circulate .... to other people in the department, but these days I just e-mail them on the Intranet or stick a .... on their desk.

j   In my job I have to design market research ...., which usually means putting together some kind of .... afterwards.

COMMUNICATION CHANNELS

What would you do first in situations a–l below?

- write a letter
- speak to the person face to face
- send an e-mail
- send an SMS
- make a phone call
- send a fax
- arrange a meeting

Complete and discuss each point. <u>Underline</u> the correct preposition.

You want to …

a   introduce your company **to** / **for** a prospective client.
b   complain **about** / **of** the service at a hotel you stayed in.
c   give instructions **of** / **on** how to get to your office.
d   confirm an appointment **for** / **on** tomorrow morning.
e   sum **off** / **up** what was agreed at a recent meeting.
f   deal **with** / **about** a complaint from an important customer.
g   follow up **with** / **on** a sales presentation you made.
h   raise the subject **with** / **of** a salary increase with your boss.
i   thank someone you stayed with **for** / **on** their hospitality.
j   ask **with** / **for** a signature on a contract.
k   send **off** / **out** a job application and CV.
l   share a joke you found on the Internet **with** / **about** a friend!

IN A RUSH

1   Read the business letter below. The person who wrote it was in a rush to finish it and made a lot of mistakes. Work with a partner. There are 17 mistakes in all. Try to correct them.

> Xenon Communications
> In touch with technology
> 22st February
>
> Re Enquiry about the DigiCom System
>
> My dear Ms Ramalho,
>
> thank you for your letter from Feb 9 and for your interest in the new Xenon digital comunication system.
>
> I am such sorry you were disabled to attend our presentation in São Paulo last month, but I am delighted to tell you we are planning another one in Brasilia on April 30.
>
> In the mean time, I enclose a copy of our last catalogue and currant prize list.
>
> If you have any questions or would like further informations concerning our company and its products, please don't hesitate but contact me again.
>
> I look forwards to hearing from you.
>
> Yours fatefully,
>
> Rudolf Kinski
>
> pp Brian Green
>
> XENON Communications   Unit 45   Pinewood Industrial Park   Oxford OX7 T42
> tel (44) (0)1865 356 777   e-mail xenon-communications@virgin.net   website www.xenon.co.uk

2   🔊 2.33   The person who wrote the letter asked a colleague with better English to check it for him. Listen to eight extracts from their conversation. Do they make the same corrections you did?

COULD I SEE YOU A MOMENT?

Work with a partner to practise checking each other's business letters. Both speakers see page 131.

WHAT'S MISSING?

1 Work with a partner. Replace the missing words in the following sentences from business letters. In sentences a–j one word is missing. In k–t two words are missing. The first one has been done for you as an example.

a   How are things <u>with</u> you?

b   I apologise not replying sooner.

c   Further our telephone conversation yesterday, …

d   See you the weekend. Best wishes, Jim.

e   I thought I'd send you a copy this article.

f   Sorry I wasn't there meet you when you called.

g   Sincerely, Brian Green

h   It was great pleasure meeting you last week.

i   Take care yourself.

j   How's going?

k   Thank you your letter May 6.

l   Get back to me soon you can.

m   I look forward hearing you.

n   With reference your fax June 3, …

o   I am writing regard your recent advertisement.

p   I'll be touch the next couple of weeks or so.

q   I can be any further assistance, do please contact me again.

r   Let know when you're next Zagreb.

s   It was nice talking you other day.

t   Please pass my regards your sales manager, Ms Fontaine.

2 Now write the letters of the sentences in the box below according to whether they usually come at the beginning or end of a business letter and whether they are formal or informal.

	Formal	Informal
Beginning		
End		

CROSSED IN THE POST

Work in groups to practise sending and receiving letters. Every ten minutes you will have to 'mail' the letter you have written to another group and reply to the one you receive. Use the phrases and expressions below as the basis for your letters, but add extra points if you like.

Group A

1 Preparation
In your group invent a sales meeting you had with a potential client. Decide what you were trying to sell, what the main features and benefits of the product are and how it compares with the competition.

2 Following up a sales meeting
Dear • Thank you • taking the time • see us • your offices in • During our meeting • I hope • able • show you the benefits of • As you saw • really is a superior product in terms of • I think • meets your requirements very well • Need further information • feel free • contact • again

3 Putting off a potential contact
Dear • Enjoyed meeting you in • Everyone agreed • very interesting discussion • Unfortunately • not in a position • carry things further • the moment • Busy time of the year for us • When • had time • consider • more detail • will contact • again

4 Reviving a cold sales lead
Dear • As someone who • previously shown interest in • wanted you to know • now a new, improved version of the • at an even more competitive price • added features include • This means you can • Enclosed • copy • new product brochure • Look forward

5 Responding to a business opportunity
Dear • Thank • letter • Jun 15 • Now had time • discuss your proposal • head office • like • arrange • meeting • explore • more detail...
OR
Dear • Thank • letter • Having considered • proposal more fully • sorry • inform you • not able • proceed at this time...

Group B

1 Preparation
In your group invent a company you met at a conference who might be interested in using your service. Decide what the service is and how you compare with your competitors.

2 Following up a business contact
Dear • A pleasure meeting you in • Hope you got back safely • I was wondering • you'd like • discuss further what we talked about • conference reception • I've spoken • my boss • very interested • exploring the idea further.• If you're interested • happy • set up a meeting

3 Putting off a prospective supplier
Dear • Thank you • coming • talk to us about • Very much enjoyed • presentation • extremely interested in • At the moment, however • considering several alternative products • haven't yet • final decision • Be in touch in due course • Thank you once again

4 Reviving a cold contact
Dear • How are things? • Hope • got over your busy period • As • haven't been in touch • a while • wondering • had more time • consider our conversation • conference • January • In fact • have some news • might be • great interest to you • When • convenient time • talk?

5 Responding to a sales pitch
Dear • Thank • your letter • copy new product brochure • Very impressed • specifications • like • place • initial order for...
OR
Dear • Thank • letter • Afraid • decided • purchase • another supplier this time • Have kept • product details • file...

Jan

Feb

Jun

Jul

If necessary, phone the other group to confirm your arrangements with them.

LANGUAGE LINKS

Vocabulary: Prepositions

Prepositions (*in, at, of, for, through*, etc.) are a restricted group of short words, each having many different purposes. They usually take their precise meaning from the words around them.

Apart from their standard uses to refer to time, place and movement, prepositions also combine with verbs, nouns and adjectives to form a lot of useful phrases and expressions. Such phrases are best learned 'whole' as items of vocabulary.

Prepositional phrases

Twenty-two prepositions are missing from the following letter. Write them in.

> Dear Mr Savage
>
> Thank you your letter 12th April. I'm very sorry the difficulties you've had getting one our engineers come and repair the alarm system we installed January. Please accept my apologies. I am as concerned the delay as you are.
>
> The manager who is responsible our after-sales service is new the department and not yet familiar all our procedures, but this is no excuse such a long delay. Rest assured, he is now aware the problem and will arrange an engineer call whatever time is most convenient you. Obviously, this will be free charge. I have also authorised a 10% refund the purchase price. If you are still not fully satisfied the system, please contact me personally and I shall be happy supply you a replacement.
>
> My apologies once again the inconvenience this has caused you.

Preposition + noun + preposition

Complete the following extracts from business letters, faxes and e-mails using the nouns in the box. Pay particular attention to the prepositions on either side of each noun.

> accordance   account   addition   agreement   behalf
> case   effect   favour   pressure   regard   terms
> touch   view

a   I am writing with .... to your advertisement in *Marketing Week*.

b   We are basically in .... with the main points in your proposal.

c   I've been in .... with our distributors in Poland concerning your enquiry.

d   There are one or two points in .... to those we discussed which we now need to address.

e   No one at the meeting was in .... of the idea.

f   The goods have been insured in .... of damage in transit.

g   There will be a 3% price increase with .... from January 1st.

h   Plan A has been rejected on .... of the considerable costs involved.

i   We decided, in .... of the political difficulties, not to export to Iraq.

j   We are again under .... from head office to reduce overheads.

k   Certainly, in .... of experience, she's the best candidate we've seen so far.

l   We are investigating the complaints in .... with our normal procedures.

m   May I, on .... of myself and the whole team, thank you for making our visit so enjoyable.

Grammar: Multi-verb expressions

When we combine two verbs in a sentence, the second verb can follow several patterns:

1   Modal verbs are followed by the infinitive without *to*:
- We **must make** a decision on this today.

2   Non-modal verbs are followed either by the infinitive with *to*:
- We **agreed to review** the situation in a month.
or by the *-ing* form:
- They **regretted borrowing** the money.
If in doubt, use the infinitive with *to*. It's much more common.

3   Some verbs, normally followed by the *-ing* form, change when there's an indirect object:
- I *advise repackaging* the product.
- I *advise **you** to repackage* the product.
- I *suggest breaking off* the meeting here.
- I *suggest **we** break off* the meeting here.

4   Some non-modal verbs can be followed by both the infinitive with *to* and the *-ing* form. But be careful. The meaning often changes – sometimes completely – as in these examples:
- They **stopped to talk**. (= they stopped doing something else so that they could talk)
- They **stopped talking**. (= the talking stopped)
- I **didn't remember to e-mail** you the report. (= there was no e-mail)
- I **don't remember e-mailing** you the report. (= I may have e-mailed it to you, but I don't remember)

5   When a verb is followed by a preposition other than *to*, the *-ing* form is usually used:
- We **succeeded in getting** the loan.
- I'm **thinking of changing** my job.

When it isn't, the meaning changes:
- He **went on talking** for over an hour! (= he wouldn't shut up)
- He **went on to talk** about profits. (= he changed the subject)

Study the information on page 91 and complete the following advice on how to produce professional letters and faxes by combining the verbs, prepositions and pronouns in brackets.

a   Reply to incoming mail promptly. Don't _____ for more than a couple of days. (put off / write back)

b   Always _____ with a proper salutation. (remember / open)

c   Don't _____ a subject line. (forget / include)

d   _____ a lot of time on social chit-chat at the beginning of the letter. (forget about / spend)

e   Most writing experts _____ lots of subheadings and bullet points to make your message clearer. (recommend / use)

f   But they don't _____ a lot of old-fashioned formal expressions. (suggest you / use)

g   Ideally, you _____ neither too formal nor too friendly. (should / aim / sound)

h   You _____ your sentences short and simple. (should / try / keep)

i   Some people _____ 10–15 words per sentence. (advise you / not exceed)

j   Also _____ long complicated words when short ones will do. (avoid / use)

k   If you have a lot of information, _____ a separate document. (consider / enclose)

l   Beware the spell check! You really _____ all your mistakes. (can't / trust it / pick up)

m   Grammar checks are even worse. You'll certainly _____ on them. (regret / rely)

n   If you _____ your whole message into less than 200 words, you've done well. (can / manage / get)

o   Reread before you send. _____ your own letter – what impression would it give? (imagine / receive)

p   _____ a difficult letter several times before you send it. (think about / redraft)

Phrase bank: Standard letter-writing expressions

You have been given responsibility for a very good customer your boss knows personally, but you don't. See what your boss would write below and make what you write a little more formal.

Informal	Formal
Dear Nick,	Dear Mr Salzmann,
How are things?	a (hope, well) _____
I got your letter, thanks.	b (thank, letter of, January 12) _____
Sorry I haven't got back to you sooner.	c (apologies, not replying) _____
About our phone call the other day, …	d (Further to, conversation, last Friday) _____
Great to meet you last week!	e (pleasure, meeting) _____
I'm writing about our contract renewal.	f (writing, regard) _____
I'm afraid I can't give you a bigger discount.	g (unfortunately, unable, increase) _____
But how about a higher credit limit?	h (what, can do, offer) _____
Let's meet and have a chat about this.	i (perhaps, meet, discuss) _____
I'll give you a call sometime next week.	j (in touch) _____
I dropped in a copy of our new catalogue.	k (enclose) _____
If you need any help, just let me know.	l (any further assistance, please do contact) _____
See you at the conference!	m (look forward, meeting, again) _____
Let's talk soon.	n (look forward, hearing) _____
Best wishes, Tony.	o (Yours) _____

16 SOLVING PROBLEMS

Problem solving is finding ways of getting from where we are to where we want to be.

ALAN BARKER, *HOW TO HOLD BETTER MEETINGS*

1 How good are you at problem-solving? Where and when do you get your best ideas?

Complete the following phrases and tick those that are true for you.

> bath book course court daydreaming desk drinks
> holiday meetings morning music night shower work

a first thing in the ....
b in the middle of the ....
c travelling to and from ....
d on ....
e at my ....
f lying in a nice hot ....
g while I'm taking a ....

h listening to ....
i on the golf ....
j on the tennis ....
k after a few ....
l relaxing with a good ....
m in problem-solving ....
n while I'm ....!

2 Compare the phrases you ticked in 1 with a partner.

3 There is a Japanese expression: *None of us is as smart as all of us.* Following this idea, one American company regularly posts questions on a bulletin board and invites its staff to brainstorm suggestions. Read the bulletin board on the left.

Today's question:

In what ways, big or small, could this company save money?

Write your suggestions below. $100 bonus for all suggestions we adopt.

Work with a partner. Think of as many ways as possible your company could save money. Then compare your ideas with the rest of the group.

4 ⊙ 3.01 Listen to the first idea the company awarded a $100 bonus to.

5 Work in groups to solve some problems three real companies faced. Speaker A see page 132. Speaker B see page 137. Speaker C see page 138.

6 ⊙ 3.02 Listen and compare each company's solution with yours. What do you think of the real solutions?

SUGGESTIONS

1 Problem-solving meetings should start with clear objectives and end with clear actions. Look at the problems and objectives in the box. Complete the suggestions in column 3 using the phrases below.

a to shift production to somewhere like South-East Asia
b to sell it direct online
c delay the new product launch
d offered it on a sale or return basis
e encrypting our most confidential information
f sell it off at a discount
g raising prices
h we involved the police
i bought the company out
j just manufacture our own components

	What's the problem?	What's our objective?	What action can we take?
1	We can't get retail outlets to stock our new product.	to get access to the customer	What if we _____? Another option would be _____.
2	Our sole supplier is about to go bankrupt!	to get the supplies we need	Supposing we _____? Alternatively, we could _____.
3	Rising labour costs are reducing profits.	to maintain our profit margins	How about _____? The answer could be _____.
4	Old unsold stock is starting to pile up in the warehouses.	to create space for new product	Why don't we _____? Couldn't we just _____?
5	Someone in the company is passing on information to the competition!	to protect our competitive advantage	What about _____? Maybe it's time _____.

2 3.03–3.07 Listen to extracts from the meetings above and check your answers.

3 Listen again and answer the following questions.

Extract 1 Which of the two suggestions is better received?
Extract 2 What will happen if a solution isn't found?
Extract 3 Why isn't a price increase an option?
Extract 4 How is product development affecting the stock situation?
Extract 5 What do you think the last speaker means when he says 'Perhaps we can even turn the situation to our advantage'?

4 Go back and underline the five most useful collocations in 1 (e.g. *retail outlet*, *stock a product*, *labour costs*). What are the equivalent expressions in your own language?

5 Complete the sentences. They were all in the extracts you just listened to.

> 'd been + wouldn't be   'd discounted + wouldn't have   'd known + could have
> would have + 'd thought   wouldn't have + 'd priced

a   We .... this problem if we .... the product more sensibly in the first place.

b   If we .... this was going to happen, we .... had our own production plant up and running by now.

c   If we .... able to get the unions to accept a lower pay offer, John, we .... considering outsourcing to Asia.

d   If we .... it sooner, we .... had to be so generous.

e   I .... called the police in already if I .... it would do any good.

Which of the sentences above refer

1   to the past and present?   ☐ ☐ ☐
2   only to the past?   ☐ ☐

PROBLEM-SOLVING TECHNIQUES

1 Do you have a special procedure for dealing with more complex problems? Complete the checklist below using the verbs in the boxes.

> a – d   brainstorm   define   review   select
>
> e – l   assign   break   criticise   draw up   eliminate   explore   invite   restate

Step One:	.... the basic problem (a)	.... the problem down into parts (e)
		.... the problem as a challenge (f)
Step Two:	.... ideas (b)	.... everyone to speak (g)
		.... nothing at this stage (h)
Step Three:	.... your ideas so far (c)	.... the possibilities of each idea (i)
		.... impractical suggestions (j)
Step Four:	.... the best solution (d)	.... an action plan (k)
		.... different tasks to different people (l)

2 The following sentences were used in a problem-solving meeting. Decide at which step in 1 each sentence was used.

1   Now, what we need are as many ideas as possible.   ☐
2   How could we make this idea work?   ☐
3   On balance, I think we should go with this idea.   ☐
4   Let's think about what we can do, instead of what we can't.   ☐
5   I'd like to hear what you all have to say.   ☐
6   OK, basically, the problem is this.   ☐

7   OK, let's see what we've got so far.   ☐
8   I think we'll have to reject this idea for now.   ☐
9   Now, how do we implement this?   ☐
10   OK, that's a nice idea.   ☐
11   Joanne, can I leave the details to you?   ☐
12   I think there are three main aspects to the problem.   ☐

EVERYDAY PROBLEMS

1 Work in groups. What sort of everyday problems do you face at work? Write down on separate slips of paper two or three of the toughest problems you have to deal with. Be specific.

2 Swap papers with another group. Read out the problems one by one and discuss with your group how they could be solved. Write down any suggestions on the back of the papers.

3 Return the papers to their original owners. Was any of the advice useful?

CREATIVITY

1 How important is creativity in problem-solving? Work in groups. Each group reads a different piece of advice on how to solve problems creatively.

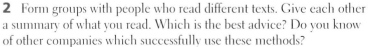

How to solve problems

1 Change your perspective

A lot of problems can be solved simply by looking at them in a different way. Try problem reversal. Don't ask how you can sell more of your products. Ask how you could sell fewer and see where that idea takes you. Perhaps you could create a totally new market where exclusivity was more important than sales volume. As marketing and communications specialist Ros Jay points out: 'Many companies have done well out of problem reversal. Businesses like Apple Computers have looked at the market and, instead of saying 'how can we compete with all these big players', have asked themselves "what can we do that all these other companies aren't doing?" In the late 90s the mighty IBM's slogan was 'Think'. Apple's was 'Think different'.

2 Be playful

Must work always feel like work? John Quelch, Dean of the London School of Business, asks: 'How many times a day does the average five-year-old laugh? Answer: 150. How many times a day does the average 45-year-old executive laugh? Answer: five. Who is having more fun? Who is, therefore, likely to be more creative? Need we ask?' At ?What *If!*, a London-based innovation consultancy, they've worked out that most people get their best ideas away from the office, so they've made the office look like home, complete with armchairs, kitchen and even table football. ?What *If!* is now a £3 million company whose clients include Pepsi Co, ICI and British Airways, so they must be doing something right.

3 Make connections

Jonas Ridderstråle and Kjell Nordström of the Stockholm School of Economics have put forward the idea that 'as everything that ever will be invented has been invented, the only way forward is to combine what is already there'. So we get 'e-mail','edu-tainment', 'TV dinners', 'distance-learning' and 'bio-tech'. Sometimes the combinations are impossible. Yamaha, for example, hasn't yet worked out a way to combine motorbikes with musical instruments – perhaps it will. But Jake Burton had more success when he gave up his job on Wall Street in 1977 to pioneer a new sport. Bringing together two quite separate things – snow and surfboards – he developed the modern snowboard. Today there are nearly four million snowboarders breaking their necks all over the world in the name of fun!

2 Form groups with people who read different texts. Give each other a summary of what you read. Which is the best advice? Do you know of other companies which successfully use these methods?

A PROBLEM-SOLVING MEETING

1 Work in groups. Group A see below. Group B see page 132. Choose a chairperson. Using the procedure on page 95, hold a meeting to solve the problem.

- Read paragraph one. What else do you know about this business?
- Read paragraph two. What's your immediate response to the problem?
- Read paragraph three. It should give you some extra ideas on how to solve the problem.
- Conduct a problem-solving meeting with your group.
- Summarise the problem and your solutions for the other group or groups. Find out if they agree with you.

1 An image problem at Hennessy Cognac

The company

Hennessy Cognac has a long and colourful history going back to 1765 when Irishman and war hero, Richard Hennessy, left the army and started the company in France. Today it is one of the premium brands owned by food and drinks giant, Diageo, whose other famous names include Guinness, Gordon's gin, Dom Perignon champagne and Johnnie Walker whisky.

The challenge

But in America in the mid 90s Hennessy had a serious image problem. Perhaps because of its great tradition, Hennessy was regarded as an after-dinner drink for old men, bores, snobs – everything the young ambitious American professional definitely did not want to become. Compared with the ever-popular gin and tonic and other more exotic cocktails, sales of Hennessy looked positively horizontal. Conventional advertising and point-of-sale promotions seemed to have little effect. The marketing team at Diageo needed to devise a truly original campaign if they were going to reverse a slow decline in sales.

The opportunity

You're not paying attention. Nobody is. These days there's so much marketing hype it's impossible to take it all in. It's estimated that we all see around 3,000 advertising messages every day from billboards to T-shirts, bumper stickers to webpage banners, and the net result is that we take no notice at all. Particularly in sophisticated luxury goods markets, straight advertising just doesn't work anymore. What does seem to work is peer pressure – seeing what our friends and colleagues are doing and doing the same. Busy people, especially, don't like their lives being interrupted by stupid commercials. But that doesn't mean they can't be persuaded, as Diageo discovered.

2 🔊 3.08 Listen to the recording to find out what the companies actually did. Were your suggestions similar? Is there anything in the case studies which is relevant to your own line of business?

LANGUAGE LINKS

Vocabulary: People and products

Decide whether the adjectives below can be used to describe people (staff), products or both. Tick the correct boxes.

	staff	products			staff	products
a	best-selling	☐ ☐	g	unique	☐ ☐
b	efficient	☐ ☐	h	luxury	☐ ☐
c	high-quality	☐ ☐	i	loyal	☐ ☐
d	well qualified	☐ ☐	j	permanent	☐ ☐
e	household	☐ ☐	k	part-time	☐ ☐
f	dedicated	☐ ☐	l	reliable	☐ ☐

The workforce

1 List the verbs and verb phrases in the box with those below which have a similar meaning.

> down tools   dismiss   inspire   instruct   lay off   motivate
> quit   recruit   relocate   resign   take industrial action
> take on   teach   transfer

hire	train	move	leave
a	c	e	g ....
b	d	f	h ....

fire	encourage	go on strike
i	k	m ....
j	l	n ....

2 The adjectives below can all be used to describe people in a company. Change each adjective into its opposite by adding *un-*, *in-*, *im-*, *ir-* or *dis-*.

a .... reliable
b .... flexible
c .... organised
d .... patient
e .... responsible
f .... creative
g .... consistent
h .... inspiring
i .... committed
j .... practical
k .... articulate
l .... honest
m .... rational
n .... decisive
o .... supportive
p .... competent
q .... assertive
r .... sociable
s .... considerate
t .... competitive

3 Complete the following staff appraisals using an appropriate positive or negative adjective from 2.

a Laura's a real ideas person. She's exceptionally ....
b Brian can only do things his way. He's a bit ....
c Max is always there to give people a hand when they need it. He's really very ....
d With Olaf it's just one mistake after another. He's completely ....
e Greta tends to take no notice of other people's needs. She's rather ....
f Richard's office looks like a bomb hit it – papers everywhere! He's totally ....
g With Miyumi the job always comes first. She's totally ....
h Sam can never make up his mind about anything. He's extremely ....
i Callum really knows how to motivate his staff. He's incredibly ....
j You can never depend on Leo to do what he's supposed to do. He's totally ....
k Elena meets all her targets month after month. She's incredibly ....
l Jeanette too often allows her personal life to interfere with her work. She's rather ....
m Eric always has to be the best at everything. He's extremely ....
n Gareth tends to keep himself to himself. He's a bit ....

The production line

1 Match the verbs and verb phrases in the box with those below which mean the opposite.

> go out of   halt   reduce   reintroduce   scale down
> withdraw

go into	◄──►	a	
start	◄──►	b	production
step up	◄──►	c	
launch	◄──►	d	
discontinue	◄──►	e	a product
boost	◄──►	f	productivity

2 Complete the following sentences using appropriate words and phrases from 1.

a We always .... new products in January at the annual Trade Fair.
b We'll need to .... production to keep up with demand.
c A staff incentive scheme helped us to .... productivity.
d We had to .... production completely until we'd found the fault.
e There were some complaints about the product, so we had to .... it to make the necessary modifications. We'll .... it next month.

Grammar: Conditionals (past reference)

You can use *if* to speculate about the likely effects of things being different in the past. You often use this type of conditional to talk about regrets and make accusations.

- If we **hadn't invested** so heavily in dotcoms, we'd **have saved** ourselves a fortune! (1)
  (but we invested heavily and we didn't save a fortune)
- You **could have got** an interview with that company if only you'd **taken** my advice. (2)
  (but you didn't get an interview because you didn't take my advice)
- If our lawyers **hadn't spotted** that mistake in the contract, we'd **be** in a real mess! (3)
  (but they spotted it and so we are not in a real mess)
- If you'd **told** me about it sooner, I **might have been able to** do something. (4)
  (but you didn't tell me sooner so I couldn't do anything)
- He **might** never **have been able to** start his own business if his father **hadn't helped** him. (5)
  (but he started his own business because his father helped him)
- If she'd **taken** her studies more seriously, she **wouldn't be flipping** burgers at McDonald's. (6)
  (but she didn't take her studies seriously and now she's working at McDonald's)

1 Study the information above and answer the questions.

a   What grammatical tense is used in the *if*-clause of all the examples?
b   What modal verbs are used in the main clause?
c   What tenses follow the modal verbs in the examples?
d   Which sentences directly refer to the effects of the past on the present?
e   Which sentences directly refer to the effects of the past on the more recent past?

2 Complete the conversation using the pairs of words in the box.

> could + tried   done + have   hadn't + wouldn't
> have + known   promised + would   would + could

Two colleagues are having an argument.
A All I'm saying is, if you'd (a) .... something about it sooner, we could .... prevented this whole nightmare from happening.
B I know, I know. And I (b) .... have if I .... have, but I couldn't.
A You (c) .... have if you'd .... , you mean.
B Maybe if I hadn't already (d) .... , I .... be able to put them all off.
A Well, anyway, it's too late now. You know, I'd never (e) .... asked you to organise these visits if I'd .... you weren't clear about it.

B Well, if you (f) .... said you wanted us to get involved in the local community more, I probably .... have had the idea in the first place.
A I mean, what were you thinking of? You've organised factory tours for three infant schools, an old people's home and the Bulgarian Embassy all on the same morning!

Which example above does not contain the Past Perfect?

Phrase bank: Problem-solving

Match each of the four stages of a problem-solving meeting to two things you might say.

a   Defining the problem

b   Brainstorming ideas

c   Reviewing ideas

d   Selecting the solution

1   OK, let's see what we've got so far.
2   On balance, I think we should go with …
3   I think there are three main aspects to the problem.
4   I think we'll have to reject this idea for now.
5   I'd like to hear what you all have to say.
6   Now, how do we implement this?
7   OK, basically the problem is this.
8   Let's keep the ideas coming.

a ☐ ☐   b ☐ ☐   c ☐ ☐   d ☐ ☐

Brainstorming

Complete the brainstorming phrases with one of the following. For two of the phrases there are two possibilities with a difference in meaning. What's the difference?

> sell it online   selling it online
> sold it online   to sell it online

a   What if we .... ?
b   Another option would be ....
c   Supposing we .... ?
d   Alternatively, we could ....
e   How about .... ?
f   The answer could be ....
g   Why don't we .... ?
h   Couldn't we just .... ?
i   What about .... ?
j   Maybe it's time ....

ADVERSE REACTIONS

1 According to Charles Darwin, 'it is not the strongest species that survive, nor the most intelligent, but the ones who are most responsive to change.' What has been the biggest change in your (working) life so far?

2 If your company was to be taken over by a foreign competitor tomorrow, which of the following would you be concerned about?

> losing your job   getting a new boss   losing authority   having to prove yourself all over again
> being promoted to a position you don't really want   a negative work atmosphere
> doing more work for no more money   being asked to fire some of your team
> being transferred abroad   having to speak more English!

3 Read the extract from news website Rosberg.com describing an international takeover and answer the questions.

a What do you think Jason Roth means by 'the strategic importance of a presence in Turkey'?

b When he says 'a certain amount of rationalization may be necessary and some assets may need to be realized to help finance the acquisition', what exactly do you think he means?

Rosberg.com

LOG IN / REGISTER

Updated: **New York** Jan 17 10:42   **London** Jan 17 15:42   **Tokyo** Jan 17 23:42   **Search news** [   ] Go

News
- Exclusive
- ◉ Worldwide
- Regions
- Markets
- Economy
- Politics
- Science
- Opinion
- Sports
- Special report

Zantis Pharmaceuticals acquires Nilay Medical
by Alistair Jay

May 17 (Rosberg) – The takeover of Turkish Nilay Medical (NIL) for an undisclosed sum by US Zantis Pharmaceuticals (ZAN) was confirmed this morning by Jason Roth, spokesperson for the North Carolina-based conglomerate. Speaking at a press conference to announce the acquisition, Zantis's first in either Europe or Asia, Roth emphasized the strong performance of Nilay and the strategic importance of a presence in Turkey. The future of the company had been in some doubt since the founding Nilay family sold its 30% stake in the firm 18 months ago. In response to news of the takeover, Nilay's share price went up by 29% on the Istanbul Stock Exchange (ISE). But Roth's admission that 'a certain amount of rationalization may be necessary and some assets may need to be realized to help finance the acquisition' was not universally welcomed amongst board members and shareholders. Ahmet Barak is to be replaced as CEO by Yvonne Latimer.

The production line at Nilay Medical

◉ Interview with Zantis CEO Yvonne Latimer
click here

4 🎧 3.09 Now listen to the podcast interview with Yvonne Latimer, CEO of the newly formed Zantis-Nilay, check your predictions in 3 and complete the information chart below.

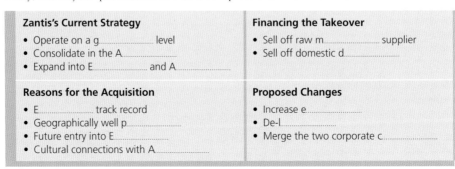

Zantis's Current Strategy	**Financing the Takeover**
• Operate on a g............... level	• Sell off raw m............... supplier
• Consolidate in the A...............	• Sell off domestic d...............
• Expand into E............... and A...............	
Reasons for the Acquisition	**Proposed Changes**
• E............... track record	• Increase e...............
• Geographically well p...............	• De-l...............
• Future entry into E...............	• Merge the two corporate c...............
• Cultural connections with A...............	

Diagram showing flat and hierarchical corporate cultures:

USA > Sweden > Germany > Japan > France > Brazil > Turkey

Source: Fons Trompenaars and Charles Hampden-Turner,
Riding the Waves of Culture

Individualism

 Turkey   Score = 37

USA   Score = 91

The higher the score, the less people consider the needs of the group or team in comparison with their own goals.

Uncertainty avoidance

Turkey   Score = 85

USA   Score = 46

The higher the score, the less people like to take risks, break rules or face change.

Source: Geert Hofstede, *Culture's Consequences*

5 Look at the cross-cultural comparison of Turkish and North American leadership and management styles. Where would you place your own culture? With a partner, try to predict some of the problems the newly merged company might face.

6 After a strong start, it's been an extremely disappointing first year for Zantis-Nilay. Read the following extract from an e-mail from Yvonne Latimer to her head of human resources, Yasemin Yetiş and answer the questions.

a   How would you describe the tone of the e-mail?
b   What do you think is the most serious piece of bad news for the company? Why?
c   Do you think it's fair of Yvonne to hold the HR department responsible for all the problems?
d   With a partner, draft some of the questions you'd want to ask your key staff at their appraisal interviews.
e   Compare questions with the rest of your group.

From:	Yvonne Latimer
Date:	Tuesday, Dec 19, 9:22am
To:	Yasemin Yetis
Subject:	Appraisals

🖉 YearInFigures.pdf

Yasemin,

The annual accounts have yet to be published, but it's already clear that we have badly underperformed in our first year. We're not hitting any of our sales targets. Several new products which were scheduled to be launched onto the market by Q4 are still stuck in clinical trials due to problems in the R&D department. The staff cuts and new procedures we introduced do not seem to have improved efficiency – quite the opposite! Market share and turnover are both well down (see attachment). And I see this morning that our share price has fallen another 12 points, making for a 35% decline since it peaked just after the takeover in January.

Most worryingly of all, we appear to be losing key members of staff at an alarming rate – both managers and research scientists. Acquiring a company is about acquiring the expertise of its people, but I would almost say we are suffering a full-scale brain drain!

I don't need to tell you that these are not the kind of results I was sent here to achieve. I think what we have here is an HR problem and I'd like to meet with you as soon as possible to discuss the upcoming annual appraisals in more detail.

7 🔊 **3.10** Listen to extracts from the annual appraisal interviews and take notes on the complaints, concerns and suggestions of some of the Turkish and American members of staff. How many of the problems were you able to predict?

8 Work in small teams. As change management consultants, you have been called in by Yasemin Yetiş to suggest ways of turning the situation around. Areas of particular importance she has asked you to look at include:

> communication problems   low morale   team-building   goal-sharing   knowledge management
> loyalty incentives   redundancy planning   intercultural training   English as the official company language

9 Draft an agenda and hold a problem-solving meeting with the rest of your team to discuss the options.

10 The board of the Zantis parent company has asked you to e-mail a summary of your recommendations to its headquarters in Charlotte, North Carolina, prior to addressing the management team in Istanbul. So you can be frank!

17 GOING GREEN

A business that makes nothing but money is a poor kind of business.

HENRY FORD, AMERICAN INDUSTRIALIST

1 Look at the web ad for environmental organisation Friends of the Earth and discuss the questions with a partner. Some of the phrases in the Discussion phrase bank may help you.

a Who do companies have a responsibility to? Their shareholders? Their customers? Their employees? Anyone else?

b Isn't it governments who should be taking care of the planet?

c Is it possible to *make* business more socially and environmentally responsible? If so, how?

Make business work for people and planet

Friends of
the Earth

> **Discussion phrase bank**
>
> There's no question that …
>
> On balance, I'd say …
>
> On the one hand …, but on the other hand …
>
> It's not so much a question of … as of …
>
> Another way of looking at this is to …

2 Complete the following newspaper headlines using the pairs of words in the box.

> accountability + transparency   biofuels + emissions   business + thing   change + agenda
> neutrality + reality   recycling + PCs   responsibility + difference   safety + conditions

A

Corporate social _____: how the world's
biggest companies can make a _____

F | Climate _____ tops political _____

G Virgin first airline to use _____
in bid to cut carbon

B ethics: doing the right _____

C Dell offers free _____
of used _____

D Carbon _____:
Myth or _____?

H Monitoring _____ standards and
working _____ at The Gap

E NEED FOR MORE _____ AND
_____ IN POST-ENRON WORLD

3 🔊 3.11–3.14 Listen to some business people talking about their attitudes to corporate social responsibility. Which two headlines in 2 are they each talking about?

Speaker 1 ☐ ☐   Speaker 2 ☐ ☐
Speaker 3 ☐ ☐   Speaker 4 ☐ ☐

4 The speakers in 3 mentioned the following terms. Can you work out what they mean?

> carbon footprint   corporate governance   greenwashing
> microcredit   stakeholders

> **Discussion phrase bank**
>
> I totally disagree with the point about …
>
> For one thing, …
>
> And for another, …
>
> The speaker has clearly misunderstood …
>
> I think they are completely wrong about …
>
> And what they fail to take account of is …
>
> If you ask me, it's more a question of … than of …
>
> The fact is, …
>
> So, all in all …

5 With a partner decide where you stand on the following issues. Then compare your views with those in the articles below.

> "Firms can no longer hide a poor ethical record behind an impressive set of accounts.
> Being green gives you a distinct competitive advantage – just pursuing profits at all costs is very 'uncool'.
> When it comes to green issues, big business is both the main problem and the only practical solution.
> For big brands motivated by profit teaming up with a celebrity for a good cause is great PR. "

Being good is good for business

Being profitable and having **a solid balance sheet** are no longer enough for banks and corporates anywhere in the world to be assured of success. Investors, the media, politicians and regulators are focusing increasingly on their willingness and ability to **comply with stricter ethical and community standards**. Being nice is no longer optional – it is becoming a business necessity.

Mauricio Villaraín, Santander Santiago's president, says that excellence goes beyond just making money. 'If you want to become a top company in the long term, you need to focus on **financial targets**. They are a necessary but not sufficient condition for success. You also need to achieve excellence in ethics and corporate social responsibility. You have to define what you want, communicate it, measure it and stick to it, no matter what, for years.' Ultimately, he says, this is good for business. 'Ethics and transparency pays. I think it's a mistake that you can defeat competition by doing wrong, we believe that more disclosure, increased transparency increases trust and that it pays.'

www.latinfinance.com

Bono Seeing 'Red' Over AIDS

Rock star and activist Bono **launched a new push** to fight HIV and AIDS in Africa, announcing a partnership with American Express and other companies to offer products under a brand called 'Red'.

'Red' will market red-themed products from Converse footwear, Gap clothing and Giorgio Armani, as well as a red American Express card. Products branded 'Red' will include sports shoes, T-shirts and sunglasses — some produced in Africa, some with African materials. **A slice of the revenue** will go to the Global Fund to Fight AIDS, Tuberculosis and Malaria.

Says Bono: 'I'm calling it **conscious commerce** for people who think about their **spending power** and say: 'I've got two jeans I can buy. One I know is made in Africa and is going to make a difference and the other isn't. What am I going to buy?'

In an interview with The Associated Press, Bono referred to the **potential discomfort** with his new alliances. 'Some people will be very upset,' he said. 'We're working with big business. But the problem just has to be sorted and we can't do it just with governments alone. We could fail. If people are cynical or genuinely not interested, then we fail. But we've tried. I think we've come up with a sexy, smart idea that will save people's lives. It is sexy to want to change the world, not to leave it as it is.'

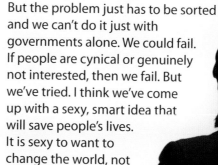

www.cbsnews.com

6 With a partner try to guess the meanings of the words and expressions in **bold** from their context.

7 When's the last time you consciously made a green consumer choice? If you can remember, tell a partner about it.

8 How has Corporate Social Responsibility (CSR) affected your company or a company you know?

18 EATING OUT

Conversation is the enemy of good wine and food.

ALFRED HITCHCOCK, FILM DIRECTOR

1 Work with a partner and discuss the following questions.

a Is lunch an important meal for you?
b Do you ever have business lunches?
c Which of the following are you most likely to say to a foreign colleague visiting your country?

I thought you might like to try some of our local cuisine.
I thought we could just grab a quick pizza or something.
I thought we'd just work through lunch and eat later.

2 What kind of restaurants do you like? Add the phrases in the box to the diagram below to make twelve useful expressions.

| does an excellent lasagne   down the road   a fantastic view of the city   five minutes from here |
| I sometimes go   specialises in fish   round the corner   a superb menu   they know me |
| a very pleasant atmosphere   you can get fresh oysters   you might like |

There's a	really nice pretty good great new	place	just	a b c	....
			which	d e f	....
			where	g h i	....
			with	j k l	....

3 Do you have a favourite place where you take clients and colleagues? If so, tell a partner about it.

4 Look at the buffet in the photograph. How many of the dishes can you name? Discuss the food with a partner. Use the phrases and expressions below to help you.

WHO SAID IT?

1 The following things were said during a business lunch. Who do you think probably said them – the host, the guest or could it be either? Write H, G or E next to each sentence.

a Nice place. Do you come here often?
b Now, what would you like to drink?
c I'll just see if our table's ready.
d This is their standard menu.
e It all looks very good.
f And those are the specials.
g Let me know if you want me to explain anything.
h So, what do you recommend?
i Well, they do a great lasagne.
j Is there anything you don't eat?

k I'm allergic to mussels.
l You could try the lamb. That's very good here.
m That sounds nice.
n Shall we order a bottle of the house red?
o Could we order some mineral water, too?
p This is absolutely delicious. How's yours?
q Now, how about a dessert?
r Better not. I'm on a diet.
s I'll get this.
t No, no, I insist. You're my guest.

2 3.15 Now compare your answers with the conversation in the restaurant. The man is the host.

TABLE MANNERS

1 In Russia they sit down at cocktail parties. In China the most important guest is seated facing the door. In Japan a tip is not expected; in France it is an insult not to leave one. How culturally aware are you at the table? Try the quiz below. <u>Underline</u> the correct information.

Cross-cultural quiz

a In **Greece** / **Finland** people frequently stop for lunch at 11.30 in the morning.

b In **Switzerland** / **Brazil** it's common to be up to two hours late for a party.

c In **Portugal** / **the USA** a business lunch can last up to three and half hours.

d In **Japan** / **Russia** the soup is often eaten at the end of the meal.

e In **France** / **Britain** cheese is normally served after the dessert.

f In **American** / **German** restaurants you may be asked if you want a bag for the food you can't eat.

g In **Arab** / **Asian** countries you must wait for your host to serve you the main meat dish.

h In **Mexico** / **Belgium** you should keep both hands on the dinner table where they can be seen.

i At a **Turkish** / **Chinese** dinner table it is extremely impolite to say how hungry you are.

j The **Japanese** / **British** sometimes need to be offered more food three times before they will accept.

k **American** / **Latin** executives like to be invited to your home for dinner.

l In **Belgium** / **Spain** an 11 o'clock dinner is quite normal.

m In **Asian** / **Arab** countries food is usually eaten with just three fingers of the right hand.

n In **Poland** / **Japan** you should keep filling other guests' glasses until they turn them over.

o In **African** / **Asian** countries it is the host who decides when the guests should leave.

Check your answers on page 132.

2 Find seven examples of the passive in the quiz in 1.

*… the soup **is** often **eaten** …*

STICKY SITUATIONS

🔊 **3.16–3.18** Listen to business people from different countries chatting over lunch and answer the questions.

Conversation 1

a   What is Hiro worried about?

b   Hiro uses different expressions to stop his colleague choosing the fugu. Complete them.
   1   It's rather ....
   2   It's a little ....
   3   You may ....
   4   I think you'd ....
   5   Really, I think you should ....

c   What does David say when he decides to change his mind?

Conversation 2

a   What is Hans's problem?

b   The Spaniards use different expressions to encourage Hans to try the squid. Complete them.
   1   We thought you might ....
   2   You'll ....
   3   You'll really ....
   4   This is something ....
   5   It's really ....

c   What does Hans say when he refuses the Spaniards' offer?

Conversation 3

a   Why does Louise have a problem choosing what to eat?

b   Jean-Claude and Louise mention lots of different cooking methods. Complete them.
   1   fr............   4   gr............
   2   bo............   5   ba............
   3   ro............

c   Complete these extracts from the conversation:
   1   … nothing made .... pastry.
   2   … nothing cooked .... oil.
   3   It comes .... potatoes and fresh vegetables.

d   Have you ever had lunch with anyone like Louise?

THE BUSINESS LUNCH

Work with a partner. You are going to talk business over lunch. Speaker A see page 132. Speaker B see below.

Your partner (Speaker A) is a good friend from abroad, whom you've also worked with in the past. You are visiting their city for a few days and they have invited you out for a nice lunch.

You called them about a week ago and mentioned a business idea you'd like to discuss with them over lunch. If they are interested, you'd like them to be involved, so prepare a short business plan to help you describe your idea. You should include:

- an outline of your basic idea (one or two sentences)
- why you think it has great business potential (have at least one good reason!)
- how you'd like your friend to be involved (time, money, expertise, contacts)
- how you see the idea developing in the future

Make sure you get a chance to talk business over lunch, but don't be a bore and talk about nothing else! Be a good guest. Show interest in the restaurant and the food (remember, you're a foreigner and don't know about the cuisine!). Try to keep the conversation moving.

If the lunch goes well, offer to pay!

> **Useful phrases**
>
> Showing interest:
> Nice place. Do you come here a lot?
> It all looks delicious.
>
> Changing the subject:
> **By the way,** I wanted to talk to you about my business idea.
> **Anyway, getting back to** this idea of mine.
> **So,** what do you think about the idea?

BASIC BUSINESS IDEA:
_____

Why it has great potential:
_____
_____

How my partner could help:
_____
_____

Future of the business:
_____

LANGUAGE LINKS

Vocabulary: Food and drink

What's it like?

1 What do the following adjectives describe? Choose nouns from the box.

> dish   fish   lunch   meat   salad   steak   vegetables

a   heavy/light/late/three-course ....
b   fillet/rare/medium/well-done ....
c   green/side/Waldorf/fruit ....
d   fried/raw/smoked/freshly-caught ....
e   roast/tough/tender/juicy ....
f   fresh/frozen/seasonal/mixed ....
g   traditional/exotic/local/vegetarian ....

> beer   bread   cheese   coffee   dessert   food   fruit

h   rich/spicy/plain/fast ....
i   dried/tropical/ripe/tinned ....
j   crusty/stale/garlic/wholemeal ....
k   strong/mild/blue/cream ....
l   fattening/refreshing/light/chocolatey ....
m   draught/light/bottled/local ....
n   liqueur/strong/instant/black ....

2 You can often turn a food noun into an adjective by adding -y.
- containing lots of salt = salty
- containing lots of sugar = sugary

a   Find five more food adjectives ending in -y in the lists above.
b   How would you describe a dish with lots of
   oil?   fruit?   taste?
   fat?   pepper?   nuts?

How to sound intelligent about wine!

1 Complete the description of a wine below using the words in the box.

> from   of   with   with

It's a crisp, dry white wine (a) .... a delicate bouquet.
It comes (b) .... the Napa valley region
(c) .... California and goes very well (d) .... fish.
1995 was a reasonable year.

2 Think of a wine you like and prepare a description of it using the words below.

Try some of the other food and drink adjectives as well. Don't worry if you sound a bit strange – so do wine experts!

> a disappointing year   an excellent year
> an exceptional year   classic   dark red   flowery   fruity
> heavy   light   light golden   medium-bodied
> medium-dry   peppery   robust   rosé   smooth
> sparkling   sweet   the smell of blackcurrants
> the taste of apples   vintage   young

Grammar: The passive

You form the passive with the appropriate tense of the verb *to be* + past participle.

- *The components for Ford cars **are manufactured** in fifteen different countries.*
- *In Spain dinner often **isn't eaten** until 10 or 11 in the evening.*
- *Steve Jobs **was re-appointed** head of Apple Computers in 1997.*
- *When **was** the euro first **introduced**?*
- *As an exporter of computer software, the USA **has been overtaken** by the Republic of Ireland.*

You can also use the passive with modal verbs:

A *How soon **will** the project **be completed**?*
B *Well, it **must be finished** by the end of the year.*
A *Yes, but **can** it **be speeded up**, do you think?*
B *Well, we'd **have to be given** a bigger budget.*
A *I think that **could be arranged**.*

You use the passive when it is unimportant or obvious who or what does something. It is, therefore, common to use the passive to talk about **processes** and **procedures**.

1 Look at these two examples:

Active: *These days, e-mail has largely superseded the fax machine.*
Passive: *These days, the fax machine has been largely superseded by e-mail.*

a   What's the subject of the first sentence?
b   What's the subject of the second sentence?
c   In the second sentence what word comes before the performer of the action?
d   Which of the sentences are you more likely to hear in a conversation about fax machines?

In both examples above our attention is focused on the subject of the sentence. You use the passive when you're more interested in the subject than the performer of the action.

2 Complete the article using the correct passive form of the verbs in brackets.

Lloyd's: Insuring the famous and the bizarre

Virtually anything (a) _____ (can / insure) at Lloyd's. In fact, over the last hundred years London's most celebrated insurance company (b) _____ _____ (ask) to issue some of the most bizarre policies ever! Here are just a few.

Car insurance is big business these days. But the very first car (c) _____ (insure) at Lloyd's (d) _____ (cover) by a marine policy. Cars were such a novelty in those days, motor policies (e) _____ (write) on the basis that cars were just ships that sailed on the land!

Actors have always been paranoid. Hollywood film idol, Betty Grable, was so worried her famous legs (f) _____ (might / injure) during filming, they (g) _____ (insure) by Lloyd's for a million dollars.

Multi-millionaire rock stars worry too. Bob Dylan, Eric Clapton, Michael Jackson, Elton John, Rod Stewart and the Rolling Stones have all insured their voices. Bruce Springsteen's (h) _____ (believe) to be worth £3.5 million.

Food critic and gourmet Egon Ronay runs a different risk. Obviously, his career (i) _____ (would / destroy) if he was ever to lose his sense of taste. So a Lloyd's policy for £250,000 (j) _____ _____ (take out) to protect him against waking up one day not knowing a haggis from a hamburger.

Insuring works of art is nothing new, but the laughter (k) _____ (could / hear) all over the city when a grain of rice with a portrait of the Queen and the Duke of Edinburgh engraved on it (l) _____ _____ (estimate) to be worth $20,000. The question is: worth $20,000 to whom?

A few years ago, a killer whale called Namu (m) _____ (capture) off the Canadian coast and (n) _____ (drag) to Seattle for display in an aquarium. The captors insured themselves for $8,000 against Namu (o) _____ (rescue) by other whales! Unfortunately, he wasn't.

One rather confident comedy theatre group insured itself against the risk of a member of the audience dying laughing. So far, however, the insurance (p) _____ (not / claim) ...

Phrase bank: Eating out

Label the following groups of phrases and expressions according to their purpose:

Avoiding disasters   Being a good host
Complimenting your host   Describing dishes
Fighting over the bill   Ordering the meal
Recommending dishes   Talking shop

a	_____	Nice place. Do you come here often?
		It was a good choice of restaurant.
		It all looks delicious.
b	_____	It's basically a fish pie.
		It comes with a salad.
		It's cooked in wine.
c	_____	If you like seafood, you'll love it.
		The lamb's very good here.
		You could try the goulash.
d	_____	It's a bit unusual – you may not like it.
		Is there anything you don't eat?
		Maybe you should try something else.
e	_____	I'll just see if our table's ready.
		Shall we have another bottle?
		Is everything all right?
f	_____	I'm going to have the steak. Rare, please.
		I'd like the vegetarian lasagne.
		Could we have a bottle of the house red?
g	_____	About this business idea of mine.
		As I was saying, we should have a meeting.
		Going back to what we were talking about.
h	_____	Let me get this. My treat.
		This one's on me. You paid last time.
		I insist ... OK, let's split it, then.

I've experienced virtual meetings that were actually more effective than any face-to-face meeting I've been in.

KATE HARPER, EXECUTIVE COACH

1 Have you ever taken part in a video- or audio-conference? How is it different from a face-to-face meeting? Do you agree with Kate Harper?

2 Look at the advertisements below for web conferencing company Connect. What advantages of web conferencing are the ads referring to? Think about your work-life balance, your department's travel budget, your company's 'carbon footprint'.

Simply Connect

... and stop your business travel costing the earth

Simply Connect

... and kiss goodbye to so much business travel

3 Read these two short reports. How do they support or contradict the messages in the advertisements?

A new report from the American Consumer Institute has calculated that the world will save roughly one billion tons of carbon in the next ten years by operating on the Internet. The trends break down like this:

E-commerce will reduce carbon emissions by 200 million tons

Telecommuting will prevent 250 million tons of emissions from reduced driving

Teleconferencing could prevent 200 million tons of emissions (if it replaces 10% of face-to-face meetings)

www.ecogeek.org

The 11th Barclaycard Business Travel survey has shown that about three-quarters of all business travellers enjoy spending time away from home. Of the 72% that enjoy business travel:

Over 50% say business travel gives them a chance to see the world

Over 30% say they have timed work trips to coincide with meeting a partner; 15% admitted to organising a business trip to see a particular destination

Only 12% said that they suffered from stress while travelling

www.dancewithshadows.com

4 Do any of the statistics in the reports surprise you?

5 Is teleconferencing the future? What sort of meetings (if any) do you think absolutely have to be face to face?

appraisal interviews   complex negotiations   crisis meetings   job interviews
multinational team briefings   new product demonstrations   project meeting updates
routine decision-making   sales presentations   team-building sessions

TELECONFERENCE: A PROJECT MEETING

Ritterberger is a large and successful construction company based in Essen, Germany. At the moment it is building a marina complex in Dubai, managing a multinational team of engineers, skilled and semi-skilled workers from Germany, Poland and Pakistan. But the project has been hit by series of problems and is now running three months behind schedule. The client, Dubai entrepreneur Ali Al-Fulani, is unhappy with progress and demanding that penalty clauses in the contract be enforced if solutions cannot be found.

1 🔊 **3.19–3.20** Ritterberger CEO Peter Kessler has set up a teleconference to clarify the situation. Read the e-mail attachment below to see who will be participating and what the main items on the agenda are. Then listen to the meeting and answer the questions.

RITTERBERGER GMBH
AUDIO-CONFERENCE TUE, NOV 29, 9:00-10:30 (CET)
Participants:
Peter Kessler (CEO, Ritterberger, Essen)
Jarek Gorsky (Chief engineer, Ritterberger, Warsaw)
Ernst Neumann (Project director, Ritterberger, Dubai)
Karim Ibadulla (Foreman, Pakistani team, Dubai)
Feliks Nowakowski (Foreman, Polish team, Dubai)
Sulaiman Al-Fahim (Site manager, Dubai)
Agenda:
1 Supply hold-ups
2 Communication problems
3 Specification changes

Extract 1
a Where is Sulaiman Al-Fahim?
b Why is Jarek Gorsky at the meeting?
c What's the situation with Ali Al-Fulani?

Extract 2
a What is the communication problem?
b What's the situation at the seaports?
c What is Karim's point about the client?
d What is Peter Kessler's conclusion?

2 Complete the teleconferencing expressions you just heard using the words in the box.

agenda agreed come covered finish finished getting
hear inputs interrupt introduce item join leave meeting
minimum objectives recap skip started time waiting

a Sorry, I had a bit of a problem _____ through.
b We're just _____ for Sulaiman.
c Let's go ahead and start. Welcome to the _____ .
d Did everyone get a copy of the _____ ?
e Before we start, let me _____ Jarek Gorsky.
f I've asked him to _____ us today because …
g All right, then, let's get _____ .
h As you can see, we have several _____ today.
i I'd like to be _____ by 10.30, if that's OK.
j Can we keep our _____ quite short?
k And let's also try to keep interruptions to a _____ .
l Sorry to _____ , but …
m I suggest we _____ item one on our agenda until …
n Let's move straight on to _____ two.
o So, just to _____ on what we've said.
p So, are we all _____ that …?
q Sorry, I can't _____ you very well.
r Could I just _____ in here?
s Right, we're running short of _____ .
t Ernst, Jarek, can I _____ that with you?
u I think we've _____ everything for now.
v We'll have to _____ there.

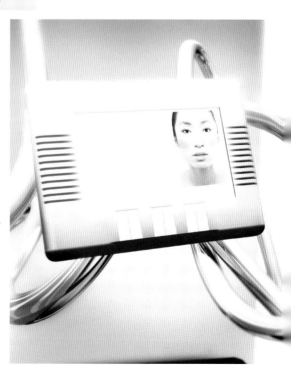

3 After the teleconference, Ernst circulated notes to the engineering team on what had been discussed. Put his notes in the correct order. Some have been done for you.

1	Peter Kessler opened the meeting and informed us that
	join us later. He then introduced
	might have to be renegotiated. Ernst and Jarek agreed to
5	that the main objective of the meeting was to get the Dubai Project back
	we skip item one on the agenda until Sulaiman could join us and went on
	have another look at overall logistics and to report back to Peter. Another teleconference
	to outline the communication problems the two work teams had
15	to bring this to the client's attention and that the contract with Al-Fulani
	joined the meeting at this point and described
	Sulaiman had gone to Port Rashid to check on deliveries and would
	the situation at the ports as serious. He explained that
12	nothing was moving and that our back-up supplies were insufficient to cope with
	been having. Peter recommended onsite training as a possible solution. Sulaiman
	the present situation. Karim reminded us that
	on schedule. Ernst suggested that
	Jarek Gorsky, Ritterman's new chief engineer in Warsaw, and emphasised
	constant changes to the building plan were also a major problem. Peter promised
18	was scheduled for next week.

4 Work in a group. You're going to hold a short teleconference. Turn to page 133 for instructions.

AN URGENT MATTER

1 A management consultancy is putting together a proposal for a major new client, pharmaceutical giant, Hoechst. Put the following e-mails between two of their consultants into the correct order. Read all the e-mails first – a and h are in the right place.

A

Subject: Hoechst report – progress?
Attachments: none

Sam
This is just a quick reminder to let you know that the Hoechst report was due yesterday.
E-mail me if you're having problems.
Jonathan

B

Subject: Costing for Hoechst
Attachments: none

Jonathan
I see your point. Estimates would give us more room to negotiate on fees, but I think the client will appreciate that we've fully itemised all the costs.
Sam

C

Subject: So you are alive after all!
Attachments: none

Sam
Thanks for the report. At last! Actually, you've done a great job on it. Just one thing. Should we be quoting precise figures at this stage or just giving a rough estimate?
Jonathan

D

Subject: Costing for Hoechst
Attachments: HoechstRepAlt

Sam
Yeah, you're probably right. It looks better if we show that we can set and stick to a budget.
Can you just make a few alterations (see attachment) and then e-mail me another copy? Oh, and cc one to Lisa as well. Thanks.
Jonathan

E

Subject: Hoechst report
Attachments: HoechstRep
CostBrkdn

Jonathan
Sorry for the delay in getting back to you. Our server's been down again. I'm sending a first draft of the report as an attachment together with a detailed breakdown of costs for the whole project. Could you have a look at them and tell me if there's anything you want changing?
Sam

F

Subject: HELLO?
Attachments: none

SAM!
Haven't you received my previous two e-mails? This is getting urgent. I've tried to phone, but you're never in. Look, I'm under a lot of pressure from head office to get this proposal in on schedule. Don't let me down, Sam.
Jonathan

G

Subject: Hoechst report – update please
Attachments: none

Sam
Just had a call from Lisa. She wants to know what the hold-up is with the Hoechst report. Did you get my last e-mail? Please let me know what the position is asap.
Jonathan

H

Subject: Revised Hoechst Report
Attachments: HoechstRep2
ConJoke

Jonathan
Here's the revised version of the report. OK, so I just missed the deadline, but only two days late. Give me a break. By the way, I found a joke on the Internet the other day that might appeal to your sense of humour: You could use it in your presentation to Hoechst: Why are they using consultants instead of rats in laboratory experiments these days? See attachment for answer :)
Sam

2 What do you think the punchline to Sam's joke is? See page 133 for the answer.

3 Match up the words and phrases below to make fifteen complete expressions. If you need to, refer to the e-mails you read in 1, where they all appeared in the same order as here.

a	this is just	if you're having	problems
b	the report	to negotiate	costs
c	e-mail me	was due	reminder
d	room	itemised	on fees
e	fully	a quick	yesterday

f	quote	the delay in	estimate
g	give	precise	report as an attachment
h	sorry for	a rough	getting back to you
i	send a	breakdown of costs	figures
j	a detailed	first draft of the	for the project

k	be under	proposal in	a budget
l	get a	stick to	head office
m	set and	missed	the deadline
n	let me	pressure from	position is asap
o	I just	know what the	on schedule

DEALING WITH MESSAGES

1   Work in groups to produce a short profile of a company, a department in that company and an executive who works in that department. Invent the whole thing or use the names of real people and companies if you prefer.

> ### PROFILE
>
> Name of company:
>
> Location:
>
> Main business activity:
>
> Department:
>
> Name of executive:
>
> Position in company:

2   Prepare five e-mail messages and (if you can) five voicemail messages that the executive you invented might receive on a typical (or not so typical) working day. Keep each message fairly short. Include personal ones if you like.

Message ideas:

good news	an apology	a rumour
bad news	an offer	an invitation
a reprimand	a complaint	a request
an ultimatum	a crisis	

3   When you are ready, write out your e-mail messages or print them off on a PC. Record your voicemail messages.

4   Swap your profile, voicemail messages and e-mails with another group.

5   Read and listen to the messages the other group gave you and decide how you are going to respond to each. Classify the messages as 'important', 'urgent', 'postpone', 'delegate' or 'bin'.

6   Write replies to the messages and return them to the group you swapped with.

7   Report back to the class how you dealt with the messages you received.

LANGUAGE LINKS

Vocabulary: Managing a project

Look at the following extracts from e-mails written by members of an international project team. The last word in each expression has been switched with another. Switch them back. The first one has been done for you.

a This is just a quick **deadline**. ◄
b E-mail me if you're having **costs**.
c I can't quote you a precise **schedule**.
d Can you give me a rough **report**?
e We're working to a very tight **figure**.
f I've attached a detailed breakdown of **problems**.
g We need to stick to our **teleconference**.
h Let me know if there's going to be a **loop**.
i We're in danger of missing our **reminder**.
j Let's set up a **budget**.
k Thanks for the situation **estimate**.
l Keep me in the **delay**.

Grammar: Reporting

In business it is important to be able to report accurately what people said in meetings, on the phone and in private conversation. Occasionally we repeat the exact words someone used, but usually it is sufficient to report the basic message.

Original statement: *There's no way I'm going to accept cuts.*
Direct speech: *He said: 'There's no way I'm going to accept cuts.'* (1)
Reported speech: *He says there's no way he's going to accept cuts.* (2)
He said there was no way he was going to accept cuts. (3)
Reporting verb: *He refused to accept cuts.* (4)

1 Study the information above and answer the questions. Which expression would you use to:

a quote exactly what the speaker said in a meeting?
b report exactly what the speaker said in a meeting?
c summarise the general idea?
d tell someone in the meeting what the speaker just said?
NB When the reporting verb is in the past, you often put the reported speech in the past too:
I'm under a lot of pressure.
Reported speech: *He said he was under a lot of pressure.*

2 Change the statements below into reported speech.

a Fritz: I'm ready.
   Fritz said he was ready.
b Akio: I'm going to wait and see.
c Claire: I've had enough.
d Philippe: I must be going.
e Maria: I'll be in touch.
f Sergio: I just can't face it.

Reporting the general idea of what someone said (e.g. offering, inviting, complaining, thanking, suggesting) is often more useful than reporting their exact words. To do this, you can use the verbs *say*, *tell* and *ask*, as well as many other verbs. It is important to learn which prepositions, objects and verb forms follow these reporting verbs.

3 Decide how the following sentences (a–j) were later reported (1–10). Write your answers in the boxes.

a Don't forget to do it.
b Have you done it?
c Could you do it, please?
d It was you who did it!
e Why don't you do it?
f Would you like me to do it?
g I'm not doing it!
h Sorry, I did it.
i I'm sorry I did it.
j I didn't do it.

1 She suggested I do it.
2 He regretted doing it.
3 She apologised for doing it.
4 He denied doing it.
5 She reminded me to do it.
6 He refused to do it.
7 She asked me to do it.
8 He accused me of doing it.
9 She asked me if I'd done it.
10 He offered to do it.

a ☐ b ☐ c ☐ d ☐ e ☐ f ☐ g ☐ h ☐ i ☐ j ☐

4 Do you have a favourite line from a movie? Read the following collection of quotes from some of the twentieth century's most famous films. Report each one using a combination of reporting verbs and reported speech. Use the words in brackets to help you. There are different possibilities.

a *Bond, James Bond.* Sean Connery, Dr No (1962)
   (say/name) ....
b *Play it Sam.* Humphrey Bogart, Casablanca (1942)
   (ask/Sam) ....
c *Mrs Robinson, I can't do this. It's all terribly wrong.* Dustin Hoffman, The Graduate (1967)
   (say/because) ....
d *Are you talking to me?* Robert De Niro, Taxi Driver (1976)
   (ask/me) ....
e *Frankly, my dear, I don't give a damn.* Clark Gable, Gone with the Wind (1939)
   (inform/her) ....
f *Come up and see me some time.* Mae West, Goin' to Town (1935)
   (invite/me) ....
g *Hang on, lads. I've got a great idea.* Michael Caine, The Italian Job (1969)
   (tell/us) ....
h *What have the Romans ever done for us?* John Cleese, The Life of Brian (1979)
   (want/know) ....
i *Go ahead. Make my day.* Clint Eastwood, Dirty Harry (1971)
   (invite) ....

5 The human resources department of a medium-sized company is deciding how much money to allocate to training. Read the following short extract from their meeting.

Gerry OK, now, about our training budget for next year. What does everybody think?

Anna Well, I think we really must spend more on advanced IT skills training.

Ingmar Hm, I'm not so sure that's what's needed. In fact, it's basic computer skills that most of our people still lack.

Gerry Yes, I think so too. But isn't this really a recruitment problem? I think we should require all new recruits to be computer literate before we employ them.

Anna Now, just a minute. We're forgetting that these are our entry-level staff we're talking about.

Ingmar And?

Anna Well, if you look at the salaries we're paying new recruits, you'll see that we simply don't pay them enough to expect computer skills. IT training is our responsibility.

Gerry Well, if we don't change our recruitment policy, we'll have to spend a fortune on training.

Anna Actually, the current cost of training is negligible, Gerry. That's why I say we should be spending more.

Now complete a report of the meeting using the verbs in the box.

a – e	doubted insisted invited pointed out raised
f – j	agreed came in reminded suggested wondered
k – o	added assured explained recommended warned

······················· **Report** ·······················

Gerry (a) ···············the issue of the training budget and (b) ···············comments from the group. Anna (c) ···············that we spend more on advanced IT skills, but Ingmar (d) ···············that was what was needed. He (e) ···············that it was basic computer skills that most of our personnel lack. Gerry (f) ···············and (g) ···············if it wasn't a recruitment problem. He (h) ···············we make computer literacy a requirement for employment. Anna (i) ···············at this point and (j) ···············everyone that we were talking about entry-level staff. She (k) ···············that we didn't pay sufficient to expect computer skills and (l) ···············that IT training was the company's responsibility. Gerry (m) ···············us that if we didn't change our recruitment policy, we'd have to spend a fortune on training, but Anna (n) ···············him the current cost of training was negligible and (o) ···············we spend more.

Phrase bank: Teleconferencing

Label the teleconferencing expressions below according to their function.

closing   handling the technology   interrupting
managing the agenda   managing the discussion
opening   time-keeping

a ··············· Welcome to the meeting.
Did everyone get a copy of the agenda?
Let's get started.

b ··············· As you can see, we have several objectives today.
Let's skip item two.
Let's move on to item three.

c ··············· Could I just come in here?
I just want to say one thing.
Sorry to interrupt, but …

d ··············· Can we keep our inputs quite short?
Let's try to keep interruption to a minimum.
Sorry, I can't hear you very well.

e ··············· So, just to recap on what we've said.
So, are we all agreed that …?
Any comments on that?

f ··············· I'd like to be finished by 10.30.
Right, we're running short of time.
We'll have to speed up, I'm afraid.

g ··············· I think we've covered everything for now.
We'll have to stop it there, I'm afraid.
We'll have to finish there. Thanks everybody.

20 NEGOTIATING

Never begin a deal, a battle or a love affair if the fear of losing overshadows the prospect of winning.

ARISTOTLE ONASSIS, SHIPPING TYCOON

1 William Ury is co-author of the world's most famous book on negotiating, *Getting to Yes*. Read the following extract from his best-selling sequel, *Getting Past No* and answer the questions.

a Which of the situations remind you of something that's happened to you? Compare experiences with a partner.

b What would you say in response to each of the people in the text?

> Daily life is full of negotiations that can drive you crazy. Over breakfast you get into an argument with your spouse about buying a new car. You think it's time, but your spouse says: 'Don't be ridiculous! You know we can't afford it right now.'
> A morning meeting with your boss. You present him with a carefully prepared proposal for a new project, but he interrupts you after a minute and says: 'We already tried that and it didn't work. Next item.'
> During your lunch hour you try to return a defective toaster-oven, but the salesperson refuses to refund your money because you don't have the sales slip: 'It's store policy.'
> In the evening you need to return some phone calls, but the line is tied up by your thirteen-year-old daughter. Exasperated, you ask her to get off the phone. She yells: 'Why don't you get me my own phone line? All my friends have them.'

2 Work with a partner. Decide who's who in the following short negotiations. In each case you have just three minutes to reach a deal if you can. When you've finished negotiating, compare your results with others in the class.

Situation 1: The favour

Negotiator A: You have been working extremely hard lately, doing a lot of overtime and are really looking forward to a relaxing weekend at the beach with friends. It's been raining for weeks, but the forecast for Saturday is for sunshine all day. You can't wait!

Negotiator B: You were supposed to be doing some overtime on Saturday morning and then having a barbecue at your house in the afternoon to celebrate the installation of your new swimming pool! But your favourite grandmother has been taken very ill and you'd really like to fly out and visit her for the weekend. Your boss has said it's OK if you can find someone else to do the overtime.

Situation 2: The unwanted gift

Negotiator A: You bought a digital camera for a friend's birthday last week, but, rather embarrassingly, someone else gave them a much better one! Take it back to the department store where you bought it and ask for your money back, so you can buy them something else more expensive. Unfortunately, you can't find the receipt, but you still have the box which clearly has the store's price label on it.

Negotiator B: You are the manager of the camera department at a large department store. It's company policy not to give refunds on returned products, but you do give gift vouchers to the value of the returned goods, which can be used throughout the store, provided the customer has their receipt. At the moment your store has a massive sale on.

Situation 3: The mobile phone

Negotiator A: You are the parent of a seven-year-old who has been asking you for months to buy them a mobile phone so they can talk to and SMS their friends. You think they are a bit young to have their own phone and have heard all sorts of stories about children spending a fortune on calls and buying expensive music downloads. Try to dissuade them.

Negotiator B: You are a seven-year-old child but very intelligent for your age! All your friends at school have mobile phones and you'd like one too. You know your parents are not keen on the idea. But SMS messages are very cheap and having a phone is a very good security measure for kids. Try to persuade your father/mother that it's a good investment.

3 Complete the following sentence in not more than five words: 'A good negotiator …'. Compare sentences with other people in the class.

4 🔊 3.21–3.23 Listen to three business people sharing their views on how to negotiate and answer the questions below.

a   Put the following stages in a negotiation into the order Speaker 1 mentions them.

have lunch	☐	set out proposals	☐
agree on a procedure	☐	agree terms	☐
bargain	☐	celebrate	☐
close	☐	listen and take notes	☐
create rapport	☐	make counter-proposals	☐

b   Speaker 2 refers to the following acronyms. What do they mean?
OP   TP   WAP   FBP   BATNA

c   According to Speaker 3, why doesn't 'win–win' usually work?

d   Complete the five pieces of advice Speaker 3 offers.
Don't get pe……………………
Don't agree to an…………………… until you've discussed ev…………………… .
Don't make any co…………………… without asking for something in re…………………… .
Ask a lot of qu…………………… .
Don't gi…………………… in to pr…………………… .

DIRECTNESS

1 Read the joke. Is there a lesson to be learned from it?

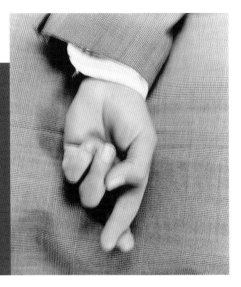

Two priests were so addicted to smoking that they desperately needed to puff on cigarettes even while they prayed. Both developed guilty consciences and decided to ask their superior for permission to smoke.
The first asked if it was OK to smoke while he was praying. Permission was denied. The second priest asked if he was allowed to pray while he was smoking. His superior found his dedication admirable and immediately granted his request.

2 How direct you want to be in a negotiation is a matter of both cultural background and personal choice. On which side of the line below would you place people from your own culture? How about you personally?

prefer the diplomatic approach ◄───────────────► prefer straight-talking

3 Find someone in your group who put themselves on the other side of the line from you. Try to persuade each other that your side is better.

4 The following thoughts passed through the minds of two negotiators during a negotiation. Use the words and phrases in brackets to reproduce what they actually said.

a   That's impossible.
(*unfortunately / would not / possible*) ....
b   We can't go higher than 7%.
(*would find / quite difficult*) ....
c   We won't accept less than $5 a unit.
(*afraid / not in a position / this stage*) ....
d   You'll have to pay more if you want that.
(*may / slightly*) ....
e   We need a commitment from you now.
(*would / some kind*) ....
f   We should spend more time looking for a compromise here.
(*shouldn't / little?*) ....
g   It would be a good idea to agree on a price before we go any further.
(*wouldn't / better?*) ....
h   We hoped you'd pay a deposit today.
(*were hoping / able*) ....
i   It will be difficult to get my boss to agree to this.
(*might not / very easy*) ....
j   That's as far as we can go.
(*think / about / the moment*) ....

5 What do the negotiators do to make their statements more diplomatic? Do you prefer the direct or diplomatic versions?

THE LANGUAGE OF NEGOTIATIONS

1 3.24 Listen to an extract from a negotiation and take notes.

2 Work with a partner. Use the notes you took in 1 to prepare to continue the negotiation. When you're ready, see if you can reach an agreement!

3 3.25 Listen to another negotiation extract and take notes.

4 Do you think you've just listened to a win–win negotiation?

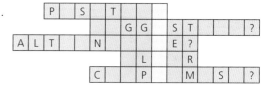

Mammoth Construction plc

Schumann Tender

Our original bid: 7.8m euros
Client counter-offer: _____ euros
Project to be completed within _____
Plant to be operational by _____
Our revised bid:
_____ euros in advance
_____ euros mid-contract
_____ euros on completion
TOTAL: _____ euros
Schedule overrun penalty: _____ euros per week

Smart Move plc

THE COMMUNICATION SKILLS SPECIALISTS

Telesales training (2-day seminar)
no. seminars: _____ over _____-month period
no. trainers _____
_____ to be approved
max. no. participants per seminar: _____
Full fee: £_____
Discount: _____% = £_____
Final fee: £_____
_____% non-refundable deposit = £_____

5 You heard most of the following expressions in the negotiations you just listened to, but some letters are missing from the final words. When you have completed them, the letters down the middle spell out some good advice for a negotiator.

a Perhaps we should begin by outlining our initial …
b Can I make a …
c What if we offered you an …
d Let me get this quite …
e Would you be willing to accept a …

f I'm afraid this doesn't really solve our …
g We may be in a position to revise our …
h I think that's about as far as we can go at this …
i Are these terms broadly …

j Let me just check I understand you …
k I'm afraid we could only accept this on one …
l What sort of figure are we talking …
m Could you give us an idea of what you're looking …

n What sort of time-scale are we looking …
o We'd like to see some movement on …
p Can we just run through the main points once …
q At the moment, we do not see this as a viable …
r We seem to be nearing …
s Well, that's it. I think we've earned ourselves a …

THE TRANSFER

1 Footballers are today's rock stars and some of the most spectacular negotiations lead to multi-million dollar packages for the world's top players. Match up the collocations below and read the article.

a	current market	industry	d	stock market	coverage	g	bluechip	brand
b	corporate	value	e	media	outlets	h	sponsorship	deal
c	money-making	image	f	merchandising	flotation	i	strong	company

Business **goals**

A recent news report tells the story of an anthropologist who discovered a lost tribe in the Amazon. Their way of life had hardly changed since the Stone Age and they had never seen a car or met a foreigner. What shocked her most about the natives, however, was not their strange social customs or mysterious religious rituals, but the fact that several of them were wearing Manchester United football shirts!

Whether or not that report is true, what is certain is that Manchester United stopped being just a famous football team several years ago and became a highly successful multinational corporation. The words 'football' and 'club' were officially dropped from the players' badges in 2000 in an effort to strengthen corporate image. With a successful stock market flotation in 1991 and a current market value of over $1.4 billion, Manchester United is as much a triumph of the media as of great soccer.

Since 1990 the club has won – to date – nine League titles, two League Cups, five FA Cups, one European Cup Winners' Cup, two UEFA Champions' League Cups, one UEFA Super Cup and one Intercontinental Cup. But it was the media coverage of the 1990 World Cup and the arrival of SkyTV in 1993 that really transformed the game into the money-making industry it is today. 'Top clubs have grown on the back of television contracts,' says Richard Baldwin of accountants Deloitte & Touche. Teams like Bayern Munich, Arsenal, Real Madrid and AC Milan turn profits many bluechip companies would envy.

'It's an oil well,' says Manchester United's former head of merchandising. He should know. The team's megastore at Old Trafford, which stocks 1,500 different items, is constantly packed, and merchandising outlets as far away as Singapore, Hong Kong and Sydney attract thousands of fans who couldn't even tell you where Manchester is on the map. 'United look and behave very much like a traditional business from a corporate point of view,' says financial analyst Nigel Hawkins. 'They have a strong brand and they have worked to maximise it by bringing in good people.'

They certainly have. One sponsorship deal alone – with Vodafone – netted Manchester £36 million, and American insurance group AIG just paid £56.5 million for a similar four-year deal. What's in it for the sponsors? Clearly, the glamour and glory of being part of the ManU legend. And let's face it, not even Vodafone has its logo in the Amazon rainforest!

2 With a partner, choose a word or phrase from each of the four paragraphs of the article to write a paragraph heading.

3 Do you support a football team? Find someone who doesn't and try to persuade them to go to a match with you.

4 3.26 You are going to work in two teams to negotiate an international transfer deal. First, listen to a brief description of how such deals are put together and take notes. When you're ready, Team 1 see page 134. Team 2 see page 137.

LANGUAGE LINKS

Vocabulary: Negotiations

Conducting negotiations

Complete the collocations by writing the nouns and noun phrases in the right-hand boxes. They are all things you might do during a negotiation.

> a breakthrough   a deadlock   options   pressure
> terms   time out

reach break	(a)	negotiate agree	(d)
look for make	(b)	apply give in to	(e)
call take	(c)	generate weigh up	(f)

Sales negotiations

1 The following things were said in a sales negotiation. Who do you think probably said them – the buyer, the seller or could it be either?

a What kind of a guarantee can you give us?
b Would that be a regular order?
c Is that your best price?
d There are no hidden extras.
e I'm afraid it's not really what we're looking for.
f Would you like to have the product on a trial basis?
g What sort of quantity were you thinking of?
h How flexible can you be on delivery times?
i I'd like to think it over.
j I can't be any fairer than that.
k What immediate benefits could we expect to see?
l Supposing we were to offer you deferred payment?
m We'll match any price you've been quoted.
n What sort of discount could you offer us on that?
o Could we rely on you to meet all our deadlines?
p Now, we'll just need to sort out one or two details.
q So, if you'd just like to sign here.

2 The following collocations all appeared in the negotiation in 1. Try to find the other half of each one in under 90 seconds!

a a regular ....
b .... benefits
c offer ....
d .... a guarantee
e delivery ....
f .... deadlines
g quote a ....
h .... extras
i deferred ....
j .... the details
k match a ....
l a .... basis

Grammar: Language of diplomacy

Your choice of language can have a powerful effect on the outcome of a negotiation. Compare the following:

We reject your offer. > I'm afraid at this point we would be unable to accept your offer.

The use of softeners (*I'm afraid*), restrictive phrases (*at this point*), modal verbs (*would*) and rephrased negatives (*unable to accept*) in the second sentence make the rejection sound more acceptable.

Look at the following ways of making what you say in a negotiation more diplomatic:

1 **Modals**: *would, could, may, might*
- *This is a problem. > This **would** be a problem.*
- *Of course, there's a disadvantage to this. > Of course, there **could** be a disadvantage to this.*

In both examples above the speaker sounds less direct, but in the first example the basic message doesn't change. *This would be a problem* still means it is a problem! But it sounds better.

2 **Qualifiers**: *slight, a bit, rather, a few*, etc.
- *There may be a delay. > There may be a **slight** delay.*
- *We're disappointed with the discount on offer. > We're **rather** disappointed with the discount on offer.*

Qualifiers soften the impact of bad news, but don't actually change it.

3 **Rephrased negatives 1**: *not very, totally, completely* + positive adjective
- *We're unhappy with this arrangement. > We're **not very happy** with this arrangement.*
- *I'm unconvinced. > I'm **not totally convinced**.*

Using positive adjectives makes you sound more positive – even when you use them in the negative!

4 **Rephrased negatives 2**: *unable, not able, not in a position to*
- *We can't go any higher than 7%. > We're **unable to** go any higher than 7%.*
- *We won't accept anything less. > We're **not in a position to** accept anything less.*

Try to avoid using *can't* and *won't*. They make you sound powerless and obstructive.

5 **Negative question forms**: *shouldn't we …?, wouldn't you …?* etc.
- *We should be working together on this. > **Shouldn't we** be working together on this?*
- *You'd be taking an enormous risk. > **Wouldn't you** be taking an enormous risk?*

Negative question forms are incredibly powerful in negotiations. Questions sound more tentative than statements and also more persuasive. Use them to make suggestions and give warnings.

6 Comparatives: -er, more, less

- We're looking for something cheap. > We're looking for something **cheaper**.
- Would you be prepared to consider this? > Would you be **more prepared** to consider this?

The use of comparatives makes what you say sound more negotiable.

7 Softeners: unfortunately, I'm afraid, to be honest, with respect, etc.

- This doesn't meet our needs. > **Unfortunately**, this doesn't meet our needs.
- You don't quite understand. > **With respect**, you don't quite understand.

Softeners at the beginning of a statement signal bad news. With respect is a particularly bad sign!

8 Restrictive phrases: at the moment, at this stage, so far, etc.

- That's our position. > That's our position **at the moment**.
- I don't think we can go any further. > I don't think we can go any further **at this stage**.

Using a restrictive phrase does not exclude the possibility of future movement.

9 The passive: it was understood, it was assumed, etc.

- You said you were ready to sign. > **It was understood** you were ready to sign.
- We thought you had accepted these terms. > **It was assumed** you had accepted these terms.

By avoiding the use of statements beginning You said … and We thought … and using passive forms instead, you depersonalise the situation and reduce the amount of personal responsibility or blame.

10 The -ing form: were aiming, had been hoping

- We aimed to reach agreement today. > We **were aiming** to reach agreement by today.
- We had hoped to see some movement on price. > We **had been hoping** to see some movement on price.

Using the Past Continuous keeps your options open – you were aiming to reach agreement and still are. The Past Perfect Continuous closes the door a little more – you've stopped hoping, but could be persuaded to hope again.

Study the information above and make the direct remarks below more diplomatic using the words in brackets to help you.

a   This is too expensive. (unfortunately / would)
b   We're not interested in your economy model. (would / less)
c   It will be difficult to sell the idea to my boss. (unfortunately / may / very easy)
d   We should be near a decision by now. (shouldn't / a bit nearer?)
e   We can't pay straight away. (afraid / might not / able)
f   I won't make any promises. (not / position / this stage)
g   This is difficult for us to accept. (would / a little / the moment)
h   You said you wanted immediate delivery. (understood)
i   We hoped you would provide after-sales service. (honest / hoping)
j   Our discussions have been unproductive. (not very / so far)
k   A fixed interest rate would be a good idea. (wouldn't / better?)
l   We had aimed to get further than this this morning. (aiming / slightly)

Phrase bank: Negotiating

Complete the six stages of a negotiation using the verbs in the box.
Then match each to two things you might say.

| agree   check   create   enter   put   work |

1 .... rapport
2 .... a procedure
3 .... forward proposals
4 .... the facts
5 .... the bargaining phase
6 .... out the details

a   So what you're saying is this …
b   Thank you all for coming.
c   We'd like to see some movement on price.
d   Great, I think that's everything.
e   I'm afraid we could only accept this on one condition.
f   Perhaps we could begin by outlining our initial position.
g   OK, let's just tie up a few loose ends.
h   What we're looking for here is this …
i   Would you like to set out your requirements first?
j   Ideally, we'd like to see …
k   We're looking forward to a productive meeting.
l   Let me just check I understand you correctly.

1 ☐☐   2 ☐☐   3 ☐☐   4 ☐☐   5 ☐☐   6 ☐☐

GOING UNDER?

1 Do you know anyone who works for their family business? How would you like to be in their position?

2 Which family member would you most / least like to go into business with? Why / why not?

3 What do you think are the main advantages and disadvantages of a family business? Think about:

> dedication to the business   divisions within the family   short- v long-term thinking   resistance to change

4 Read the advertisement for Corelli Motorboats. What kind of customer is it aiming to attract? How do you imagine this kind of family business is run? What sort of challenges do you think it has to face?

Sit at the wheel of the Corelli Pantera and experience true perfection – classic Italian design and over sixty years of wooden boat-building tradition.

No two Panteras are alike. Each customised craft is as individual as you are. Creating your dream is a labour of love at our family boatyard on the shores of Lake Como.

You accept no compromise. And neither do we.

Corelli – live the life!

5 Look at the trade magazine article below. What do you think the title means?

6 Now read the whole article and underline any positive and negative information about the company.

Corelli Motorboats: Drowning in its own success

In the hand-built wooden powerboat industry, few names command so much attention and loyalty as Corelli. For many, the prize-winning Pantera is naturally associated with the millionaire lifestyle of oil sheikhs, aristocrats and movie stars.

The classic appeal of the product is not the creation of a clever marketing department, but of the charismatic Lazzaro Corelli (son of founder Giorgio), his son and chief engineer, Fabio, and his Australian son-in-law and export sales manager, Mark Chambers. In a world of fibreglass hulls and on-board computers, the Corelli family has always stuck to traditional materials and construction techniques. And there has been no shortage of customers. With an output of just 400 boats a year, the order books are always full. In a recent interview with this magazine Lazzaro cheerfully declared that 'business has never been better!'

But that's only half the story. Demand may be increasing, but Corelli's traditional labour-intensive production methods have led to five-year waiting lists. Rumour has it that up to 20% of orders end in cancellation when wealthy customers lose patience with the Corelli obsession with perfection.

Analysts also express doubts about the profitability of the Lombardian firm. Soaring production costs mean that margins on even the pricey Pantera are tight. With strong competition from the States, Corelli is faced with the seemingly impossible task of increasing production without compromising on its reputation for quality.

And even quality is something Corelli can no longer take for granted. The level of craftsmanship is unquestionable, but the boats have so far failed to meet official ISO standards.

Lazzaro Corelli makes light of his company's problems. 'In this business' he says, 'we don't play by the normal rules.' And certainly the firm has survived in a fiercely competitive market for well over half a century.

But at 67 and with a question mark over his health, how long can it be before Lazzaro steps down? And if the rumoured divisions within the family are true, will Corelli soon be sending out an SOS?

The Corelli boatyard

ISO = International Organisation for Standardisation

SOS = a signal sent out by ships in difficulty at sea

7 What are the strengths and weaknesses of Corelli as a business? What opportunities might it have and what threats does it face? Transfer the information from the article you just read to the SWOT analysis below and compare with a partner.

STRENGTHS	WEAKNESSES
What does the company do well? What unique resources does it have? What do others see as its strengths?	What could the company improve? Where is it lacking resources? What are others likely to see as weaknesses?
OPPORTUNITIES	**THREATS**
What opportunities are open to the company? What trends could it take advantage of? How can it turn strengths into opportunities?	What trends could harm the company? What is the competition doing? What threats do the company's weaknesses expose it to?

8 3.27 Listen to a conversation overheard in the Corelli boatyard between Lazzaro and his son-in-law, Mark. Take notes and add any useful information to the SWOT matrix above.

9 Do you see the offer from Cascadia Inc. more as an opportunity or as a threat?

10 Study the report below. With a partner decide what the figures say about the current state of the business. Look for general trends, opportunities and danger signs and make a list of key points.

Output: 400 boats pa
Price range €90,000–280,000

Market: competitive global market
85% of production is for export

Ownership: Lazzaro & Claudia 50:50

Marketing: highly personalized sales, boat shows, magazine adverts

Average market growth: 5%pa (last 3 yrs)

Market prospects: Europe 11–12% growth
Asia 7–8% growth
USA 4–5% growth
Middle East 9–10% growth

Financial history	Yr-2	Yr-1	Yr0	Yr+1	Industry average
Sales (€m):	59	62	68	70	60
Pre-tax profit (€m):	7.7	7.0	6.0	4.5	8.8
Profit margin (%):	13.1	11.4	8.9	6.5	14.6
Debt/Assets Ratio:	28%	34%	41%	50%	27%

Cost structure: increasing cost of sales caused by large factory capacity
highly skilled workforce
high degree of customisation

Economic factors: strong euro, rising oil prices

Corelli sales by country

Italy 15% Other 18% Middle East 32% USA 35%

Powerboat market trends

Large high-tech boats ▲ 10%
Hand-built wooden boats ▲ 15%
Small hand-built boats ▼ 5%
Small fibreglass boats ▲ 25%

Mark Chambers, 36
Son-in-law, sales manager

Lazzaro Corelli, 60
Head of the family

Fabio Corelli, 32
Son, chief engineer

Claudia Corelli, 54
Lazzaro's wife

Chiara Corelli, 23
Daughter, industrial designer

Sofia Chambers, 29
Daughter, artist, Mark's wife

11 3.28 You have been brought in as consultants to the Corelli family business. You conduct private interviews with each of the family members. Listen to extracts from those interviews and take notes.

12 To what extent do you think the problems are about:

generations?	Lazzaro and Claudia want to keep things the way they are	The younger generation want to see some changes
culture?	The Italians are very passionate about what they do	The Australian is very practical and direct
gender?	The men have very fixed ideas about how things should be done	The women are more open to creative options

13 Work in small consultancy teams. Using all the information you have, prepare a short presentation outlining your recommendations to the Corellis. Use the SWOT analysis you carried out as your main visual aid if you like and/or prepare others.

Try to take equal account of both business and personal issues. If the company stays in the family, who should take over from Lazzaro?

02 MAKING CONTACTS

Conference advice

Speaker A

> One way to stand out at conferences, even if you're a bit shy, is to wear one subtle but interesting thing. It could be an unusual tie, watch or piece of jewellery or just a flower in your lapel. You'll be surprised how many people comment on it and it's a great way to start a conversation! Don't be afraid to hand out your business cards. I always run out by the second day. So take plenty! Eat in the conference centre. Don't be put off by long lunch queues – they're a great place to meet people. As for which presentations you should attend, the best way to make sure you're keeping up with the latest trends is by going to all the big talks by the industry leaders. Find out who the stars (and bores) are before you go. BTW don't be embarrassed about walking out of boring presentations halfway through. Your boss isn't paying you to waste your time. Hate to disappoint you, but 80% of the talks will be BORING. Don't be tempted to do the tourist stuff. You don't have time. You can always go back there on holiday. And avoid the hotel bar in the evenings. Find a nice quiet place to relax at the end of what will feel like very long days. Oh, and don't forget to pack comfortable shoes – you're going to do a lot of walking! Hope this is some help. Good luck!
>
> Posted by Angelina Wasserman at 4:23PM on October 4

04 KEEPING TRACK

Sorry?

Speaker A

1 Read out the text below to your partner.

When you read the information in **bold**, whisper so they cannot hear!
Your partner should ask you for the exact information they missed. If not, keep reading!
If your partner just says 'Sorry?', reply 'Sorry what?'

The famous Budweiser Company

Budweiser is the world's bestselling brand of beer. In the USA it represents **22 per cent** of total beer sales. The American company that makes it is the biggest brewery in the world with 50 per cent greater **output** than its nearest competitor, the Dutch multinational, **Heineken**. Budweiser is the all-American beer. With its enormous **marketing budget**, it spent more than **32 million** dollars to be 'an official partner' in the soccer World Cup. Over the last 40 years, the company has had many **advertising slogans**. But by far the most successful is 'Budweiser: the King of **Beers**'.

2 Listen to your partner reading out a similar text. Ask them to clarify anything you don't understand. When you're clear about what the information is, write it down in full. Check each point you clarified with your partner at the end.

04 KEEPING TRACK

Quiz answers

1 1.3 billion
2 Exxon Mobil
3 the Toyota Corolla
4 KLM
5 the Yomiuri Shimbun
6 Louis Vuitton
7 Barbie
8 the electric light bulb
9 Ireland
10 Hewlett-Packard
11 Luxembourg
12 Proctor & Gamble

04 KEEPING TRACK

Didn't I say that?

Speaker A

1 Read out the following sentences to your partner. Each one contains a silly discrepancy. Can he/she spot it?

a I love Scotland, especially Dublin.
b I always drink German wine. Bordeaux's my favourite.
c I first met Ulrike yesterday. She's one of my closest friends.
d I've nearly given up smoking. I'm down to about 30 a day now.
e Let me introduce you to my wife. And then I'll introduce you to her husband.

2 Listen to your partner reading out some sentences. Can you spot the discrepancies? Query any you hear using some of the expressions on page 24.

05 WHAT WOMEN WANT

Gender spenders quiz

The answer to all the quiz questions is 'Women'.

05 WHAT WOMEN WANT

Case studies

X2 Stylebooks

Computer manufacturer X2 went for the standard colour makeover by launching a range of laptops called Stylebooks, which came in green, powder blue, and pink, as well as black and silver. They also weighed less than 1.8kg. But, significantly, they had all the usual features, including a full-size keyboard, the latest mobile processor, and Wi-Fi wireless networking built in. No compromise on technology.

Burberry iPod case

iPod digital music players which come in several colours have predictably drawn more women buyers than the standard black and white models. But the real growth has been in fashionable accessories. Even up-market fashion houses like Burberry have custom-designed carry cases for the world's bestselling MP3 player in their signature plaid pattern.

Barbara K Toolkit

These days 75% of women carry out home improvements by themselves. Barbara K's 30-piece tool kit, which sells through the usual DIY and department stores, is specially designed to help them. The tools look good, but also weigh a little less than regular tools with the grips and handles sized to better fit a woman's hand.

Harry's Ale

19-year-old Harriet Easton has taken on the male-dominated world of traditional English beer by developing with a local brewery a light, fruity ale that appeals to women of all ages. 'A lot of women I know,' she says, 'particularly young women, think real ale is unsophisticated, fattening, unhealthy and unfeminine, but pint for pint it's less fattening than orange juice'. So as not to alienate male drinkers she decided to call it Harry's Ale.

Nike Goddess

In its 30-year history Nike has developed something of a macho image, but its slogan, 'Just do it', doesn't really do it for most women. So global creative director John Hoke came up with Nike Goddess. 'Women weren't comfortable in our stores,' he says. 'So I figured out where they would be comfortable - most likely their own homes. The Goddess store has more of a residential feel. I wanted it to have furnishings, not fixtures. But, above all, I didn't want it to be girlie.'

Frauenbank

Astrid Hastreiter, a 41-year-old IT specialist, has launched a bank for women in Germany which offers a full range of financial services and credit facilities. 'It is extraordinary how many German women avoid talking about their money and what to do with it, simply because they are not keen to sit opposite a sharp-suited banker who has little understanding of their needs,' she said. Frauenbank's customers are typically university-educated women between 30 and 55. There are also a small number of male clients. 'We are women-friendly, but that does not mean that we are hostile to men'.

CASE STUDY: HIGH FLIER

From: Shavi Kumar
Subject: I forgot to mention …

Hi guys

Had a bit of fall in the mountains. Don't worry. Nothing serious. Fortunately, I landed on one of the other climbers, which was very considerate of him. Jamil, check my insurance for that. Anyway, I'm on my way back to Mumbai now and should be in tomorrow as planned. But I just remembered a few things I probably should have mentioned last Fri.

First of all, if a guy from the Indian Embassy in Washington gets in touch, whatever you do, don't agree to anything. He's been trying to get me to give a talk there for weeks. He's a real pain. And it's a complete waste of time. Please get rid of him!

On the other hand, I've been expecting a call from Callum Brody, my financial adviser in NY. If he does call about a deal he's organising for me, just say yes to whatever he asks you to do. Don't wait for me to come back or it may be too late!

You may hear from Hanna or Lukas in Berlin. They always want me to OK big decisions before they go ahead. I think it's just cultural. Anyway, I'll leave it to you to decide what to do. Just make sure we get Baumann Studios. I want to sell off our old studios in Germany as soon as the Baumann deal goes through.

I have a horrible feeling that I told my parents I'd be at some deadly party they're arranging this week, but if it clashes with anything important, please think of an excuse for me not to be there!

Basically, nothing must interfere with our meetings with the bank and with Sony. Those are our big priorities over the coming weeks. Of course, if the Sony deal goes through, it would be nice to have a chance to get some publicity for that. So let me know if any opportunities to talk to the media come up.

BTW, I was only joking when I said I didn't want to speak at the MTV Awards. Of course, it would look very bad to cancel that now. Public speaking goes with the job.

One thing you could all be doing is thinking about our meeting on internet advertising a week on Fri. We really need some fresh ideas. Our current agency is hopeless and I'd like to see us doing something different.

Hope there haven't been any disasters while I've been away!

OK, speak to you all tomorrow.

Shavi

06 BUSINESS TRAVEL

The nightmare journey

Speaker A

Work with a partner. In each of the situations below you are a business traveller. Your partner is the other speaker.

06.00
Business traveller: You didn't get your five o'clock alarm call at your hotel this morning, so you overslept! Now you've missed your taxi to the airport. Your plane leaves in 90 minutes and it's at least half an hour to the airport. Go and complain at the reception desk. Get them to book you another taxi and telephone Heathrow airport to say you are on your way. You start: *What happened to my alarm call?*

06.15
Business traveller: Your taxi has finally arrived. Explain that your plane leaves in an hour and a quarter and that you must be on it. If you miss the Zurich meeting at 11.00, your boss is going to kill you! You thought about taking the Underground, but you have a very heavy bag of product samples to carry. You start: *Heathrow airport. Terminal 1. And please hurry!*

07.00
Business traveller: By some miracle, you have arrived at Heathrow! But your plane leaves in half an hour. You'll have to run! You didn't have time to change any money at the hotel, so you only have three £50 notes and your credit cards. Pay the taxi driver and go!

07.15
Business traveller: You are at check-in with your case of product samples for the Zurich meeting and your hand luggage. Fortunately, the hotel phoned the airport and they were expecting you. Thank god you're travelling business class!

07.30
Business traveller: After all the panic to get to the airport, your British Airways flight is going to be delayed for an hour and a half! You wanted to fly Crossair, but they only had economy class seats left. Now there's nothing to do but wait. Luckily, your meeting is three hours away, so you can still just make it.

09.15
Business traveller: You managed to get a seat in economy on the Crossair flight. You're scheduled to arrive in Zurich in an hour, which gives you another 45 minutes to get to your meeting. You might just do it! Suddenly, you hear the following announcement: 'Good morning, ladies and gentlemen. This is your captain speaking. I'm afraid I've just been notified that, due to bad weather over Zurich, we've been diverted to Geneva. I am very sorry for the inconvenience this may cause, and will keep you informed of any further changes to our schedule.' You must call Zurich! Ask a flight attendant if it's OK to use your mobile. You start: *Er, excuse me!*

06 BUSINESS TRAVEL

In arrivals

Speaker A

It is 9.30pm. You are in the crowded arrivals area at Newark airport in New York. There has just been a terrible thunderstorm and it is still pouring with rain.

You are picking up a senior colleague who works in your Cologne office. Because of the weather, their flight is two hours late, but your boss told you to 'look after them well' – take them out to a top-class restaurant, maybe a nightclub or two. You have never met them before, so you are holding up a large piece of card with their name written on it.

Your car is just five minutes away in the car park. You have booked a table at Guastavino's, a fabulous restaurant in Manhattan and are looking forward to an enjoyable evening. According to your boss, 'money is no object'. If he can, he's going to join you both later for drinks.

You've been working very hard recently. Tonight you are going to relax and have fun!

07 HANDLING CALLS

Asking politely

Speaker A

Your partner is a colleague at the same level in the company as you.

Call them (they always seem to be very busy!) and ask them to:

Call 1 organise the itinerary for a visit by some Chinese government officials next week (your partner is much better at this kind of thing than you are).
Call 2 e-mail you a copy of the Warsaw report (it's a week late!).
Call 3 get on to your IT department (the system's down on the whole of the first floor).
Call 4 take a look at the Hamburg project proposal (you're too busy with the Milan proposal).

How often did you get your partner to do what you want?

You'll receive calls from your partner asking you to do things for them. Respond according to how important and/or urgent it is and how busy you are.

Call 1 You're doing a cost breakdown for the Budapest contract but you can't finish it until the Hungarians send you more detailed figures.

Call 2 You keep calling your London office to check the arrangements for the big presentation you and your partner are giving next Friday, but can't get through.

Call 3 You're in the middle of a difficult meeting with a group of union officials who are unhappy about working conditions.

Call 4 You've worked through two Saturdays in a row and are about to leave the office early.

07 HANDLING CALLS

Unexpected phone calls

Speaker A

Call 1 You make the call 1730 local time
You work in the marketing department of Shiseido Cosmetics, Tokyo. Phone the advertising department of Cosmopolitan magazine, Paris. You want to speak to either Monique Leblanc or Philippe Roussel about the cost of a full-page advertisement.

Call 2 You receive the call 1030 local time
You work for Barclays Global Mutual Funds in New York and deal with corporate investment. Your colleague, Neil Thomas, deals with company pension schemes, but you have no idea where he is. He went out to get a bagel an hour and a half ago and hasn't been seen since. You're very busy and have to keep putting Speaker B on hold to deal with different problems. Neil's mobile number is 181 650 777.

Call 3 You make the call 1500 local time
You are a sales representative for Fujitsu computers, UK. You're calling Speaker B at General Accident Insurance with a quote for 25 laptops, which they asked for by responding to one of your company's internet advertisements. You have a range of discounted prices you can offer from $19,000 to $48,000 depending on the model. You could e-mail these, but prefer to phone because it gives you a chance to get an appointment.

Call 4 You receive the call 1045 local time
You work for Burson-Marsteller, the world's biggest public relations company, and are based in Boston, USA. In the course of your job, you get to go to a lot of conferences and meet a lot of people. You can't always remember them all, although it's an important part of your job to pretend to do so. You've just got a new boss, who you don't like very much, and are on your way to a meeting with her now.

08 MAKING DECISIONS

Questionnaire analysis (page 45)

Whether you wrote yes or no is unimportant.

If you wrote *it depends* to five or more questions you are a reflective decision-maker. You like to take your time thinking things through before coming to a final decision. In some jobs this is a good strategy. But we live in a world of rapid change – be careful you don't take too long to make up your mind!

If you wrote *it depends* to two or fewer questions, you are a reflexive decision-maker. You'd rather think fast and make the wrong decision occasionally than take so long to decide you miss an opportunity. This can be a vital skill for a manager. Just make sure you're right more often than you're wrong!

If you wrote *it depends* to three or four questions, you are a balanced decision-maker. You don't waste time agonising over simple decisions, but you don't rush decisions that have serious implications either. You seem to be in control of both your head and your heart. But are you so in control you never take a risk?

08 MACHING DECISIONS

08 MAKING DECISIONS

The decision-making meeting

Plan B

🔊 **1.40** If you are unable to reach a decision on the new Bond, perhaps it is because the film series itself needs to be brought into the 21st century. Why not break with tradition altogether and make the Bond character a woman? You could reverse all the stereotypes and attract a completely new audience. You know the actress below is interested in the idea. Read her profile, then listen to an interview extract.

name and age
Diane Fairchild 26
nationality
Anglo-French
marital status
single
height and build
1.78m slim, athletic
physical pursuits
Swam for her university. Black belt Taekwondo.
experience
Did a law degree at Cambridge before going into acting. A rising star who has become 'hot property' in Hollywood after her huge success in the action thriller *Spider-Web*. Just completed a twelve-week run on Broadway. Though 'typically British', the Americans love her.
achievements
Won a Golden Palm at the Cannes Film Festival for her first Hollywood film.
usual fee
Diane's 'bankability' has increased dramatically in the last two years. Now earns at least $2 million a film.
comments
Likes to combine serious theatre work with escapist films. Says she thinks a female Bond is just what the 007 series needs.

10 SMALL TALK

Cultural sensitivity test

Speaker A

Work with a partner. You have three intercultural dilemmas and they have three different ones. Take turns to describe the dilemmas to each other and discuss what you'd do in each situation. Do you agree on what you *should* do? Is that what you'd both *really* do?

Dilemma 1: You meet a Spanish business contact you haven't seen for ages who wants to stop and chat, but you're running late for an appointment. Do you stay or do you make your excuses and go?

Dilemma 3: A British salesman is giving you a demonstration of a new office product. He seems to like telling a lot of jokes. Do you join in the joke-telling or wait until he gets to the point?

Dilemma 5: You are having a pre-negotiation coffee at a potential client's headquarters in Berlin. Do you mingle with the opposing team or stick with your own people?

For comments on your answers see page 138.

14 BEING HEARD

Hang on a minute!

Speaker A

Read the short article below about intercultural business etiquette. In a few minutes you are going to try to read it aloud to your partner in under a minute, so first check you understand everything and mark places where you can pause for breath!

Your partner is preparing to read a similar article aloud to you. So, when you are both ready, decide who will read first. Read as fast as you can, but try to make sense!

As you listen to your partner read, you should interrupt them as often as possible to clarify anything which isn't absolutely clear. Your objective is to stop them reaching the end of the text in a minute. See who can get further. Good luck!

Do business across culture and you'll be faced with a minefield of *dos* and *don't*s. But whose *dos* should you do? And whose *don't*s should you avoid? The Chinese, for example, traditionally enter a room in order of seniority, whereas in Spain the boss will usually make a late entrance. So who goes first in a Spanish–Chinese meeting? In Singapore strong eye contact is considered aggressive. But, according to Austro–German superstition, you must look people directly in the eye whenever you say cheers in a bar. If you don't, you'll have seven years' bad sex. Is it worth breaking a rule to be lucky in love? And, in these times of globalisation and the networked economy, can there really be such a thing as a business lunch when in New York it's all about business and in Paris it's all about lunch? They say 'When in Rome, do as the Romans do'. But what if the Romans are meeting the Koreans in Krakow?

INTERRUPTOMETER

↑ You're hopeless!

Learn to be more assertive.

OK, but avoid doing business in Latin America.

Pretty good. You could be a politician.

↓ Excellent! Nobody else can get a word in.

14 BEING HEARD

The questionnaire shows what type of 'animal' you are in meetings. First add up your total number of points.

a   Agree = 0 points   Disagree = 1 point
b   Agree = 1 point   Disagree = 0 points
c   Agree = 1 point   Disagree = 0 points
d   Agree = 0 points   Disagree = 1 point
e   Agree = 0 points   Disagree = 1 point
f   Agree = 1 point   Disagree = 0 points
g   Agree = 1 point   Disagree = 0 points
h   Agree = 1 point   Disagree = 0 points

If you scored:

0–2 points
You're a mouse at meetings – shy, quiet, you don't like to be the centre of attention. You make a very good listener, but need to say what you really think more often.

3–4 points
You're a fox at meetings – sly, patient and sudden in your attacks on other people's points of view. You don't say much, preferring to let others give you all the information you need to destroy their arguments.

5–6 points
You're a horse at meetings – enthusiastic and full of energy, it takes a strong person to keep you under control. You work very hard to get your ideas across, but will sometimes do as you're told just to keep the peace.

7–8 points
You're a bulldog at meetings – loud, proud and fond of the sound of your own voice. People know you always mean what you say, but you need to listen to what they're saying a bit more often.

15 SNAIL MAIL

Speakers A and B

Situation 1

Speaker A, you are the boss. Your secretary, Speaker B, just gave you this letter to sign. Point out the mistakes in it and tell him/her how to rewrite it. There are 23 mistakes in all. Don't sign anything until he/she writes it properly!

Speaker B, defend yourself! You were in a rush when you wrote the letter and can probably correct a lot of it without your boss's help.

> **Useful language**
> You don't need …
> That's spelled …
> That should be …, not …
> With an 's' / without 's'
> ff = double f
> ABC = capital letters
> abc = lower case letters
> , = comma
> ' = apostrophe
> Mr, Ms, Dr = abbreviation
> ? = question mark
> . = full stop/period
> ( ) = brackets

Speaker A starts: *Could I see you a moment …?*

> Dezember 3RD
>
> Daer Mister Barghiel.
>
> I'am writing to confirm our apointment on Dec 7. Off course, I have your adress, but I am wonder if you could to send to me instruction on how to get to your office for that I will be come by my car.
>
> A lot of thanks. I very much am look forward to meet you.
>
> Yours faithlessly,

Situation 2

Repeat the previous activity. This time, Speaker B is the boss and Speaker A is the secretary. There are 23 mistakes in the letter.

Speaker B starts: *Could I see you a moment …?*

> Mai 7th
>
> Dear Doc Jane Garland,
>
> With referrance to your order (ref NO. 606-1, I am regretting informing you that the the DCS1 is currantly out of stock May I suggest you consider to upgrade to the DCS2? When you are interesting, I would be happy to send you detales.
>
> Letting me know if I can to be of any furthest help?
>
> You're sincere,

16 SOLVING PROBLEMS

Three real companies

Speaker A

Read the business dilemma below. Then summarise the basic problem to the rest of your group and brainstorm some solutions.

The owner of a Mexican restaurant in San Francisco faced a dilemma. She wanted to advertise but couldn't afford to pay for space in the local newspaper or for airtime on the local radio station.

16 SOLVING PROBLEMS

A problem-solving meeting

Group B

Using the procedure on page 95, hold a meeting to solve the problem below.

- Read paragraph one. What else do you know about this business?
- Read paragraph two. What's your immediate response to the problem?
- Read paragraph three. It should give you some extra ideas on how to solve the problem.
- Conduct a problem-solving meeting with your group.
- Summarise the problem and your solutions for the other group or groups. Find out if they agree with you.

A quality problem at Harley-Davidson

The company
Harley-Davidson is more than just a motorcycle company. It's a legend. The firm's website says it all: 'It's one thing for customers to buy your product. It's another for them to tattoo your name on their bodies.' Featured in cult movies like *Easy Rider* and brandstretched to include everything from cowboy hats to deodorant, the Harley is an American icon to stand alongside Coke, Levis and Marlboro.

The challenge
But in the mid 80s the company was in big trouble. Faced with strong competition from Japan and unable to keep costs down without affecting quality, Harley was steadily losing market share to copycat models manufactured by Honda, Yamaha and Kawasaki. Thanks to just-in-time production methods and a simpler management structure, it seemed that everything the Americans could do the Japanese could do better and more cheaply. A flood of Japanese imports was even starting to worry the Reagan administration in Washington. New Harley-Davidson CEO Richard Teerlink had to come up with a rescue plan – and fast!

The opportunity
One thing Teerlink knew was that the average age of the Harley rider was increasing. It was no longer a young blue-collar worker's bike. High prices had seen to that. Now middle-aged bankers, accountants and lawyers wanted to swap their business suits for biker leathers at the weekend and go in search of freedom. These people weren't in a hurry to take delivery of their bikes, as long as it was worth the wait, and 75% of them made repeat purchases. They admired the superior engineering of the Japanese bikes, but they really didn't want to buy Japanese – they just needed a good reason not to.

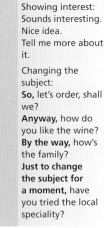

18 EATING OUT

Table manners

Answers to quiz

a	Finland	i	Chinese
b	Brazil	j	Japanese
c	Portugal	k	American
d	Japan	l	Spain
e	Britain	m	Arab
f	America	n	Japan
g	Arab	o	Asian
h	Mexico		

18 EATING OUT

The business lunch

Speaker A

Your partner (Speaker B) is a good friend from abroad, whom you've also worked with in the past. They are only in town for a few days, so you've invited them out for a really nice lunch.

Think of a local restaurant you like and prepare a short menu of dishes and a drinks list to explain to your guest. Write the names of the dishes and drinks in your own language. You should include:

> **Useful phrases**
> Showing interest:
> Sounds interesting.
> Nice idea.
> Tell me more about it.
>
> Changing the subject:
> **So,** let's order, shall we?
> **Anyway,** how do you like the wine?
> **By the way,** how's the family?
> **Just to change the subject for a moment,** have you tried the local speciality?

- at least one dish which you really like and think everyone should try
- one dish which most people don't like very much and which you don't recommend
- one dish, if you can, which is a little difficult to explain to a foreigner (prepare for this)
- one dish or drink (wine, beer or a soft drink) which is a speciality of the region (prepare an appetising description)

Your partner phoned you a week ago and mentioned a business idea they wanted to talk to you about. Perhaps they will tell you more over lunch, but do your best to be the perfect host and don't just 'talk shop'! Try to keep the conversation moving.

You're the host, so insist on paying!

Menu

Starters

....

....

Main courses

....

....

Desserts

....

....

....

Drinks

Wines

....

....

Beers

....

....

Soft drinks

....

....

19 TELECOMMUNICATIONS

Teleconference: a project meeting

Work in the largest group possible. You are all human resources directors of different branches of a multinational IT solutions company. You want to send 30 of your staff on a team-building weekend. You've drawn up a shortlist of options. Things you should consider include: the practical training element, the fun factor, safety, cost.

1 Dragon boat racing followed by riverside barbecue and evening firework display

Teams of 15-20 take part in three boat races during this fun-filled, action-packed day! After an initial team-briefing and training session, teams spend the morning practising their rowing technique and working out a winning race strategy. Then it's off to the races! Food, drink and fireworks on the river round off the day.
Venue: Macau, China
Cost: $140

2 Lapland dog-sledding followed by banquet at mountain lodge and wolf-watch

Teams of three build their own traditional dog-sleds from construction plans and materials supplied on site. After a short dog-handling session they set off with a local expert on a wilderness trail in search of treasure buried deep in the forest. The day ends with a fabulous banquet by roaring fires! Optional night trip to hear the howling wolves!
Venue: Rovaniemi, Finnish Lapland
Cost: $190

3 Italian 'bank robbery' followed by pasta and Chianti celebration and cabaret

Teams of 10 compete to carry out a simulated bank robbery right in the heart of Rome! After a planning session and team presentation at the 5-star Lord Byron Hotel, 'controllers' take to the sky in helicopters whilst teams take the wheel of our special Mini Coopers. At stake: $50m in gold bullion! The evening ends with music and wine.
Venue: Rome
Cost: $320

Note: prices are all per person and do NOT include flights or accommodation.

Choose a chairperson. You have just 15–20 mins for the teleconference. Try to stick to the following agenda:

1. Open the meeting and explain its objective.
2. Ask participants to briefly introduce themselves.
3. Give each participant a chance to present their preference, but keep inputs short and try to discourage too much interruption.
4. Allow some time for participants to discuss their preferences, but prevent arguments and digressions.
5. Ask each participant to vote for their preferred event and announce the group's final decision. If a clear decision cannot be made, choose the cheapest of the preferred options.
6. Thank participants and close the meeting.

When you are ready, sit in a circle, a metre apart if possible, facing outwards, so that you cannot see the other speakers and hold your teleconference.

19 TELECOMMUNICATIONS

An urgent matter

Answer:

Consultants are more common that rats, the lab technicians get less attached to them, and there are things a consultant will do that a rat won't.

20 NEGOTIATING

The transfer

Negotiating team 1: The player's agents

You represent the interests of _____ (*choose or invent a name*), the eighteen-year-old superstar striker who plays for _____ (*choose or invent a club*). Already a member of his national squad, your client clearly has a brilliant career ahead of him. His current team has set a transfer fee of £10 million, which is quite a lot for such a young player, but fair considering his enormous potential. The final transfer fee will be agreed between the two clubs and is nothing to do with you. Your job is to negotiate your client's financial package with the management of Manchester United.

You do not have to reach an agreement with Manchester. Barcelona, Juventus and Arsenal are also very interested in your client. But you do know he particularly wants to play for them, so you have approached them first.

It is in your interests to:

- get a higher than average wage for such a superb player of international status (more than £80,000 per week)
- get a good annual fee (your agent's commission will be calculated on the basis of this!)
- go for the shortest contract you can get or one with a very low termination penalty (your client may not be as happy at Manchester as he hoped)
- secure a fair percentage of merchandising profits (maybe 15% – the fans are sure to want to buy products with your client's name on).

But you may need to be flexible on some of these points.

Your client has also asked you to try to get:

- a penthouse apartment in central Manchester (he wants to enjoy the nightlife)
- two left-hand drive sports cars (preferably Ferraris or Porsches) for himself and his new wife
- first-class air tickets for his immediate family (eight people) to come and visit him occasionally plus half a dozen trips home for himself every year.

At present your client has a £1m a year sponsorship deal with Nike, which he would like to keep.

The negotiation is scheduled to be held at Old Trafford. First, with your team, work out your opening, target and walk away positions for each of the following points. When the other team is ready, they will invite you into the boardroom. You may take two five-minute time-outs during the meeting, if you need them. Write down any terms you agree to.

	OP	TP	WAP
Basic wage			
Annual fee			
Length of contract			
Contract termination fee			
Percentage of merchandising profits			
Accommodation			
Car			
Flights home			

02 MAKING CONTACTS

Conference advice

Speaker B

One thing I've learned about conferences is always to carry 'useful stuff' – spare change, an extra pen and paper. You'd be surprised how many people don't have the right money for the coffee machine or turn up to a talk without a pen. Lending them yours is a great way to start a conversation! But, whatever you do, don't give your business card to everyone you meet or you'll have a mountain of e-mail when you get back! Make a few notes on the back of useful cards and make sure you throw away useless ones at the end of each day. Also use lunch and coffee breaks to take notes on what you've learned and who you've met or you'll forget it all later. It may sound strange, but I'd skip the big presentations. You can network much better at workshops and small group sessions where people have similar interests to you and you can talk more easily. A word about audience etiquette. It's very bad manners to walk out of a talk halfway through, even if you're not enjoying it. Think how you'd feel! Make sure you get to see something of Rome while you're there – shouldn't be all work and no play! On the subject of work, remember, the hotel bar is where the real networking gets done. Just be careful how much you drink!!! Finally, dress to impress. Best suit, best accessories, best shoes = best results.

Posted by Gianni Corbucci at 8:06PM on October 7

04 KEEPING TRACK

Speaker B

1 Listen to your partner reading out a text. Ask them to clarify anything you don't understand. When you're clear about what the information is, write it down in full. Check each point you clarified with your partner at the end.

2 Read out the text below to your partner.

When you read the information in **bold**, whisper so they cannot hear!

Your partner should ask you for the exact information they missed. If not, keep reading!

If your partner just says 'Sorry?', reply 'Sorry what?'

The original Budweiser Company

Budweiser is one of the Czech Republic's oldest and most famous beers. In fact, the brewery which makes it is over **700** years old. It shares its name with the best-known US brand because in **1876** the Americans decided to name their product after the small Hungarian town of **Budweis**.

After a long **legal dispute**, the Czech company now markets its product under the Budweiser name in more than **40** different countries. Obviously, this has confused some **consumers**. So the Czechs, with far fewer resources than the Americans, have responded by advertising it simply as 'Budweiser: the beer of **Kings**'.

04 KEEPING TRACK

Speaker B

1 Listen to your partner reading out some sentences. Can you spot the discrepancies? Query any you hear using some of the expressions on page 24.

2 Read out the following sentences to your partner. Each one contains a silly discrepancy. Can he/she spot it?

a I've got three children – one of each.
b We met the French negotiating team at their headquarters in Lisbon.
c I'm worried about this trip to Denmark. For one thing, I don't speak a word of Dutch.
d The managing director must be at least 70. But it's his grandfather who really runs the company.
e I work for a firm called Network Software. We make washing machines, fridges, that kind of thing.

06 BUSINESS TRAVEL

Speaker B

Work with a partner. In each of the situations below your partner is a business traveller. You are the other speaker.

06.00
Hotel receptionist: You have just come on duty at the Novotel reception desk. Your colleague, who went home five minutes ago, says there has been a problem with the internal telephone system all night. Since you arrived it's been one complaint after another!

06.15
Taxi driver: You have just picked up someone at the Novotel who wants to go to Heathrow airport. On your way to the hotel you heard this on the radio: 'Traffic news now, and there's been a major accident on the M25 this morning involving three lorries and eight cars. Police say to expect delays of up to an hour. If you're travelling to Heathrow this morning, you're advised to take the Underground to Paddington station and then the Heathrow Express …'

07.00
Taxi driver: Fortunately, the traffic was not as bad as you expected. But your last two passengers paid you in £50 notes and took nearly all your change – you only have a £10 note and three pound coins. There is a cashpoint machine in the airport terminal if you need it, but another customer is waiting to get into your taxi. You start: *Well, we made it! That's £23, please.*

07.15
Check-in clerk: You are checking in a late business class passenger. Their hand luggage is OK, but their suitcase is well over the 25 kilo limit – 38 kilos! The flight is full and due to depart in 15 minutes. You cannot accept their luggage. You could book it onto a later flight if they pay excess baggage. You start: *I'm sorry but your case is too heavy.*

07.30
BA representative: You are at Gate 42, Heathrow airport. Flight BA922 to Zurich is delayed and you have a lot of unhappy passengers sitting in the departure lounge. A few have already asked for seats on the 8.30 Crossair flight. You have just received this message on your mobile: 'The plane has serious mechanical problems and cannot leave London today. Another plane is flying out from Zurich, but there will now be a delay of approximately four hours.' You start: *British Airways regrets to announce …*

09.15
Flight attendant: You are the chief steward on Crossair flight 711 from London Heathrow to Zurich. Unfortunately, your flight has just been diverted to Geneva because of bad weather. A lot of passengers are getting angry and insisting they make phone calls. The use of mobile phones is strictly prohibited on aircraft and in-flight phones are only available in business class.

06 BUSINESS TRAVEL

In arrivals

Speaker B

It is 9.30pm. You are in the crowded arrivals area at Newark airport in New York. There has just been a terrible thunderstorm and it is still pouring with rain.

You have just arrived two hours late after a nightmare flight from Cologne. Normally, you are a good flier, but there was so much turbulence you were almost sick on the plane. You don't know who is meeting you, so you are looking for a sign with your name on it.

To be honest, you don't feel like talking much and would just like to go straight to your hotel, have a shower and go to bed. But maybe you should eat something light first – it's a long day of meetings tomorrow and you want to be on good form.

This is your first time in New York. It's a pity you feel so ill.

07 HANDLING CALLS

Asking politely

Speaker B

Your partner is a colleague at the same level in the company as you.

You'll receive calls from your partner asking you to do things for them. Respond according to how important and/or urgent it is and how busy you are.

Call 1 You're in the middle of trying to do your quarterly accounts for the third time this week and don't want to be disturbed!

Call 2 You're a few days late with the Warsaw report and need about another day to finish it.

Call 3 You've been having computer problems all day and haven't got any work done.

Call 4 You've been doing paperwork all day. You've just finished going through the 100-page Milan project proposal and need a break!

Call your partner (they always seem to be very busy!) and ask them to:

Call 1 e-mail you a cost breakdown for the Budapest contract (you need it for a meeting next week).

Call 2 make sure everything is arranged for the big presentation you and your partner are giving in London next Friday.

Call 3 set up a meeting with head office to discuss complaints about working conditions at the plant.

Call 4 get on to the telephone company about faulty phone lines (your customer service department is in chaos!)

How often did you get your partner to do what you want?

07 HANDLING CALLS

Unexpected phone calls

Speaker B

Call 1 You receive the call 0930 local time
You are a student of journalism in Paris working for *Cosmopolitan* magazine during your summer vacation. There was no one in the office when the phone rang, so you picked it up. You've never spoken English on the phone before and misunderstand everything Speaker A tells you. After a minute or so, end the call by offering to get someone who speaks better English.

Call 2 You make the call 1630 local time
You work in the finance department at Daimler-Chrysler in Stuttgart and are responsible for the management of the company pension scheme. You want to query something with the fund manager at Barclay's Global Mutual Funds in New York, Neil Thomas. It's rather urgent. You finish work at six.

Call 3 You receive the call 1500 local time
You work in the sales department of General Accident Insurance, UK. You are holding a meeting in your office to discuss the training programme for your new intake of 25 sales personnel. At first, you have no idea who Speaker A is when he/she calls – probably a sales rep from one of the computer companies you contacted on the Internet the other day. Be civil, but get him/her off the phone.

Call 4 You make the call 1045 local time
You work for a small public relations company in Bath, UK. 18 months ago you met Speaker A at an international conference in Chicago. He/She works for Burson-Marsteller, the world's biggest PR firm. You got on very well and stayed up till three in the morning. You mentioned you'd love to work for a bigger company and he/she offered to introduce you to his/her boss if you ever came to Boston. You're in Boston, at the Logan Airport Hotel. Your mobile number is 751 533 200.

10 SMALL TALK

Speaker B

Work with a partner. You have three intercultural dilemmas and they have three different ones. Take it in turns to describe the dilemmas to each other and discuss what you'd do in each situation. Do you agree on what you *should* do? Is that what you'd both *really* do?

Dilemma 2: Your new American boss organises a weekend barbecue. You find yourself amongst a lot of people you've never met. Do you join in the fun or leave as early as you can?

Dilemma 4: A Finnish colleague invites you to conduct the final stages of an important meeting in the sauna. Do you accept or politely decline?

Dilemma 6: You are in a meeting with a group of Chinese business people. The senior executive seems to be bored by what you have to say. Do you ignore him and concentrate on his deputy or persevere?

For comments on your answers see page 138.

14 BEING HEARD

Hang on a minute!

Speaker B

Read the short article below about intercultural business etiquette. In a few minutes you are going to try to read it aloud to your partner in under a minute, so first check you understand everything and mark places where you can pause for breath!

Your partner is preparing to read a similar article aloud to you. So, when you are both ready, decide who will read first. Read as fast as you can, but try to make sense!

As you listen to your partner read, you should interrupt them as often as possible to clarify anything which isn't absolutely clear. Your objective is to stop them reaching the end of the text in a minute. See who can get further. Good luck!

16 SOLVING PROBLEMS

Three real companies

Speaker B

Read the business dilemma below. Then summarise the basic problem to the rest of your group and brainstorm some solutions.

The manager of a bank in the UK had become alarmed at the number of stolen cheques being cashed. Signatures were simply too easy to forge. Something had to be done.

20 NEGOTIATING

The transfer

Negotiating team 2: Manchester United

You represent the management of Manchester United Football Club and are interested in buying an 18-year-old superstar striker .... (*ask Team 1 for his name*) who plays for .... (*ask Team 1 for the name of his club*). His current team is asking for a transfer fee of £10 million, which is quite a lot for such a young player, but fair considering his enormous potential. However, you are not negotiating the transfer fee today. Your job is to negotiate the financial package on offer.

You do not have to sign this player. There is no shortage of young internationals wanting to play for the world's most famous football club. But he is something special. With the right training, he could become one of the world's top players within the next five years.

It's in your interests to:

- pay no more than the standard wage (already high at £70,000)
- keep the annual fee as low as possible (it could always be raised on renewal of contract if your new player lives up to his potential)
- go for a five-year contract with a heavy penalty for early termination (you don't want to invest in the development of a player who disappears to another club after just a few seasons)

It's said there's a universal language of business, but if so, it's not too clear what it is. Just saying hello can get you off to a bad start, with well-qualified Germans wanting you to call them Herr Doktor Professor and Americans wanting you to just call them Chad or Brianna. Even 'Yes' and 'No' can cause problems. To most of us, a nod is 'Yes' and a shake of the head is 'No'. But in Bulgaria, Greece and Turkey the opposite is true. In Mexico and Japan the word 'No' is often avoided altogether. In Monterrey they may just be anxious not to disappoint. In Nagoya it's the harmony of the meeting they don't want to disrupt. In Britain the best route to harmony is thought to be humour. And with bad weather, bad government and bad public transport, they certainly have plenty to joke about. Perhaps there's a cultural universal there, after all. Cultures that have less fun feel the need to be funny.

INTERRUPTOMETER

↑ You're hopeless!

Learn to be more assertive.

OK, but avoid doing business in Latin America.

Pretty good. You could be a politician.

↓ Excellent! Nobody else can get a word in.

- pay as low a percentage of merchandising profits as possible (perhaps 5% – you don't know how popular the new player will be with supporters).

But you may need to be flexible on some of these points.

You can also offer:
- the use of a £2.5m house with six bedrooms and swimming pool, in a quiet suburb twelve miles outside Manchester
- a brand-new, top-of-the-range 4-wheel-drive Jeep for driving to and from matches and training sessions
- three first-class flights home with British Airways.

You understand the player currently has a sponsorship deal with Nike, which would have to be cancelled. Nike sponsor your main rivals in the Premier League, Arsenal.

The negotiation is scheduled to be held at Old Trafford. First, with your team, work out your opening, target and walk away positions for each of the following points. When you are ready, welcome the player's agents into your boardroom. You may take two five-minute time-outs during the meeting, if you need them. Write down any terms you agree to.

	OP	TP	WAP
Basic wage			
Annual fee			
Length of contract			
Contract termination fee			
Percentage of merchandising profits			
Accommodation			
Car			
Flights home			

16 SOLVING PROBLEMS

Three real companies

Speaker C

Read the business dilemma below. Then summarise the basic problem to the rest of your group and brainstorm some solutions.

A company that makes industrial cleaners and sells them by direct mail had an obvious problem – boring product, boring market. The question was: how could they get noticed?

10 SMALL TALK

Comments on questionnaire (pages 130 and 137)

Dilemma 1 Business people from Latin and Arab countries tend to have a more flexible, 'polychronic' attitude to time than their 'monochronic' North American and North European counterparts, for whom time really is money. Their 'high-context' culture also places greater emphasis on personal relationships than 'low-context' Northerners do. The message? Try not to be too busy for Brazilians or Italians and don't mess up Americans' tight schedules.

Dilemma 2 A good sense of humour is an admired quality in many cultures – notably British, American and most Latin countries – though the type of humour may vary from wordplay to sharp sarcasm to innuendo and even the surreal. In other cultures, however – particularly Germanic ones – humour is not usually considered appropriate in a business context. The message? You don't have to be a comedian with the British, but always smile at their attempts at humour. With Germans or Swiss, leave the jokes for the bar after the meeting.

Dilemma 3 The amount of socialising you do prior to and during a negotiation will depend both on your own and the opposing team's negotiating styles and where the negotiation is being held. In Japan, for example, the negotiation process is long and relationship-building plays an important part. The same is true of the Middle East. In the USA things move faster and their negotiating style tends to be both more informal and adversarial. In Germany there may be little time for small talk. The message? Follow your opponents' lead, but do all you can to create rapport.

Dilemma 4 Mixing with colleagues out of work-hours is an integral part of business in America where many companies are run like sports teams with the boss as both captain and coach. Elsewhere, there may be a strong dividing line between work and home. The message? In social situations simply be yourself. Neither do anything that offends you nor that you think may offend your hosts.

Dilemma 5 Different people have different ideas about where is an appropriate place to do business. For some, talking about golf all morning at the office, and business all afternoon on the golf course is quite normal. Others do more business in bars than boardrooms. But these days people are more culturally aware and don't usually expect foreigners to observe their own business customs. The message? A polite refusal to go to a Finnish sauna or a Spanish bullfight will not usually offend.

Dilemma 6 When doing business with Chinese and most other Southeast Asian cultures, you should be aware of their strong sense of hierarchy. The senior figure present must, of course, be shown respect at all times. The fact that they are present at the meeting shows that they take you and your business proposition seriously. But don't expect them to show much interest in the details. So, whilst appearing to address 'the boss' directly, it is the deputy you should be concentrating on, since this is almost certainly the actual decision-maker. Of course, any decision will be made after the meeting in small informal groups, so never rush things.

LISTENING SCRIPTS

01 GLOBAL ENGLISH

 1.01

Speaker 1

Well, to be honest, learning English isn't my idea of fun. I mean, rock concerts are fun. Motorbikes are fun. Snowboarding is fun. Learning English isn't fun. It's hard work. But it's worth it. I don't need English every day in my job right now. But if I want to get on in my career, I know I'm going to need it more and more. English is where the money is, so I just think of it as an investment in my future. We Swiss are very practical like that.

Speaker 2

Hm, well, I accept that English is the language of the media, but I'm not so sure about business. Personally, I know a lot of business people who speak almost no English at all. Twenty-five per cent of the world speaks English. OK, but that means 75% don't. The way I see it, if I'm trying to sell you something, I should speak your language. But if you come to Ecuador to sell me something, then you should speak Spanish.

Speaker 3

Coming from a tiny country like the Netherlands means we've always had to speak foreign languages. So it's nothing new for us. The same goes for people from Luxembourg, Belgium, Scandinavia. Eighty per cent of Dutch people speak English. Most of us speak some German too, or French. We certainly don't expect anybody to speak Dutch! In fact, the firm I work for recently introduced English as the official company language. So now I speak English all day – to other Dutch people!

Speaker 4

I'm afraid I really don't like English that much. I find the pronunciation very difficult. It's certainly not as beautiful a language as my language, which is Italian. And, anyway, I think it's more difficult as you get older to learn foreign languages. But my company wants me to learn English, so I don't really have much choice. If a quarter of the world speaks it, I suppose I must too. But I'll always think in Italian. My brain works in Italian.

Speaker 5

I don't know why people who speak European languages complain about learning English. Try learning it when your native language is Korean! Actually, I find I can speak English OK, if I'm doing business with other non-native speakers, like Argentinians or Japanese. But with native English speakers, I do feel at a disadvantage. I've heard that 66% of British people don't speak a foreign language at all. Hardly surprising when so many of us have to learn English.

Speaker 6

Well, actually, I love English. It's true the pronunciation is quite hard to get right, but the grammar is much simpler than my language, Hungarian – at least at the beginning. That's the thing about English – it's easy to speak a little quite quickly. It gets harder later, of course. Frankly, I don't know why some French and Germans are against using English words. It seems to me that English is full of foreign words – especially French and German!

02 MAKING CONTACTS

 1.02

Extract 1

Half an hour from the world's most romantic city and rated by conference organisers the 'hottest' venue in Europe, Disneyland Paris's corporate clients include American Express, Unilever and MCI. If you think business and the Lion King don't mix, the Disney magic will soon change your mind. With its unique atmosphere and superb fully equipped convention centre for 2,300 people, its 95 meeting rooms and 3,000 square metres of exhibition space, Disney's theme park is sure to be a huge success with both you and your family. As well as fabulous banqueting facilities for over a thousand people, Disney is able to arrange special private events, such as the amazing 'Journey through Time' and the 'Cape Caribbean' adventure or, if you prefer, golf tournaments and team-building activities. Walt Disney's aim was always 'to make people happy' and that aim now extends to corporate hospitality in the cultural heart of Europe.

Extract 2

Two thousand years ago it was the home of the ancient Mayan civilisation. Today Cancun is the most popular resort in Mexico, its unspoilt coastline a watersports paradise. With its 426 rooms overlooking the Caribbean, 24-hour room service, express checkout, outdoor pools, residents-only health club and 200 metres of exclusive private beach, the Hilton Cancun is rated among the three best hotels in Latin America. Whether swimming with the dolphins or playing roulette in its own offshore casino, you can be sure of an experience to remember. Or why not take advantage of the Hilton's car rental service and explore the nearby ruins of Chichen Itza? Whatever your company's needs, send them your requirements and they will plan the logistics for you. What's more, if you book on special value dates, you'll get a generous 10–30% discount. This year, why not let your annual conference be part of Cancun's 2,000-year-old tradition?

Extract 3

At 321 metres high, higher than the Eiffel Tower and only 60 metres shorter than the Empire State Building, the magnificent Burj Al Arab is the world's tallest and most luxurious hotel. Diamond white by day and a rainbow of colours at night, occupying a central location in Dubai with flight connections to all the major cities of the world, the Burj Al Arab combines the latest technology with the finest traditions of the past. Spacious deluxe suites from 170 to 780 square metres, in-room laptops with Internet access, full conference facilities on the 27th floor, a VIP helipad on the 28th, a golden domed ballroom and a world-class restaurant with spectacular views across the Arabian Gulf all go to make this the ultimate business venue. As they say in the Emirates, 'Welcome, honoured guest'.

 1.03

Conversation 1

A   Oh, hi, David. How are things? We were just talking about the guy over there.

B   Who?

A   The big tall guy in the green tie behind those women. The guy standing at the bar.

B   Oh, yeah.

A   You know him?

B   Yes, that's Karl Schelling.

A   Karl who?

B   Schelling. He's the new director of R&D at Siemens.

A   In Munich?

B   Yeah, that's right. Nice guy. I was talking to him last night in the bar.

A   Oh, he's at the Hilton?

B   Yeah. He was telling me about how he got the job.

A   Really?

B   Yeah, apparently he was headhunted from Philips. They made him an offer he couldn't refuse. Doubled his salary.

A   Headhunted? Don't expect Philips are too happy, then. All that sensitive information.

B   Well, no, quite.

A   He's presenting, isn't he?

B   Yeah, he's on this afternoon. He's talking about data security.

A   You're joking.

B   No, here he is on the programme: Data Security in the Connected Economy.

 1.04

Conversation 2

C   Chris, who's that man over there in the light suit?

D   You mean the grey suit?

C   No, not him! Over there, standing by the entrance. Talking to that woman in black.

D   Oh, yes, that's, er, what's-his-name? William Hill. Hall. William Hall, that's it. He's at the Sheraton where I'm staying, actually. He's head of research at Sony UK. Yes, he's giving a talk on … where's my programme? … Ah, yes, here it is. Erm, …yes, on New Generation Gaming Systems. 10 o'clock on Saturday. I think I'm going to that.

C   Mm, sounds interesting. He doesn't look very happy, though, does he?

D   Well, no. Neither would you in his position.

C   How do you mean?

D   Well, this is just a rumour, mind you, but, erm, I've heard they may be moving R&D to Frankfurt.

C   Really? Are you sure?

D   Well, no, but that's what I heard.

C   And he doesn't want to make that move?

D   Well, the thing is: I'm not sure they're keeping him on. I think they want a German to lead the team.

C   Oh, I see. Well, no wonder he's unhappy…

 1.05

Conversation 3

E   Anne, you know nearly everybody here. Who's that woman in the brown jacket with the long red hair? She's talking to that other woman, the one in the white dress.

F   Oh, you mean, Irena, Irena Stefanowitz?

E   Yes, who is she? I saw her coming out of the Marriott last night with a whole group of people. Going to some dinner party, by the look of it. Sounded like they were speaking Polish.

F Yes, she's a professor at the Warsaw University of Technology. And I think she does quite a lot of consultancy work as well. Amazing speaker. You should go to her talk.

E Really? What's she talking about?

F I think she's doing a session this year on innovation strategies.

E Interesting. You know, I'm going to be working on a project in Krakow next year.

F Krakow? Oh, you'll love it there. Very nice city.

E Yes, if all goes well, there might be a lot more work in Poland.

F Oh, well, in that case, perhaps you should meet Irena. I'm sure she'd be interested in talking to you.

E Yes, perhaps you're right.

F I should warn you, though …

E What?

F Well, she's quite influential in Warsaw.

E Oh, yes?

F Yes. Let's just say it doesn't pay to get on the wrong side of her. A friend of mine knew her well. They had a bit of a disagreement, and his latest project proposal was rejected by the authorities.

E Hm. OK, I'll remember that.

F But you must meet her. In fact, why don't I introduce you now?

E Erm, well, OK then …

 1.06

Conversation 4

G … So, anyway, that's how it ended up costing me 75 euros just to get from the airport to the hotel!

H Oh, dear. Well, I did I warn you about some of those mini-cab drivers.

G Yes, yes, I know. I'll wait in the queue with the rest of you next time. … Anyway, let's change the subject … Who's that blonde woman over there?

H Hm?

G The one in the black dress. Over there, talking to those two guys.

H Which two guys?

G Those two. The woman with her back to us!

H Oh, her! That's Margo Timmerman.

G Ah, so that's Margo Timmerman. I thought so. She still works for Cisco, right?

H Yeah. Heads up their technical department in the Netherlands.

G Isn't she giving the keynote presentation tomorrow morning?

H Uhuh. She's talking about new server technology or something. Why?

G Hm, I'd quite like to talk to her if I get the chance. Is she staying at the Marriott, do you know? I might leave her a message.

H Erm, no, she's probably over at the Hyatt. That's where most of the Cisco people are staying.

G Ah, right … Listen, you seem to know her. You couldn't introduce us could you?

H Er, well, to tell you the truth, I'm really not the best person to ask.

G Oh?

H No. She, er, used to be my boss. You know, years ago. We, er … Well, let's just say we had very different ideas about how to manage a project. And she, er, let me go.

G You mean she fired you!

H Yes, well, all right. Keep your voice down! I wasn't exactly fired …

 1.07

Conversation a

A Is this your first visit to Russia?

B Er, yes it is, actually. Fascinating place.

A Yes, isn't it? I come here quite a lot. **What do you do**, by the way? I see you work for Glaxo.

B How did you know? … Oh, yeah, my badge. Yeah, I'm in R&D. Molecular modelling to be precise.

A Really? We should talk. **Can I get you a drink?**

B Er, no thanks. I'm fine.

A Sure?

B Well, just a top-up, then. Thanks.

A What are you drinking? The Chardonnay, isn't it?

B Erm, yeah. So, what line of business are you in?

 1.08

Conversation b

C Hi, Fiona Hunt. SunMicrosystems. Mind if I join you?

D Erm, no. Er, Michael Steele.

C Pleased to meet you, Mike. Try one of these – they're delicious.

D Er, thanks, but seafood doesn't agree with me.

C Oh, then try the cheese dips instead. They're good too. Have we met somewhere before? Oslo, perhaps?

D I don't think so.

C Mm. I was sure I recognised you … You're an Aquarius, aren't you? I can tell.

D Well, I don't know. I'm not really into horoscopes, I'm afraid.

C When's your birthday?

D Oh, er, February the 2nd.

C I knew it! A typical Aquarius.

D Er, yes. Geez, is that the time? **If you'll excuse me, I have to make a phone call. It's been nice talking to you.**

 1.09

Conversation c

E I really enjoyed your talk this morning.

F Oh, thanks. Yeah, it went quite well, I think.

E You had some very interesting things to say. I'm Amy Cooper, by the way. Yes, I'd like to talk to you about some of your ideas. My company may be interested in your product. **Where are you staying?**

F At the Regency.

E I'm at the Hyatt. Why don't we fix up a time to chat over a drink? Here's my card.

F Oh, thanks. I've got mine here … somewhere.

E Don't worry. I know who you are. So, **how are you enjoying the conference?**

F Well, it's been good so far. More people than ever this year. But, er, **isn't this weather awful?** Half a metre of snow this morning, I heard.

E Yeah, it gets pretty cold here in Moscow, that's for sure.

F Erm, would you excuse me a moment? I'll be right back.

 1.10

Conversation d

G So, how's business?

H Fine. This merger's meant quite a lot of work for us, but, fine.

G Hm. Well, mergers are often difficult. So, er, **what do you think about** the Middle-East situation?

H I'm sorry?

G The crisis in the Middle East. It was in the news again this morning.

H Er, well, I, er …

G I mean, it must affect a company like yours – you being in oil.

H Er, no, I think you've made a mistake. I'm not in oil. I work for Audi.

G Audi? Oh, sorry. Thought you were someone else.

H That's OK. Er, if you'll excuse me, I must just go and say hello to someone.

 1.11

Conversation e

J I like your watch. An Omega, isn't it?

K Er, well, to be honest, don't tell anyone, but it's a fake.

J No! Well, it looks real to me. Where did you get it?

K Turkey. It cost me twenty-five dollars.

J Amazing! So, do you know many people here?

K No, not really. It's the first time I've been to one of these conferences.

J Me too. So, what's your hotel like?

K Hm, pretty comfortable. Nothing special, but it's OK, I suppose.

J Yeah, you're at the Sheraton, aren't you? Last year they held this thing in Mexico. The Hilton Cancun. Fabulous hotel, they say.

K Cancun! A bit warmer than here, then!

J Oh, yeah. I went there on holiday once. Beautiful place. **Can I get you anything from the buffet?**

K Oh, that's all right. I'll come with you. I'd like some more of that Beluga caviar before it all goes!

03 MAKING CALLS

 1.12

A Hello?

B Hello.

A Hello. Is that Dutch Hydro?

B That's right.

A Can I have the accounts department, please?

B Yes.

A Sorry?

B This is the accounts department.

A Oh, right. Erm, I'd like to speak to Marius Pot, please.

B Yes.

A Sorry?

B That's me.

A Well, why didn't you say so?

B Can I help you?

A I hope so! I'm calling about an invoice I received.

 1.13

B Hello, accounts department. Marius Pot speaking.

A Ah, Mr Pot. Just the person I wanted to speak to. **I'm calling about** an invoice I received.

 1.14

A Good morning, Cheney & Broome. Can I help you?

B Yes, please … er, … Just a moment …

A Hello? Are you still there?

B Yes, sorry … erm …

A How can I help you?

B Oh, yes, can I speak to, er, to, er … just a minute … yes, to, er, Catherine Mellor, please?

A Certainly. Who's calling, please?

B Sorry?

A Can I have your name, please?

B Oh, yes, it's Ramon Berenguer … from Genex Pharmaceuticals.

A Thank you. Can I ask the purpose of your call, Mr Berenguer?

B Oh, yes. It's about, er … an invoice.

A Thank you, Mr Berenguer. Putting you through now.

 1.15

A Good morning, Cheney & Broome. Can I help you?

B Er, yes. This is Ramon Berenguer from Genex Pharmaceuticals. **Can I speak to Catherine Mellor, please?**

A Certainly, Mr Berenguer. Can I ask the purpose of your call?

B It's about an invoice.

A Putting you through now.

 1.16

a **Can I help you?**

b **Can I ask who's calling?**

c **Can you spell that, please?**

d **Can I give her a message?**

e **Can you tell him I called?**

f **Can you read that back to me?**

g **Can you speak up, please?**

h **Can you tell me when she will be back?**

i **Can you get back to me within the hour?**

j **Can you ask her to call me back?**

k **Can I get back to you on that?**

l **Can I leave a message?**

 1.17

Message 1
Hello. This is Cheryl. I phoned you about five times yesterday, but you weren't in. Anyway, I corrected those figures you faxed me. OK, speak to you later.

Message 2
Hi, Peter. Anne here. I wanted to talk to you about the project meeting tomorrow, but you're obviously not there. The good news is we finished Phase One on time. As I explained, I may be a little late for the meeting. So just go ahead and start without me. I'll join you about 10.

Message 3
Er, this is Zoltán. Just to let you know, I started the report this morning and just e-mailed you the first part. Oh, I included the quarterly accounts in the report, too. Let me know what you think.

Message 4
Mr Carter. It's Philip Heath. I talked to our stock control manager about the Venezuelan consignment and he says we despatched the goods a week ago. The shipping agent says they delivered them this morning. So, problem solved!

Message 5
Hello, Mr Carter. This is Ryan Hope from SilverStar. I called you a couple of weeks ago about an estimate for a contract in Malaysia. Erm, we discussed my client's requirements and, well, I expected to hear from you last week. Could you give me a call on 01865 555959 as soon as possible, please?

Message 6
Pete. It's me. Sorry, mate, I tried everything, but head office say we can't have any more time. They say they waited six months for the preliminary report, another six months for the feasibility study and now they want to see some results. Anyway, I booked the conference room for three tomorrow. Give me a call when you get in. We need to talk.

 1.18

Message a
Hi, it's Seiji. Listen, the negotiations here in Nagoya are going pretty well, but we seem to be deadlocked on price. Can you authorise me to offer them a 14% discount on 50,000? I think that should do it.

Message b
Hi, it's Jim. Listen, I'm in a bit of a panic. I'm at the Expo in Dublin and, you won't believe this, but I've lost the memory stick with my entire presentation on it! Could you e-mail over my slides as attachments as soon as possible? Thanks!

Message c
Hi. Tony here. I'm still stuck in a meeting here at head office. Are you making progress with the conference arrangements? Please make sure you contact the speakers to confirm their attendance. Cheers.

Message d
Hi, Kate here. I'm with the people from Microsoft in Seattle and they're querying our invoice for the third quarter. Can you ask someone in accounts to check the figures and reinvoice them if necessary? Thanks.

Message e
Hello, this is Alicia. This is urgent. I really need a copy of the Turin report from you by tomorrow afternoon at the latest. Call me straight back if you're having problems.

Message f
Hi there, this is Mike. Listen, I've got an appointment over at your offices on Friday. Do you want to meet up? Maybe go for a beer or something? Oh, by the way, Ian sends his regards. Catch you later. Bye.

 1.19

Call 1

B Hello. This is Patterson Meats, Sylvia Wright's office. Thank you for calling. I'm afraid I'm not able to take your call right now, but if you'd like to leave a message or send a fax, please do so after the tone, and I'll get back to you as soon as I can.

A Hello, Sylvia. It's Tim Curtis from the Sydney office. I just wanted to know how the meeting with the people from Tesco Supermarkets went. This is a really good chance for us to start exporting to Britain. I hope their visit was a success. Er, give me a ring when you get in, would you? Bye now.

 1.20

Call 2

A Hello. Tim Curtis.

B Hi, Tim. It's Sylvia here. I got your message.

A Sylvia, hi. So, how did it go?

B It went pretty well, I think. They sent three people in the end.

A Three? Well, that's a good sign.

B Yeah, there was Bill Andrews, head of meat purchasing. I think you met him when you went to the UK last month.

A That's right. He seemed pretty interested when I spoke to him then.

B Yeah, he asked me a lot of questions about our quality control.

A Uh-huh. I thought he might. I hope you told him he's got no worries there.

B I certainly did.

A Good. So who else came? Er, did Stephanie Hughes come?

B Er, they sent Jonathan Powell from their marketing department instead, and Melanie Burns, who's in charge of imported produce.

A Oh, right. I didn't meet them in London. So, did you show them the processing plant?

B I did. There wasn't time to do a tour of the factory, but I showed them the packing department and the freezer units. Then we gave the presentation – me and Ian – and took them out to dinner afterwards.

A Great. Did they say when they'd let us know? I mean do you think they'll place an order or not?

B Well, it's too early to say. But I think they were quite impressed.

A Hm.

B They said they'd be in touch in the next couple of days or so. They were a bit worried at first about British customers accepting our product. Although they do sell other exotic meats already. Ostrich, for example, and that's quite popular.

A Erm, excuse me for a moment, Sylvia … Sorry about that. I just had to sign something. Where were we? Oh, yeah, they were worried about UK customers accepting our product, you say?

B Well, I don't think it's a problem. Er, you know what the Brits are like – animal lovers and all that. They weren't sure if people would accept kangaroo meat as an alternative to beef.

A Kangaroos are too cute and lovable to eat, huh?

B Well, something like that. But I told them they're not exactly endangered. There are twice as many kangaroos in Australia as there are Australians. Kangaroo's been on the menu here for years. They agreed it tastes good and, as I said to them, it's a really healthy option – ten times less fat than a beef steak and no chance of getting mad cow disease!

04 KEEPING TRACK

 1.21

Extract a

A The problem is money.

B Sorry, what did you say?

A The problem is money.

B Oh, as usual.

Extract b

A We have to reach a decision by next week.

B Sorry, when did you say?

A Next week.

B Oh, I see.

Extract c

A An upgrade will cost $3,000.

B Sorry, how much did you say?

A $3,000, at least.

B Oh, as much as that?

Extract d

A Ildikó Dudás spoke to me about it yesterday.

B Sorry, who did you say?

A Ildikó Dudás – from the Budapest office.

B Oh, yes, of course.

Extract e

A The company is based in Taipei.

B Sorry, where did you say?

A In Taipei.

B Oh, really?

Extract f

A The whole project might take eighteen months.

B Sorry, how long did you say?

A Eighteen months.

B Oh, as long as that?

 1.22

A OK, so, just to give you a summary of the sales figures for last month.

B Last month? Don't you mean this month?

A No, I mean last month. This month's figures aren't ready yet, are they?

B Oh, no, of course not. Sorry.

A So, overall, sales for last month are up again – by 2.6%, in fact, which is pretty good.

C Er, 2.6%? Shouldn't that be 6.2?

A Yeah, up by 6.2%. Didn't I say that?

C No, you said 2.6.

A Oh, … right. Well, you know what I mean. So, anyway, the thing is, we're getting the best results in Denmark and Norway – 30,000 units.

C 30,000? That doesn't sound right to me. 13,000, surely?

A No, the figures are here – Denmark and Norway: 30,000 units.

B Denmark and Norway? Are you sure? That can't be right. Sales have never been good in Scandinavia.

A That's just the point. Sales in Scandinavia are usually terrible, but they were excellent in June.

C June? Isn't it July we're talking about?

A July! Yes, of course, July! If you'd just let me finish! What I want to know is if we could sell product in Scandinavia in June, …

C July.

A … in July, then why can't we sell it there every month?

B Good point. Have you spoken to John about it?

A John? You mean Jim.

B Jim, yes. Whoever's in charge of Northern Europe these days.

A Jim Munroe. I couldn't. He's had to fly to Scotland. His mother's ill apparently.

C There must be some mistake.

A Hm?

C Well, I saw Jim this morning as I was coming in – on his way to play golf, by the look of it.

A What? Are you sure? Wait till I see him!

 1.23

A So, welcome to Tokyo, Matt. It's good to have you on the team.

B Thanks, Sally. It's good to be here.

A I think you're going to enjoy your three months here, Matt. Now, this is Sharon Hall. She's the person you'll mostly be working with on the project.

C Hi, Matt.

B Hi … **Sorry, I didn't catch** your name.

C Sharon. Sharon Hall.

B Hi, Sharon.

A Sharon's in charge of our corporate loan department. She's sorting out an office for you at the moment. You'll probably be working over at Empire House.

B Sorry, where did you say?

C Empire House. It's our office building on the other side of town.

B Oh, OK.

A Don't worry, I'll take you over there later. Now, you and Sharon will be reporting directly to Daniel Cash, our VP for corporate finance.

B Sorry, who?

C Daniel Cash.

B Oh, right. And he's the vice-president for …?

A Corporate finance. I thought you two had met? Anyway, Daniel's had to rush off to a meeting, but he told me to say he'd meet you both at two tomorrow.

B Sorry, I don't understand. I thought the whole team was meeting tomorrow at nine?

A We were. But, er, something came up. Anyway, Sharon can fill you in on most of it. Sharon?

C Yes, you'll have two assistants working with you, Matt. Janet White and Robin Sellers.

B OK, (writing it down) Janet White and Robin …?

C Sellers. Janet's our top mergers and acquisitions specialist. I think you two will get on well. She'll be helping you with your research. And Robin's your interpreter. He's

very familiar with business procedures here – as well as being fluent in Japanese, of course.

B **Sorry, I'm not with you**. Interpreter? What do I need an interpreter for? I thought I was just here as an advisor.

A Erm … The situation's changed a little since we last spoke, Matt. We'd now like you to lead the negotiations with the Sapporo Bank. In fact, that will be your main responsibility.

B **I don't quite see what you mean**, Sally. Erm, I'm no negotiator, especially not for a takeover as big as this. I'm the guy with the pocket calculator. I just make sure the figures add up.

C Oh, come on, Matt. You're too modest. We know your track record. Janet can take care of the figures. We want you to lead the first round of negotiations on the 13th.

B You mean the 30th, right? The 13th is next week.

A That's right. We've scheduled the first meeting for next Wednesday. Janet will be able to brief you before then. This is your big chance. I'm counting on you, Matt. I know you won't let me down.

CASE STUDY: HIGH FLIER

 1.24

A Morning, everyone. Come on in. Make yourselves comfortable. Oh, there's coffee and fruit juice if you'd like some. Danita, could you hold my calls for the next half hour, please?

B Certainly, Mr Kumar. Can I get you anything at all?

A No, I'm fine, thank you, Danita … OK, I just wanted to congratulate you all on doing a superb job on the Viacom project – really well done, everyone! – and, er, to let you know what my schedule is for the next couple of weeks. I've decided I need to get away for a few days. You know, give myself some time to think through this Pixar deal. So, I guess you need to know how I'm fixed for appointments, in case anyone calls or e-mails while I'm away. You won't be able to reach me in the Himalayas!

C You going base-jumping again, Shavi? Should I call your insurance broker?

A No, no, that won't be necessary, Jamil. I almost frightened myself to death last time. I thought I'd just do a little climbing. Get back to nature.

D Well, say hello to the mountain goats for us, Shavi!

A I will. Now, my schedule. OK, let's see. Right, I'll be away till Tuesday – that's the eighteenth – so we'll hold our usual Monday staff briefing on the Tuesday morning instead, if that's OK with everyone. Good. Then in the afternoon I've got a meeting with the people from the Bank of India. Obviously very important. I think that will probably go on into the evening. I'd like to take them somewhere special for dinner. Perhaps you could arrange that for me, Danita.

B Certainly.

A Great. Now, on Wednesday, the nineteenth, I'm flying to Delhi to speak at the MTV

Awards in the evening. So that's the whole day away from the office. Although I don't mind cancelling the talk if something better comes up. You know how I hate public speaking! But on Thursday I'm staying in Delhi to open our negotiations with Rama Gaming Systems. They're a good little company with some very exciting new products – games for mobile phones. And I think they'd make an excellent addition to our portfolio. Anyway, I'm meeting them in the morning just to get things moving and then flying home in the afternoon. Hopefully, I'll be back in time to take us all out for our monthly club night. I thought we might try the Enigma at Juhu Beach.

C Good choice. That's where all the Bollywood actresses go.

A Still looking for a Bollywood bride, Jamil?

C Who said anything about marriage?

A OK, then, let's meet there at ten. Now, I've kept Friday pretty much free of appointments. It'll give me a chance to catch up with some paperwork. OK, let's look at the following week. Monday the twenty-fourth. Right, on Monday we've got our people from Cobrax Music Online coming over to join us for a meeting with that new rock band. Who are they again, Varsha?

D The Purple Vedas.

A The Purple Vedas? … Oh, yes. I remember them now … Actually, I might miss that meeting. I'm supposed to be taking Sashi for lunch, which means shopping and lunch. And then more shopping. I'll leave that one to you, Varsha. You know more about the music side of the business than I do, anyway.

D No problem.

A Right, Tuesday and Wednesday, I'm in the office as usual. No appointments so far. Thursday I'm talking to Joe Takashi and Aaron Silverman from Sony Pictures. There's a real chance we may finally get a Hollywood studio interested in our latest movie. So I have to be here all day for that. Friday morning we're discussing our internet advertising. I'm not at all happy with what we're doing with that at the moment. And then in the afternoon, we've got a short meeting with indiamusic.com about an online promotion. I don't know if I really need to be there for that, but we'll see. OK, that's it. If I don't see you before, have a great weekend!

 1.25

Voicemail 1

Hello, Shavi! Where are you? This is Antoine. I've been trying to contact you all weekend. I have some good news. You know, of course, that your movie *Dharma* has been nominated for Best Foreign Language Film at Cannes this year. And, well, I have it on good authority – don't ask me how – that you're going to win. Yes, it's true! Let's just say I have friends in high places. Now, I know how busy you always are, but I really think you should be here in France for this. If you do win, you know it would be tremendous publicity for you in Europe. I would also like to organise something special while you are here for the paparazzi. Something which will be in all the newspapers! Just leave it to me! The dates, as you know, are 14th to 18th of May. So get back to me

as soon as you can because I have to start setting things up and there's very little time. Bye for now.

Voicemail 2

Ah, hello, Mr Kumar. This is Bhupen Chandra from the Indian Embassy in Washington. I hope you don't mind me calling. I was given your direct line by your secretary last week. I was hoping to speak to you about a forthcoming event. Perhaps you received my e-mail about this? The ambassador would like to invite you to speak to a mixed group of Indian and American entrepreneurs in about three weeks' time, er, May 5th, in fact. I realise it is rather short notice, but, er, you are not an easy man to reach. Perhaps you could give me a call when you have time. Your secretary has my number and extension. I look forward to hearing from you. Goodbye.

Voicemail 3

Shavi! It's Callum. Don't tell me you're up a mountain someplace! This is urgent. Listen, you remember that Web TV company I told you to buy shares in? Well, if you're going to buy them, you have to do it fast because the price is about to take off. You're in for twenty million, right? Just give me the go-ahead to buy them for you and I'll do the rest. Or perhaps one of your people can authorise it for you. You didn't go away without telling them I'd be calling about this deal, did you? Look, Shavi, this is a sure thing. Completely safe investment. Now, I'm in New York for the next few days, but, look, whatever time it is, just call me as soon as you get this message, OK?

Voicemail 4

Hi, Shavi. It's Lukas calling from Berlin. We've almost reached agreement with the Baumann Studio, but we're still stuck on price. They've agreed to everything else we wanted, but they're asking for another seven million euros, and I don't think they will move on that. Believe me, we've tried! However, I still think they are a very good buy and that we should go ahead and accept their terms before one of our competitors does. Still, seven million euros is seven million euros, so I'd prefer it if I had your authorisation before making the final offer. Can you get back to me on this as quickly as possible or I think we may lose this one? I'm at the Park Inn Hotel, room 303. And you have my mobile number. Bye now.

Voicemail 5

Ah, hello, Mr Kumar. This is Philippa Smith. I don't know if you remember me. We met at a London Chamber of Commerce dinner a year or so ago? I was with the BBC then. Anyway, I'm a producer now with CNBC and we're doing a new series of *Inside India*. We'd very much like to do a short documentary about you, your career and, well, about the media and entertainment industries in India, in general, really. The idea would be to spend a few days following you around with a camera – to see you in action, as it were – and then maybe we could also do a more formal interview. We'd need to do the filming within the next few months, but we can fit in around your schedule. Anyway, have a think about it and I'll call you again in a few days to see if you'd like to go ahead. Bye for now.

Voicemail 6

Shavi, it's Sharad here. Listen, you know that games company we're supposed to be meeting next week, Rama Gaming Systems? Well, I've just heard that they're already in talks with Dell India! Yes, can you believe it! They kept that very quiet! Now, we were going to meet Rama here in Delhi on Thursday, right before you flew back to Mumbai? But I suggest we make that an all-day meeting now we've got some competition. I think we may need the extra time. Let me know if you agree. Bye.

Voicemail 7

Shavi, it's your mother. Some sons actually call their mothers from time to time, but I haven't heard from you in weeks. I've been calling all your phone numbers all morning and you seem to have disappeared again. You haven't forgotten that I'm having a little party for some of your father's old university colleagues on Tuesday evening, have you? That's Tuesday the 18th, Shavi – as in the day after tomorrow! Oh, I know how you always hate my parties, but you never came to the last one and this time you promised you'd be here. So please call me and let me know if you're going to come after all – or whether you are going to disappoint me and your father once again.

Voicemail 8

Mr Kumar, it's Joe Takashi from Sony Pictures. I'm sorry to inconvenience you, but there's been a slight change of plan. Aaron can't make our meeting on Thursday 27th but he was wondering if we could bring it forward a week to Thursday 20th instead. Actually, that's almost the only time this month we can make it, I'm afraid. But if things go well, we might like to extend our meeting into the Friday as well. There's a lot to talk about. Anyway, let me know if Thursday 20th suits you or if we'll just have to reschedule for later next month or maybe June. Thanks a lot. Bye now.

05 WHAT WOMEN WANT

 1.26

Speaker 1

I work as a financial consultant in Stockholm. And what I've found is that my female clients bring me ten times more new business, more referrals, than my male clients. It took me a while to notice this, but then it hit me. When women are happy with the services they get, they tell all their friends and colleagues about it. Satisfied male clients, on the other hand, either don't think to tell anyone else or want to keep the information to themselves. Now, I pretty much concentrate on targeting women as clients, because when you do a good job for one client, you gain access to a whole network of contacts. It's perfect word-of-mouth marketing!

Speaker 2

The Chinese Confucian tradition puts men at the head of the household, chief decision-makers, but, ah, I don't think this reflects the current situation in China. Women now account for about 47% of the workforce here, so we are an important market. But, actually, in China it is young women, maybe 16 to 30, who are the real future. Young Chinese are enthusiastic adopters of all kinds of technology. And there are about 160 million young women in China. That's more than the entire population of Japan! Huge business opportunity. Mao Tse Tung used to say 'Women hold up half the sky'. I say women hold up most of the sky!

Speaker 3

There's no question that women are the main purchasing decision-makers in most families. In Spain, where I come from, especially, women rule the home! Of course, you have to remember that there are more and more single people these days. This is another important trend. The number of people living alone in northern Europe, where I work now, is approaching 50%. So there are plenty of younger men around with no-one to make those buying decisions for them! But in Spain, where people often live with their parents until they are in their late 20s, this is not so much the case. And in the older age groups, yes, it is definitely the women we need to target.

Speaker 4

Hm, well I think it depends on which school of thought you belong to – the men-and-women-are-totally-different or the we're-all-basically-the-same school of thought. Personally, I stand somewhere in between those two ideas. I mean, it's true that too many companies are run by men who have no idea what their mostly female customers want. How can they? I think it might be a good thing if more boards of directors actually looked like their customers! On the other hand, I think you can take the gender thing too far. Several companies have tried to create products specifically for women – cars, computers – and they've often failed. You end up stereotyping: women will want this, need this, like this. My advice? If you're going to target female consumers, do masses of market research first. Don't trust your intuitions. They can be very wrong!

06 BUSINESS TRAVEL

 1.27

1

A   Excuse me. Is there somewhere I could send a fax from?

B   Certainly, sir. There's a business centre on the third floor.

2

A   Did you pack your bags yourself, sir?

B   Well, no, my wife … Oh, er, I mean, yes. Yes, of course.

3

A   Could I ask you to open your luggage, please, madam?

B   Oh, … all right. Will this take long? Only someone's meeting me.

4

A   Window or aisle?

B   Er, window, please. But not near an emergency exit, if possible. You can't put the seats back.

5

A   This is your captain speaking. We're now at our cruising altitude of 11,000 metres, making good time and just passing over the Costa Brava.

B   Oh, look. There it is. Full of British tourists.

6

A   Can you tell me what time you stop serving dinner?

B   Half past ten, madam. Are you a resident? I can reserve you a table if you like.

7

A   Er, Heathrow airport, please. Terminal 1. I'm in a bit of a hurry.

B   Well, I'll do what I can, sir. But the traffic's terrible this morning. Some sort of accident it said on the radio. Might be quicker taking the Tube.

8

A   British Airways regrets to announce the late departure of flight BA761 to Buenos Aires. This is due to the late arrival of the plane from Argentina. Estimated departure time is now 15.10.

B   Oh, here we go again!

9

A   This is your captain speaking again. We're in for some turbulence, I'm afraid. So, for your own safety, would you please return to your seats and make sure your seatbelt is fastened while the 'fasten seatbelt' sign remains on. Thank you.

B   Erm, excuse me. You're sitting on my seatbelt. Thanks.

10

A   I'm sorry but this bag is too heavy to take on as hand luggage. You're only allowed six kilos. You'll have to check it in, I'm afraid, sir.

B   But I've got my computer and everything in there. And gifts for my family.

11

A   I'm afraid I'll have to check your hand luggage too, madam. Could you open this side pocket? And, er, would you mind not smoking, please?

B   Oh, I'm sorry. I didn't realise.

12

A   Have you got anything smaller, sir? Don't think I can change a twenty.

B   Uh? Oh, just a minute. I'll see.

13

A   There has been a change to the schedule for flight BA761 to Buenos Aires. This flight will now depart from Gate 59. Would all passengers travelling to Buenos Aires please go to gate 59.

B   Gate fifty-what?

14

A   Right. That's fine, thank you, madam. You can go through now.

B   What! You've just unpacked everything in my suitcase! How am I supposed to go through like this?

15

A   Could you switch off your laptop now, please, sir? We're about to land.

B   Uh? Oh, yes, of course.

16

A   Here you are. Keep the change.

B   Oh, thank you very much, madam. Have a good flight.

17

A   Excuse me. Erm, **do you think I could have an alarm call at half past six tomorrow morning?**

B   Certainly, madam. Could I have your room number, please?

18

A   Good afternoon, ladies and gentlemen. Flight BA761 to Buenos Aires is now ready for boarding. Would you please have your passports and boarding cards ready for inspection?

B   And about time too!

 1.28

1

A   Excuse me, **could you tell me where the rest room is?**

B   Certainly, sir. There's one just across the lobby, by the elevators.

A   Thank you.

B   You're welcome.

2

A   That's five quid, please, mate.

B   Erm, I've only got a ten, I'm afraid.

A   That's fine. So that's five pounds I owe you. Just a minute.

B   By the way, **could you tell me which way's the nearest Underground?**

3

A   Excuse me, am I going the right way for the shopping mall?

B   Er, no. Erm, you need to go back the way you came till you come to a big drugstore.

A   Uh-uh.

B   Turn left, then take a right at the parking lot and the mall's right in front of you.

A   Thanks.

B   Have a nice day!

4

A   Day return, please.

B   To the City?

A   Yes, please … Oh, my god!

B   Is there a problem?

A   I've just realised I left my briefcase with my wallet in the boot of that taxi!

5

A   Your bill, madam.

B   Oh, thank you. Er, who do I make the cheque out to?

A   Er, just Webster's will be fine. Did you enjoy your meal?

B   Er, yes … Everything was … fine. Er, is there a chemist's nearby, do you happen to know?

6

A   Which way you headed, ma'am?

B   Er, Liberty Street.

A   That's quite a few blocks from here. **Can I call you a cab?**

B   Won't that be expensive? Maybe I should take the subway.

A   I wouldn't at this time of night. Cab'll probably only cost you five or six bucks.

7

A One way or round trip?

B Er, one way, please. Is there a cart I could use for my baggage?

A Sure. They're over by the phone booths. You'll need two quarters.

B Oh, then **could you change this for me?**

8

A Erm, excuse me. I'm looking for a gas station.

B Oh, right. A petrol station. I think there's one at the next roundabout.

A Pardon me? … Oh, you mean a traffic circle. Great. Thanks a lot.

B No problem.

 1.29

Conversation 1

A Hello. **You must be waiting for me.**

B Mr de Jong?

A That's right.

B How do you do, sir. **Let me take those for you.** Did you have a good flight?

A Not bad, not bad. It's even colder here than Cape Town, though. And we're having our winter.

B Oh, yes. It's rained all week, I'm afraid. Always does for Wimbledon.

A Hm? Oh, the tennis. Actually, I was expecting to meet Mr Hill.

B Yes, sir. I'm afraid Mr Hill had to go to a meeting. He sends his apologies. He said to take you straight to your hotel, give you a chance to freshen up and he'll meet you in a couple of hours or so.

A Oh, right. Fine.

B **You must be tired after your long flight.**

A Oh, not too bad. Luckily, I managed to get some sleep on the plane.

 1.30

Conversation 2

C Greg! I'm over here …

D Caroline! Good to see you again! God, it's crowded here. I nearly missed you.

C I know. Didn't you see me waving? So, how are things?

D Fine, fine. Susan sends her love.

C How is she?

D Very well. Congratulations, by the way.

C Hm?

D On your promotion.

C Oh, that. Yeah, well, if you work for the same company long enough … Now, my car's just five minutes away. **Let me help you with your bags.**

D Oh, that's all right. Well, maybe the really heavy one.

C Now, I thought we could get some lunch first and then go back to the office and do some work. Oh, you're staying with us, by the way. David's dying to meet you.

D Sounds good to me. David, yes. A new job and a new husband. So, how's married life?

 1.31

Conversation 3

E Miss Sheridan?

F Yes, you must be Alan Hayes.

E That's right.

F Hello. Thanks for coming to meet me.

E Not at all. We thought it would be quicker. This way you can meet the whole team this afternoon. We thought you might just want to relax this evening.

F Oh, yes. Probably.

E So, how's business?

F Couldn't be better. So we're all set for the meeting tomorrow?

E We certainly are. Martin sends his regards, by the way.

F How is he?

E He's fine. So, **how was your flight?**

F Oh, pretty good. I got upgraded.

E Lucky you! That never seems to happen to me.

F Mm. It certainly makes a difference. I could get used to it.

E Well, now, we'll go straight to the office if that's OK with you. I'd like you to meet Graham Banks. He's the head of our legal department.

F Yes, I think I spoke to him on the phone.

E Oh, yes, of course. Now, **let's see if we can get a taxi …**

 1.32

Conversation 4

G Mr Okada?

H Er, yes.

G Hello. Welcome to London. I'm Sharon Miller.

H Er, from Sabre Holdings?

G That's right. I'm the head of the M&A department – Mergers and Acquisitions.

H I see. I was expecting … Never mind. So, Miss Miller. Pleased to meet you.

G Pleased to meet you, Mr Okada. Now, I've got a taxi waiting outside. So why don't we let the driver take those bags of yours?

H Oh, thank you very much.

G We'll drop your things off at the hotel. **We booked you into the Savoy.** I hope that's OK. I think you'll be comfortable there.

H Yes, that will be fine.

G Great. Then I thought we could meet up with my assistant Geri King and get some lunch.

H Gerry King? I don't think I know him.

G Her, actually. No, she's just joined us. She's got a lot of questions she'd like to ask you.

H Yes, of course. I wonder … It was a very long flight … Do you think I could go to my hotel first?

G Yeah, sure. **We booked a table for 1.30,** but that's OK.

H I am a little tired and I need to freshen up.

G Of course. We'll check you into your hotel and then meet in, say, three quarters of an hour?

 1.33

Call 1

A Allo!

B Oh, hello. Do you speak English?

A Er, … yes, a little. Can I help you?

B This is Anne Cook from *What Car?* magazine.

A I'm sorry?

B Anne Cook. *What Car?*

A What car?

B Yes, that's right.

A You want a car?

B No, no, sorry. I work for *What Car?* I'm a journalist. Er, can you put me through to Yves Dupont?

A I'm afraid I don't understand. Can you speak more slowly, please?

B Yes, I'd like to speak to Yves Dupont, if he's available.

A Ah … One moment, please. I'll get someone who speaks better English.

B Thank you!

 1.34

Call 2

A Hola …

B Hello. Is that Joaquín Fuentes?

A Er … Yes, speaking.

B Joaquín. It's Geoff White.

A Geoff White?

B NetWorth Systems? We spoke last week.

A Oh, yes. I'm sorry. Geoff, of course.

B Er, yes. Anyway, I'm calling about those prices you wanted, …

A Oh, yes … Listen, Geoff, I'm afraid I can't talk right now. I'm in a meeting.

B Oh, I see.

A Yeah. Can you call me back – say, in an hour?

B Erm, yeah, sure … No problem.

A OK, I'll speak to you later … No, wait, could you just e-mail me the figures instead?

B Erm, yeah, yeah, sure.

A Thanks a lot.

B I'll do that right away.

A Great. Thanks for calling.

B Yeah, bye.

A Bye.

 1.35

Call 3

C Jim, can you get that?

A Uh? Oh, OK. … Yeah?

B Hello? Is that Western Securities?

A Uh-huh. What can I do for you?

B This is Laura Como from Tricolor. I'd like to speak to Karl Lesonsky, please. It's about a pension fund.

A Just a minute. Anybody seen Karl? … He's not here.

B Do you know when he'll be back?

A No idea. He's usually in by now. Probably taken a long lunch.

B Oh, I see. Well, perhaps you can help. Who am I speaking to?

A   Er, Jim Savage. But, er, ... Oh, just a minute ... (puts her on hold)

B   Oh, come on!

A   Er, hello Ms Como?

B   Yes!

A   Look, I don't normally deal with pensions. I think you'd better wait till Karl gets back.

B   Well, when will that be?

A   I really don't know.

B   Well, that's helpful.

A   OK. Look, give me ten minutes. I'll see if I can reach him on his cellphone.

B   No, don't bother. I'll call back later.

 1.36

Call 4

A   José Senna.

B   Ah, Mr Senna. Hello. I'm sorry to bother you. Your secretary gave me your mobile number.

A   Er, that's OK. ... Can I ask who's calling?

B   Oh, I'm sorry. This is Nigel Waters. We met at the Expo in São Paolo last year.

A   Oh, yes, Mr Waters. How are you?

B   Fine, fine. You said if I was ever in Rio you'd introduce me to your boss? Remember?

A   Oh, ... Yes. Um, so you're here in Rio?

B   That's right.

A   Erm, well, it's a bit difficult right now. I'm on my way to a meeting. But ... er, **leave it with me. I'll see what I can do**.

B   Right.

A   Can you give me a contact number?

B   Oh, yes, I'm staying ...

A   Just a minute, where's my organiser? ... OK.

B   Yes, I'm staying at the Mirador in Copacabana. It's 548 8950, er, room 314.

A   3-1-4. ... OK. I'll try to make the arrangements. **Don't worry, I'll sort something out**.

B   Great.

A   And, er ... Oh, the traffic's moving. Look, **I'll get back to you tomorrow**. OK?

B   I can't hear you very well.

A   No, the signal's breaking up. Speak to you tomorrow.

B   OK, fine. I'll wait to hear from you then. Bye.

08 MAKING DECISIONS

 1.37

a

Asa Candler's best business decision was definitely deciding to buy the rights to Coca-Cola from its inventor, Dr John Styth Pemberton. Unfortunately, in one of the worst business decisions ever, Mr Candler went on to sell Coke's bottling rights for just $1. Coca-Cola's daily output is one billion bottles.

b

Between the mid-70s and the early 80s Swiss watchmaking companies saw their world market share fall from 30 to just 9%. Then, in response to strong Japanese competition, came the decision to collaborate. The result was the Swatch, and market share shot up to 50%.

c

In 1991 Dell Computers almost made its biggest mistake when it decided to expand and start selling through high street stores. Boss, Michael Dell, quickly changed his mind and returned to selling PCs direct to consumers, a strategy which has put Dell, a company that now employs 21,000 people, consistently amongst the top three PC manufacturers in the world.

d

In 1955, small record producer, Sam Phillips sold the exclusive contract he had with a young unknown singer to RCA for the grand sum of $35,000. Unfortunately for Phillips, the singer was Elvis Presley and he lost the royalties to over a billion record sales.

e

The world's bestselling toy, Barbie, is over forty years old. The decision in 1961 to give her a boyfriend, Ken, was the first step in a successful brandstretching exercise, which now includes Barbie CD-ROMs and Barbie digital cameras. As a result, the toy continues to outsell even Nintendo and Lego. Somewhere in the world a Barbie is bought every two seconds.

f

In 1938 two talented artists, Joe Shuster and Jerry Siegel, sold the rights to the comic-book character they designed to their publisher for $130. The decision cost them a fortune – the millions they would have made by retaining ownership of Superman.

g

In 1977 Steve Jobs invented what many consider to be the first personal computer – the Apple 1. Xerox, in their worst decision ever, missed a similar opportunity. Unfortunately, Apple refused to license its products to other manufacturers. By trying to keep control, Jobs lost out to Microsoft. And it was Bill Gates, not Steve Jobs, whose personal worth first broke the $100 billion barrier.

h

And finally, in what is perhaps the most tragic business decision ever, in 1886, gold prospector, Sors Hariezon, decided to stop digging for gold and sell his land to a South African mining conglomerate for $20. Over the next ninety years that land produced over a million kilos of gold a year – 70% of the gold supply to the Western world!

 1.38

A   Thanks for coming everybody. OK, let's get down to business. As you know, **we're here to talk about the relocation to the UK** and I'd like to hear what you have to say. Now, the plan is to make the final move in January, but that's a busy month for us. So, what do you think?

B   Can I just stop you there for a moment, Elke? This relocation idea – I mean, it's ridiculous. I don't think anyone here actually wants to go and live in Britain.

A   With respect, you don't quite seem to understand, Erich. The decision has already been taken.

B   Sorry, I don't quite see what you mean. I thought we were here to discuss this.

A   No, perhaps I didn't make myself clear. We are relocating to Cambridge in November. That's been decided ... .

B   So why are we having this meeting?

A   If I could just finish what I was saying. What we are discussing today is how to implement the decision. This affects our Scandinavian office too, you know. There's a lot to talk about. Now ...

C   Can I just come in here?

A   Yes, what is it Axel?

C   Well, I can see why we should have a branch in the UK, instead of Scandinavia. We do most of our business there. But we're a German company. Head office should be here in Germany, surely.

A   I'm afraid that's completely out of the question. The decision to relocate makes good logistic and economic sense. We're still a fairly small business. Having branches in different countries is just not an option.

B   I totally disagree. Our market is Northern Europe and Germany is at the heart of Northern Europe.

A   Yes, but 70% of our market is in the UK. Look, perhaps we can come back to this later. I can see some of you are not happy about it, and I agree with you up to a point, but I am not in a position to change company policy. OK, let's move on. How are we going to handle administration during the relocation? Does anyone have any suggestions? How about using the Stockholm office while we move from Bremen to Cambridge? Kjell?

D   Well, to be honest, Elke, we feel very much the same as our German colleagues here. We think the decision to close down the Bremen and Stockholm offices is a mistake.

A   I see ...

C   Look, maybe we should take a short break, Elke. I think one or two of us would like to have a word with you – in private if that's OK.

A   Right. Well, sorry everybody. We'll have to break off here, I'm afraid. Axel, Kjell, Erich, I'll see you in my office ...

 1.39

Interview 1

A   So, Peter, how do you see the Bond role?

B   Well, Richard, I see Bond as essentially a very private man. He travels the world, meets beautiful women, finds himself in dangerous situations, but we never really know him. I think too many actors want to make Bond ... erm ... an obvious superhero, a lover, even a comedian. Of course, he's all those things, but above all he's ... erm ... a man of mystery, a spy, someone outside the ordinary world. Bond is his own man. A loner. Quite cold. On one level, Bond is about simple, basic ideas like love, humour and death. He's also a fantasy, completely unreal. I think Bond himself knows he's unreal. I want to play him as a man ... erm ... living up to his legend.

Interview 2

A   Well, Sam, you're an American. Is that going to be a problem for you playing Bond?

C   No, I've played Brits before and my English accent's OK. How's this? 'The name's Bond. James Bond.' But actually, Richard, ... er ... I don't see why Bond can't be an American, or at least a Canadian. I mean, Bond's just whatever you want him to be. The music, the cars, the bad guys, … they're what make the film. Humour is the important thing. If Bond isn't funny, then it's just a silly film with lots of explosions and fast cars and women who get killed just after they sleep with Bond. Er, but Bond has a certain style … stylish, funny, but not too sexist – that's how I'd play Bond. Bond for the 21st century.

Interview 3

A   Now, Jon, how do you see yourself playing the part of Bond?

D   Well, firstly, I think over the years Bond has lost some of his danger. And I'd like to change that. Maybe people are worried about too much violence in films, but let's face it, Bond kills people, lots of them – for a living. He has a licence to kill. He's not just a pretty face. He's a dangerous man. A man who knows he could die at any moment – although we know he won't! I think people need to believe in the actor playing Bond, believe that he's capable of violence, even does his own stunts. Of course, people expect the special effects and the glamour, but that's no good unless Bond looks like he really means business. So I'd just play Bond as me, Richard. That's all I ever do anyway!

Interview 4

A   Charles, you've wanted the Bond part for a long time. How would you play him?

E   I'd like to see Bond return to the old style of those early films, Richard. I think Bond has become too techno these days. And it's difficult to compete with films like *Star Wars* and *The Matrix* on special effects. Bond shouldn't take himself too seriously, but he shouldn't be a joke either. That's difficult to get right, but a good story helps. Bond – the real Bond – belongs to the 1960s, a more optimistic, less cynical age. My Bond would be … er … traditional, intelligent, charming. He'd drive his old Aston Martin, not a BMW! He'd keep his old-fashioned values, but in a modern world of real dangers. Bond is something unique. A British institution. He shouldn't be modernised.

 1.40

A   Diane, this would be quite a professional challenge for you, taking over as Bond. Would people accept a woman in the part, do you think?

F   Well, frankly, no, I don't think they would, Richard. It'd be like having a woman play Superman or Indiana Jones. And what are you going to call her? Jane Bond? It would be ridiculous. But … erm … I don't really see myself becoming Bond … so much as replacing him. I think you've got to begin again really. Maybe have James finally killed off in one of those spectacular opening sequences before you introduce the new female character. Now, Bond is a pretty hard act to follow after forty years, so, obviously, my character has to be larger than life and twice as dangerous! The great thing would be you could do all the old sexist jokes in reverse and nobody would complain. But … erm … I think the secret of a female Bond is, she's got to have style and a wicked sense of humour or everyone will just hate her for getting James's job. What I want to know is: James always had his Bond girls; will I be getting any Bond boys?

CASE STUDY: TOY STORY

 2.01

A   Ms Sheridan?

B   Hmm. Er, yes?

A   Sorry to disturb you, ma'am. There's a call for you. A Mr Fu. Would you like to take it?

B   Erm, oh, yes, thank you. Must be urgent if it can't wait until I get to Shanghai.

A   Actually, I think Mr Fu said he was calling from Shenzhen.

B   Shenzhen? Hello, Michael.

C   Fiona?

B   Yes, speaking. Michael, what are you still doing in Shenzhen? Aren't you supposed to be in Shanghai for the meeting?

C   That's right, but I'm afraid I've had to stay at the lab. In fact, the whole team's been here all night. Fiona, I think we may have a rather serious problem. And I thought you should know right away.

B   Know what?

C   Well, you remember those customer complaints I told you about? About the zoo animal play-sets and the space stations?

B   Yes, I remember. I thought you said there was nothing to worry about.

C   Well, I didn't think there was. I mean, it was only one or two complaints at first. But then we've had about a dozen more cases of parents claiming their kids have been made sick putting the toys in their mouths.

B   What? But that can't happen. I mean, we have the strictest safety regulations in the business.

C   I know. But I ran some tests, anyway. Just to be sure. And it seems the paint on the toys is not our usual paint.

B   What do you mean, not our usual paint?

C   Well, don't ask me how it got there, but the paint on those toys has an extremely high lead content.

B   You mean it's toxic?

C   Yes. And quite seriously so.

B   Oh, my god. You're absolutely sure about this?

C   I'm absolutely sure.

B   How many toys are we talking about, Michael?

C   We could be looking at the entire output of the Hangzhou plants since the last safety check.

B   Numbers, Michael, numbers! How many toys could be toxic?

C   Off the top of my head? I'd say about one and a half million toys … Fiona? Are you still there?

B   Yes, I'm still here. Listen, I'm due to arrive in Shanghai in about, er, three hours. And the first thing I'm going to do is head straight out to the plant in Hangzhou. I suggest you get on the next plane out of Shenzhen and join me there.

C   I've already booked my flight.

B   Good. And bring those lab results with you. There's something very suspicious going on and I want all the facts in front of me before I start making accusations. But we may as well face it. Whoever's responsible for this, it's our worst nightmare come true! …

 2.02

A   Ah, Ms Sheridan. Welcome. Please, take a seat.

B   Thank you. Mr Liang, this is Simon Anderson, our head of PR. In view of what we discussed at our last meeting, I've asked him to join us this morning. Simon, this is Thomas Liang. He owns the plant here in Hangzhou.

C   How do you do, Mr Liang.

A   A pleasure to meet you, Mr Anderson. I do hope we are able to sort out this unfortunate business. As you know, our two companies have worked successfully together for many years now. It would be a great pity if this were to damage our relations.

C   Mr Liang, I'll come straight to the point. I'm here because your actions have put Thompson Toys in a very difficult position.

A   My actions, Mr Anderson?

C   Erm, I mean, of course, the actions of Liang Manufacturing …

A   I really don't think it helpful at this stage to accuse me.

B   Simon, let me handle this. Mr Liang, please excuse my colleague. We're all under a great deal of stress at the moment, as I'm sure you'll understand. Could you just explain to Mr Anderson what you explained to me on Tuesday?

A   Certainly, Ms Sheridan. Well, now, it seems that one of our subcontractors, Chen Enterprises, normally a very good company, I must say – we've worked with them for several generations – well, now, it seems they have let us down rather badly by not using the correct paint in this case.

C   Just a minute, Mr Liang. You're saying you use subcontractors to manufacture Thompson toys? Who authorised this?

B   Actually, Simon, it's common practice here. Normally, there's no problem.

C   Excuse me?

A   Mr Anderson. Perhaps I might remind you that the reason you, and indeed most of your competitors, outsource manufacturing to China is to reduce your production costs. With wages rising in China, we have to cut our own costs by subcontracting other factories to do some of the work. It seems this particular subcontractor did not use the authorised paints and so we face this very serious problem together.

C   As far as I can see, Mr Liang, you face this problem alone. Our contract is very clear about safety standards and the use of the proper materials.

A   I am very much aware of our contractual obligations, Mr Anderson. But surely it is also in the spirit of that contract that we work together to solve our present difficulties.

B   Simon, let's leave the matter of responsibility for another meeting, shall we? Mr Liang, I've decided to withdraw all one and a half million toys manufactured by this plant since our last safety inspection. I'm sure you'll see that this is a necessary precaution.

A   Ms Sheridan, I think it is highly unlikely that more than a few products have been affected. It would be very bad for Liang Manufacturing's reputation if you were to order a total product recall.

B   Nevertheless, I'm afraid I really have no option. Now, we have to move quickly …

 2.03

A   Come on Dan, where are you? …

B   Ms Sheridan? Sorry to keep you waiting. I'm putting you through to Mr Cleveland now.

C   Good morning, Fiona.

A   Dan! What are these headlines I'm reading about another product recall? And why wasn't I told?

C   Now, just a minute, Fiona. I only ordered that recall this morning. God knows how the press got to hear of it! I was going to call you. It's a separate problem. Magnets, this time.

A   Magnets?

C   The small high-powered magnets we put in some of the toys. The whole lot are defective. There's the usual danger of children swallowing them. It's the same problem we had in 2005.

A   Dan, we had to recall three million products that time.

C   It's 18 million this time, Fiona.

A   I can't believe I'm hearing this! After all the difficulties of the past few weeks. Don't tell me – the Hangzhou plant again, right?

C   Well, actually, it's more widespread than that. But, the thing is, the Chinese are saying it's not their responsibility this time. They're saying it's a design fault. In fact, they're making a political issue out of this whole business, saying we overreacted to the paint problems and have damaged their reputation.

A   Overreacted? They've damn near destroyed this company!

C   Well, they might actually be right. We have had some design problems. Listen, Fiona, these recalls have really opened us up to a lot of criticism from the media. They're starting to ask questions again about working conditions in our Chinese and Malaysian plants, about why the Chinese are subcontracting, about how much profit we're making. The stockholders are in a panic. We may even be looking at a total worldwide product ban if we don't act fast …

 2.04

Journalist 1

Tom Kravitz, USA Today. There are a lot of angry and concerned parents this morning. They're wondering how this happened and what you're doing about it?

Journalist 2

Carlos Herrera, La Vanguardia. Are you, in fact, saying that the Chinese are responsible for this whole situation?

Journalist 3

Amy Yip, South China Morning Post. Your Chinese manufacturers claim you are blaming them to cover up your own responsibility and are

demanding a public apology. Are you planning to give them this?

Journalist 4

Jean Davis, International Herald Tribune. Could I ask you how you plan to compensate parents who've already bought Thompson toys as Christmas presents and are now worried that they may be dangerous?

Journalist 5

Ellen Weissmann, Wall Street Journal. After two massive product recalls in the last month, what do you say to parents who have simply lost confidence in buying Thompson toys altogether?

Journalist 6

Martin Summers, the London Times. I'd be interested to hear why you apparently didn't know that your Chinese manufacturers were subcontracting to other factories.

Journalist 7

Louis Laforge, Le Monde. Isn't it true that Thompson makes enormous profits by outsourcing production to Asia and that your products would be safer if they were manufactured in Europe or the USA?

Journalist 8

Inge Eckschlager, Handelsblatt. Do you deny that your Chinese factories are working under such pressure to manufacture your products so quickly and at such low cost that this kind of disaster is to be expected? Isn't it the case that saving money is more important to Thompson than safety?

Journalist 9

Koichi Kanazawa, Yomiuri Shimbun. Could you just clarify exactly what the new safety procedures will be and how they will be an improvement on the old ones?

Journalist 10

Sandra White, National Enquirer. I've heard stories that Thompson keeps it's costs low by employing convicts in Chinese prisons to work for no pay. Would you care to comment on these allegations?

Journalist 11

Kyle Gray, CNN News. Is it possible that this sudden increase in serious product defects is the result of sabotage by someone within your company – perhaps being paid by one of your competitors?

Journalist 12

Vladimir Sholokhov, Bloomberg Online. I imagine that the increased cost of improving your safety procedures will mean an increase in the price of your toys as well. Will the customer have to pay more just to be sure the toys they buy are safe?

Spokesperson

Thank you, ladies and gentlemen. I'm afraid that that's all we have time for today. If you'd like to collect your press packs as you leave, you'll find more detailed information in there …

09 NEW WORLD ORDER

 2.05

For some years now, Brazil has been getting stronger as an economy. I think it's a good place to do business. In the past, we had boom-bust cycles. You know, one year things were good, next year disaster. Of course, this was very bad for international trade. Our currency, the real, it

was very unstable. Now the real is really gaining against the dollar and the euro. Inflation is falling, exports are increasing and we have much easier credit terms. Brazil is the second most populated country in the Western hemisphere. We are the world's top exporter of beef, chicken, ethanol, iron ore, sugar, coffee, orange juice. And we have a multi-billion dollar redevelopment programme to help poorer regions of the country. We still have a long way to go, but I think we are a good place to outsource business and a good trading partner – also, of course, a great place to live! The only problem is our labour laws, which are still very restrictive. Our unions are strong and somewhat inflexible. It is a major problem. But we are working on it. You wait and see, by 2050 the Brazilian economy will be as strong as the UK!

 2.06

The Russian economy is doing well. The rouble is strong. One indicator of this is house prices, which are high. I read somewhere that Moscow is now the world's most costly city for foreigners. Everywhere you look in Moscow you see new construction projects and the streets are packed with cars. Of course, everybody knows that it is the energy sector which has created the economic boom here. One third of the world's total natural gas reserves are in Russia. The company I work for, Gazprom, is the state-owned conglomerate which controls gas supplies. We are the world's third largest company, a $300 billion company. Perhaps the only problem here is that we continue to create, how shall I say, political complications. I think it was necessary for Russia to be quite hard on companies like BP and Shell, who were making big profits in Russian oil fields with little benefit for Russians. And the changeover from the Soviet energy subsidy system has not been easy. But maybe now it is time to separate politics from business. European gas reserves are declining. There is a good market for us in Europe for many years to come as friendly business partners.

 2.07

For several years now people have been talking about China as the next big world power, but more recently they are beginning to talk of India in something like the same way. The dragon and the elephant – China and India, Chindia some people call it. But I think it is important to highlight some of the differences between our two countries. Here in India we don't have the same great mega-cities and modern infrastructure as China. Here we have nothing like a Shanghai, Beijing or Guangzhou. But we have something else. We have a well educated workforce, many with a good level of English. In fields like medicine, engineering and IT we are very strong. So strong, in fact, that many Indian graduates are leaving India – brain drain. This is a problem for us, but you have to remember that the 28% of our population with the highest IQ is greater than the entire population of America! Depending on whom you ask, somewhere between one half and two-thirds of all Fortune 500 companies are already outsourcing to India. The standard of living in India has risen so much because of this that we ourselves now outsource – to places like Brazil, Ukraine, Romania and the Philippines. Still, almost half of all outsourcing these days is to India.

2.08

China is a very exciting place to be nowadays. For people in the West it can be hard to believe what we have achieved in such a short time. But, remember, 200 years ago China and India represented half of the world's GDP per capita. Soon this will be true again. Certainly most of the industry and money are concentrated in the eastern coastal regions at present. But we have 38,000 science and technology companies throughout China employing four and a half million people. We are creating 7 million new jobs every year. At this rate, in 10 to 15 years our GDP will match the USA. Of course, the USA is the biggest importer of Chinese goods. One result of this is that our banking industry is flooded with cash and this makes it difficult for government to control lending and investment. Some think the Chinese economy may, er, be growing too fast – that bust will follow boom. I think this is not a problem. 40 to 50% of our GDP goes on domestic investment. We manufacture many capital-intensive goods like petrochemicals, silicon wafers, digital displays, cars, steel, ships. We have avoided financial crises like those in South Korea and Thailand. No, the biggest problem for China now is pollution. With our industry growing so fast, we are in danger of overtaking the USA not only in GDP but also as the world's biggest polluter.

10 SMALL TALK

 2.09

Extract 1

A   Er, how do you do. I'm Tom Pearson, Export Manager, Falcon Petroleum.

B   How do you do, Mr Pearson. I am Sakamoto, Assistant Director of International Investments, Mizoguchi Bank. Please sit here opposite the door. You'll be next to Usami-san.

A   Oh, OK. I sit here, right?

B   That's right. **Have you tried green tea before**, Mr Pearson?

A   Er, yes I have. I had it last time I was here. I like it very much.

 2.10

Extract 2

A   Good morning everyone. I'd like to introduce you all to Dr Alan Winter, who's come over from the Atlanta office to spend a few days at our research centre. Welcome to Berlin, Dr Winter.

B   Thank you very much, Wolfgang. It was kind of you to invite me.

A   OK, let's get down to business, shall we?

 2.11

Extract 3

A   … And then Juventus scored the winner. It was an incredible goal! Did you see the Lazio game last night, Miss Sterling?

B   Yes, I did. Wasn't it a great match? One of the best I've ever seen. But then there's nothing like Italian football.

A   So, you like football then?

B   Oh, yeah. I love it. In fact, my father was a professional footballer.

A   Really?

B   Yes. He wasn't a superstar or anything, but he, er, played for Leeds.

A   Leeds United?

B   Yes, that's right.

A   They were a great team in the 70s, weren't they?

B   Yeah, that's when he played for them.

A   Amazing. Wait till I tell Luigi. Our new partner's father played for Leeds United, ha!

B   Where is Luigi, by the way?

A   Oh, he'll be here soon. He's never the first to arrive, not Luigi …

 2.12

Extract 4

A   Rain stopped play again yesterday, I see.

B   Sorry?

A   The cricket. They cancelled the match.

B   Oh, they didn't! Well, we certainly haven't seen much cricket this summer.

A   No. Chocolate biscuit?

B   Oh, have we got chocolate ones? Business must be good.

C   Right, everyone. Er, I suppose we'd better get started …

 2.13

Extract 5

A   Right, shall we start? First of all, this is Catherine Anderson from London. I think this is your first time in Finland, isn't it Catherine? Or **have you been here before**?

B   Actually, I came here on holiday once, but that was a long time ago.

A   Well, we hope you enjoy your stay with us. Now there's fresh coffee if you'd like some before we begin …

 2.14

Extract 6

A   OK, you guys. Thanks for coming. Now, to business … Oh, did you all get coffee?

B   Hey, wait up. I got a great one here.

C   Oh no, it's one of Marty's jokes.

B   See, there's this guy George goes for a job, right? And it's a really cool job. Right here in New York. Big money. So, anyway, he takes a test, like an aptitude test, you know, him and this woman. There's two of them. And they have to take a test to get the job.

C   Yeah, yeah, so …?

B   So they both get exactly the same score on the test, George and the woman – ninety-nine per cent.

C   Uh-huh.

B   So George goes into the interviewer's office. And the interviewer says 'Well, you both got one question wrong on the test, but, I'm sorry, we're giving the job to the other candidate.' So George says 'Hey, that's not fair! How come she gets the job?' And the interviewer says 'Well, on question 27, the question you both got wrong, she wrote "I don't know" and you wrote "Neither do I".'

C   That's a terrible joke, Marty.

B   No, you see, he copied her test, right?

A   Marty, we've heard the joke before. It's ancient. OK, everybody, time to work.

B   I thought it was funny.

 2.15

Extract 7

A   As you know, Albert, I'm the last person to talk about other people's private lives. If the president of France himself wants to have an affair, I don't care. I mean, this is not the United States.

B   Yes, quite.

A   What I do worry about is what's going on between our vice-president and our head of finance.

B   They're having an affair?

A   Haven't you heard? I thought everybody knew.

B   God, no! No one ever tells me anything.

A   I mean, it's not the affair I care about. It's how it affects our meetings. Haven't you noticed?

B   Noticed what?

A   How they always agree on everything.

B   Well, now you mention it …

11 E-MAIL

 2.16

It's instant. And efficient. That's what I like about it. I work in project teams a lot and you can just keep everybody up to date in one simple message. Perfect.

Actually, I find the more people you send an e-mail to, the less chance you have of getting a reply. Everybody thinks somebody else will answer it.

Erm, well, being cc-ed on every little thing drives me nuts. I'd say 60% of the messages I get have nothing to do with me.

Speed – that's the best thing about it. You can just get the job done and move on. Most of my e-mails are only two or three lines long.

What do I hate about e-mail? Er, well, spam, I guess. I mean, I have a filter, obviously. But I still seem to get all those Viagra and sexual enhancement offers!

What I really like is that you can just get straight down to business. There's no need for all the chat. Just get to the point.

What I can't stand is all the junk, the stupid jokes, all the meaning-of-life stuff that seems to fill my Bulk file. All those things, you know, like, 'Send this to ten more people or a disaster will hit your city'. I mean, come on!

I think all the silly stuff is quite cool, actually. The jokes, the slideshows. I mean, it's just a way of keeping in touch. It's not meant to be taken seriously!

Well, I hate the phone, not a people person! So e-mail's great for me. You don't have to deal with people.

The really neat thing is that you can go back through your e-mails and see what's been said. You have a permanent record of every discussion. Which is really useful sometimes.

What really annoys me are those little smiley things, emoticons. Just childish.

I'm a big fan of e-mail. You leave a voicemail, nobody gets back to you. You send an e-mail, it always gets through. I think people are better about answering their e-mail than their phone.

People expecting an instant reply – that really bugs me. I mean, OK, so you sent me an e-mail. Like I'm supposed to drop everything and answer it?

Well, I'm not crazy about 15-paragraph e-mails. Or those 20-megabyte attachments that take an hour to download. When do these people get any work done?

I think e-mails can sound quite impersonal at the best of times and it's easy to sound more direct than you meant. I mean, you'd never be that direct on the phone. That's how you get flames with people reacting to careless writing. I've certainly sent off plenty of angry e-mails and then regretted it!

I read somewhere that 20% of e-mail gets read by the boss, which is kind of scary. I'm not keen on the idea that Big Brother is watching me!

 2.17

Message 1

Hi Koichi, it's Sarah Greenwood here. There's been a change of plan. Peter and I were hoping to arrive in Nagoya on Monday. That's not going to be possible now, I'm afraid, because I have to be in Edinburgh that day. So, we're aiming to get there by Wednesday, but that should still give us plenty of time to get organised before the presentation.

 2.18

Message 2

Hi Koichi, it's Sarah again. Peter and I were planning to stay at the Radisson, because it's near, but apparently there's a conference next week and it's already fully booked. Sorry, I was going to e-mail you about this yesterday. Could you find us somewhere else? Thanks very much.

 2.19

Message 3

Hi Koichi, it's me again. Just one more thing, sorry. We're intending to keep the presentation itself quite short – about 45 minutes – to allow plenty of time for questions, and we're going to use PowerPoint, so we're going to need a projector and screen, if you can organise that. Thanks, see you on Wednesday.

12 PRESENTING

 2.20

1 They tried it. They liked it. So they bought it.
2 They tried it. They liked it. So they bought it.
3 We can never be the biggest, but we can be the best.
4 We can never be the biggest, but we can be the best.
5 Did you know that the whole thing was absolutely free?
6 Did you know that the whole thing was absolutely free?

 2.21

I have said that great men are a mixed lot / but there are orders of great men // There are great men / who are great men / amongst all men // but there are also great men / who are great / amongst great men // And that is the sort of great

man / whom you have amongst you tonight // I go back 2,500 years / and how many of them can I count in that period? // I can count them / on the fingers of my two hands: // Pythagoras / Ptolemy / Aristotle / Copernicus / Kepler / Galileo / Newton // Einstein // And I still have two fingers left vacant //

My lords / ladies / and gentlemen // are you ready for the toast? // Health / and length of days / to the greatest of our contemporaries // Einstein //

 2.22

Part A

A OK, this brings us on to the next item on our agenda this morning, which is online business. Now, I know some of you are concerned about the recent performance of E-Stock, our online subsidiary. So I've asked Gary Cale, our new head of e-business, to bring us up to date. Over to you, Gary.

B Thanks, Michelle. To start off, then, I know you have all seen the figures up to the last quarter – disappointing to say the least. Nine months ago, when we first went online, we were getting over 250,000 hits a day. Three months ago, when I joined this company, we were getting just 60,000 and it was obvious we were failing to attract sufficient customers to our website. So, what was going wrong? In a word, technology. The problem was not the service we were offering, but the website itself.

 2.23

Part B

B Now, three things make a good website. First, access to the website must be fast. The slow access speed of our website meant people were getting bored waiting for pages to load and simply going somewhere else. Second, a good website must be easy to use. Ours was so complicated, customers sometimes didn't know if they were buying or selling! And third, a good website must have excellent search engines. Ours didn't. To give you an example of what I mean, a fault we hadn't noticed in the programming caused fifteen hundred people to invest in a company that didn't even exist. Yes, embarrassing. I'm glad I wasn't here to take the blame for that one! **OK, to move on**. Greenbaum-Danson is unquestionably one of the world's leading financial services companies. We're the biggest, oldest and most respected firm in the business. But to succeed in online stock trading, to succeed in any area of e-business, you need a first-class website. So, creating a first-class website was our first priority. The next thing was internet advertising, winning back the customer confidence we'd lost. That's a longer job, but we're making progress. The final thing, and this always takes time in e-business, will be to actually make a profit. Well, we can dream!

 2.24

Part C

B **Have a look at this**. It's a graph showing the number of trades our customers make per day on our website. **As you can see**, the figure was fluctuating for the first three months and then fell sharply to bottom out at just 10,000 trades a day. For a company of

our size, that wasn't too impressive. But look. We're up to nearly 40,000 trades now, our highest ever, and still rising.

OK, I'm going to break off in a minute and take questions. **So, to sum up**. One, improvements in our website have led to more hits and increased trading. Two, advertising on the Internet will help us win back customers. Three, profits will follow. E-trading in stocks is the future. In the US alone it's the way a quarter of the public choose to buy their shares. This is the information age and the Internet is the ultimate information provider. I'm reminded of what banker Walter Wriston once said: 'Information about money is becoming more valuable than money itself.' Thank you.

CASE STUDY: REACHING OUT

 2.25

Hi. It's Angel. Listen, I'm really sorry. I forgot to attach the notes to the PowerPoint slides I sent you and I don't have internet access at the moment. So let me just quickly talk you through them, OK?

Right, slide one. I thought it might be quite effective to start off with a very simple visual. The idea is that it looks quite dramatic, but the audience won't know what it means until you tell them. Here's the statistic you can quote: we obviously only have one planet earth. But at the speed we're currently using up our natural resources, we actually need 1.3 earths to just replace what we use. A frightening thought.

OK, now slide two. This gives a bit more information to support slide one, figures for the last fifty years. As you can see, in the mid-1960s we were already using 70% of the earth's natural resources. We started to exceed nature's ability to regenerate in the mid-1980s. Point out the ecological capacity threshold here. These figures, by the way, come from a study by the National Academy of Sciences if anyone wants to know. You could mention a few more figures if you like – in the last fifty years, oil consumption has gone up by 700%. Meat production, fish catches and carbon emissions are all up 600%. But make sure you emphasise at this point that one world is clearly no longer enough for us! So who's consuming all the resources?

On to slide three. Answer your question from slide one with this graph. I think the figures speak for themselves. The global population has increased from two billion in 1800 to over six billion today. But what's more interesting is that it has gone up from three billion just since 1950. To put that into perspective, you could ask your audience to raise their hands if they're over forty. Then tell the over-40s that in their lifetime they have seen the number of people on the planet double! The other thing to point out here is that it is, of course, in the developing world that the population increase has been most dramatic. Does this mean that the developing world is using up all our resources? Absolutely not. In fact, the richest 1% of the global population consumes as much as the poorest 44%.

Slide four. This chart shows how the world's income is distributed. Some economists say that as the rich get richer, this eventually helps the poor get richer too. But the figures here tell a different story. This chart was actually put together by the United Nations Development

Programme. The five horizontal bands represent the richest to poorest levels of society. And, as you can see, the top fifth have 82.7% of the world's income and the bottom fifth just 1.4%. In fact, 30% of the global population lives on less than two dollars a day. All bad news. But the key point is this – with our current economic model, there will never be sufficient capital and resources for the poor to live as the rich do. If everyone wants to own a car, fly around the world and buy a new mobile phone every year, on this planet, with the resources it has, this will never be possible. What's needed is a new economic model.

Finally, on to slide five. This is where we at Equitus are trying to make a difference. Traditionally, small businesses in the developing world have had to deal with investment agencies, governments and bureaucracy – at best, inefficient. But not any more. With the power of the Internet, it's possible to connect those small businesses directly with private investors in the developed world. Even a $50 loan can make an enormous difference to a small farmer. But here's how Equitus is different from most other micro-loan companies. There's no interest payable. Lenders log on to the Equitus website and choose the business or businesses they want to invest in. Equitus transfers the funds to a local partner who gives the money to each business in the lender's portfolio. The local partner collects repayments and keeps the lender informed about how the businesses they're sponsoring are doing. When the investment matures, the lender gets their money back and can withdraw it or reinvest. It's the nearest thing to reaching out across the globe and giving a helping hand to business.

OK, that's it. I'll leave it to you to decide how to deliver the speech. Speak to you later. Good luck!

 2.26

Hi there! It's Angel. How are you all doing in Madrid?

Things are going well here in Belize. Very hot and humid, but it's a nice hotel I'm in, and I think I'm making some very useful contacts. So, anyway, how did the presentation go?

Did you manage to get the basic message across about what we do? That's the most important thing.

The opening's always really important. Were you happy with your introduction?

Really? And did it all sound clear and organised?

Mm. How was your English?

OK. And were the visuals I sent you helpful or did you make some of your own?

How did you finish? Strongly, I hope!

Uhuh. So is there anything you'd do differently if you had to give the presentation again?

I see. Well, that's good because I've arranged for you to give the same talk tomorrow in Toronto. Yes. In fact, I've booked you onto the next flight … Hello? Hello? Are you still there?

13 ENTER THE BLOGOSPHERE

 2.27

Erm, well, Web 2.0 is a term that was invented by the founder of O'Reilly Media, Tim O'Reilly, back in 2004, I think. And, er, it's really just the way in which technological changes have had an impact on the way the Internet works and what it's used for. So, on a very basic level,

whereas Web 1.0 was about dial-up charges, with everybody using conventional phone lines to access the Internet, now, obviously it's about bandwidth and bandwidth costs – what people are paying to get the fastest broadband connection. Dial-up is pretty much dead now. And, whereas Web 1.0 was about being wired, Web 2.0 is increasingly about wireless connections, so that, as Alan Cohen says, 'you can find anything, anywhere, anytime'. So, that's just the technology – faster, more mobile internet access. Actually, pretty soon the desktop computer will be dead too if you ask me and we'll all just be using laptops or handhelds.

What's more interesting to me, and what we really mean by Web 2.0, is that the Internet is no longer just about companies having websites and wanting to attract business to those websites. That's the old Web 1.0 model. Companies saying: 'Here we are. This is what we do. Are you interested?' More and more, what we're seeing now is online communities, not just companies, communities consisting of businesses, their customers, competitors and other stakeholders talking to one another online through things like blogs. The old website was just something you read – a kind of online brochure. The blog involves writing. It's a two-way thing. It's less about information than conversation – which I think is what Tim Berners-Lee, the inventor of the world wide web, originally intended it to be. And when people start talking to each other online about what they like and dislike about companies and their products, you have a very powerful force. Websites like YouTube and Flickr are basically about sharing, whether it's videos or personal photos. Companies themselves find new ways to collaborate too and so that's why, from a business point of view, Web 2.0 is less about owning than about sharing.

 2.28

Extract 1

One thing I think is happening is that search engines like Google and AltaVista are actually getting less effective now that there are more than 100 million websites on the Internet. And this is where social networking sites like Facebook and MySpace come in. I mean, if you were looking for, say, a good holiday deal in the Caribbean, you could google 'Caribbean holidays', but you're going to get about half a million results coming up. What's the use of that? Much better to ask for advice on Facebook and you'll get people who've actually been on those holidays telling you who to contact. So this is really about large groups of consumers helping each other and cutting out the advertising hype.

Extract 2

Hm, well, the problem I have with blogs is that most of them are absolute junk, just total rubbish. I mean it's all very well going on about how Web 2.0 gives us all a voice, the so-called 'democratisation' of the Net, yeah. Great, but who's going to quality control all this stuff people put out there? I read somewhere that a new blog is posted every half second. My god, that's just crazy! Some of the people publishing their views are just illiterate idiots. I don't see how their opinion on anything is worth a cent to multinational businesses. Seems to me that, nine times out of ten, posting a blog is the best way to tell a million people why you're not worth listening to!

Extract 3

Big corporations are taking a while to get used to this new platform for doing business, but it's getting there. I mean, sure, quite a lot of businesses probably use blogs and video-sharing sites just because they think it's the cool, fashionable thing to do. But there are others who see that being in direct contact with their customers is actually great for business. I mean, who better to go to to discuss product and service development than the people who are already buying your stuff? This is the 'prosumer' idea. Consumers who also produce, who have some input into the way you design and market whatever it is you're selling. It's a dialogue now – between buyers and sellers – and if you ignore your buyers, they take their business to someone who's listening.

Extract 4

Frankly, it's no use companies going on about patents, copyright and intellectual property anymore. Those days are over. If you produce a rock video, within minutes someone is going to post it on YouTube, maybe even edit it, change the music, mix it with a totally different video. You can't stop it. Look what happened with MP3 technology. All these record companies wanted to close the music download websites down. It's stealing, cheating artists etc etc. Now what? They sell songs off albums online. Bands like Radiohead give their new albums away practically for free online to see what the reaction is before they manufacture the CD. If instead of fighting media sharing, you use it to your advantage, it can actually be the best form of marketing there is. I mean, even the Queen of England's on YouTube!

Extract 5

A lot of people seem to think that viral videos are just for kids. Well, if they are, there are an awful lot of kids out there watching them. The most popular one at the moment has been viewed a billion times so far. 15% of the planet has seen it! Companies like Burger King and Dove soap have practically turned their businesses around using viral marketing. The videos are so popular, people start copying them, making fake versions and all this is actually incredibly good publicity. Say you're selling a really boring product like tins of fish. You could spend millions on TV commercials, but, let's be honest, who cares about your tinned fish? Virtually no-one. Or, like the company John West, you could put a series of very funny videos onto the Internet. And, bang, you're famous. You've created massive publicity. You've created buzz.

Extract 6

As far as I can see, the biggest benefit of Web 2.0 to the world of business is that it's possible for a company to link up with another company – whether down the road or on the other side of the planet – and collaborate on new innovative products and services. In the past, companies protected their expertise, their ideas, their intellectual capital because they saw everything in terms of competition. But in the world of academia, of science, of medicine, of engineering, all progress has been made through collaboration, not by keeping your best ideas secret. But now you've got mining companies like Goldcorp actually sharing their confidential data online in the hope that other companies and individuals can help them. In their case, thanks to networking, they went from an underperforming $100 million company into a $9 billion giant. This is co-operation mixed with competition – co-opetition – and it works!

14 BEING HEARD

 2.29

Extract 1

It's a joke, really, this idea that everyone's opinion is valued. I mean, how much can you disagree with the boss? After all, she's the boss!

Extract 2

You often leave a meeting not really knowing what you're supposed to do next, what the action plan is. I usually end up phoning people afterwards to find out what we actually agreed.

Extract 3

Nobody seems to come to the meeting properly prepared. If you want a copy of the report, they don't have it with them. Need to see the figures? They'll get back to you. It's hopeless!

Extract 4

You often get several people all talking at the same time. So no one's really listening to anyone else. They're just planning what they're going to say next. It's survival of the loudest!

Extract 5

They're usually badly organised. Nobody sticks to the point. People get sidetracked all the time. It takes ages to get down to business. As they say: 'If you fail to plan, you plan to fail.'

Extract 6

You know even before you begin who's going to argue with who. The facts don't seem to matter. It's all about scoring points, looking better than your colleagues and impressing the boss.

Extract 7

I try to stop them over-running. We sometimes hold meetings without chairs. That speeds things up a lot! I've even tried showing the red card to people who won't shut up, like in football. Not popular.

Extract 8

The same two or three people always seem to dominate. The rest of us just switch off – doodle, daydream, count the minutes. I sometimes play Tomb Raider on my laptop with the sound off.

Extract 9

Well, to be honest, everybody knows we don't actually decide anything in meetings. The boss already knows what he wants to do anyway!

Extract 10

Well, nothing interesting was ever discussed in a boardroom. That's why it's called a boardroom – people go there to be bored. Most offices are unsuitable for long meetings. And as for breakfast meetings, no way! My idea of a breakfast meeting is breakfast in bed with my wife.

 2.30

Extract 1

A   OK. You've all had a chance to look at the quarterly sales figures.

B   Yes. They're terrible.

A   Agreed, but **if I could just finish**. We're 30% down on projections. The question is why?

C   **Can I just come in here?** It seems to me that our marketing strategy is all wrong.

B   **Now, just a minute**. Are you trying to say this is our fault?

C   Well, what else can it be? We're offering generous discounts …

B   **Look, sorry to interrupt again, but** …

C   **No, hear me out**. We're offering very generous discounts to our biggest customers as part of our introductory offer. And sales are still slow. Something's going wrong, and I say it's the marketing.

B   Well, if you ask me, the problem is the product itself.

C   And what is wrong with the product? BabySlim is an innovative addition to our product line.

B   Innovative, yes. But there is no market for diet baby food. I said so at the very beginning. Who's going to admit they've got a fat baby?

A   You know, maybe he has a point …

 2.31

Extract 2

A   So, that's the position. The company has been officially declared bankrupt.

B   Yes.

A   And our chief executive officer has been arrested on charges of corruption.

B   Yes.

A   Of course, our company president has been on television to make a public apology.

B   Of course.

A   But there was nothing he could do.

B   Of course not. Gentlemen, it is a black day in our company's proud history.

A   Yes. A very black day. Very, very black.

C   **Can I just come in here?**

B   Please, do.

C   Well, it's just a suggestion, but shouldn't we all be looking for new jobs?

 2.32

Extract 3

A   Now, just a minute, just a minute!

B   There's no way we're going to accept this!

A   Could I just …?

B   They can't make English the official company language!

A   Could I just …?

B   If head office thinks we're all going to speak English from now on …

A   **Could I just finish what I was saying?**

B   Frankly, it's bad enough that we have to speak English in these meetings.

A   Please! **Let me finish**. No one is suggesting we can't speak our own language.

B   But that is exactly what they are suggesting!

C   **Can I just say something?**

B   Go ahead.

C   Well, as I understand it, this is only a proposal at this stage.

A   That's precisely what I was trying to say – before I was interrupted.

B   Now, **hang on a second** …

C   If I could just finish … . The idea is to introduce English gradually over the next two years …

B   Oh, no! Not while I'm in charge of Human Resources.

A   Yes, well, that brings us on to item two on the agenda: restructuring the Human Resources department.

15 SNAIL MAIL

 2.33

1

Erm, well, where's the address? You've completely missed the address out. And what's the twenty-twost of February, Rudi? You mean twenty-second. That should be 'nd', right?

2

'My dear Ms Ramalho' is a bit old-fashioned, don't you think? Sounds like a 19th-century love-letter, eh? I don't think you need the 'my'. 'Dear Ms Ramalho' will do. And it's a capital 'T' for 'Thank you'. I know it's after a comma, but it's a capital.

3

So that should be: 'Thank you for your letter of February ninth.' Oh, and 'communication' has got a double 'm', Rudi! Try using the spell check.

4

What's this? 'I am such sorry'? That's 'so sorry', isn't it? Actually I don't think you need the 'so'. Just 'I'm sorry' sounds better … OK … 'I'm sorry you were disabled to attend our presentation'? So this woman arrived in an ambulance, did she? 'Unable', I think you mean.

5

'In the mean time …' Oh, I think 'meantime' is one word, not two. Yeah, one word. Oh, what's gone wrong here? 'I enclose a copy of our last catalogue'? That should be 'latest'. The last one's the old one not the new one.

6

Erm, 'current' is with an 'e', not an 'a' – c-u-double r-e-n-t. And it's a price list, Rudi, not a prize list. With a 'c' not a 'z'. We're not running a lottery!

7

'Information' is singular. You don't need the 's'. So, 'If you would like further information … uh-huh … please don't hesitate but contact me again.' That should be 'don't hesitate to contact me again'.

8

Right, nearly finished. 'I look forwards to hearing from you.' That doesn't sound right to me. Wait a minute, it's 'I look forward' not 'forwards'. Yeah. And, er, 'Yours fatefully'. That's 'faithfully' not 'fatefully' – f-a-i-t-h, faithfully … Actually, it isn't, is it? It's 'Yours sincerely'. Because you've written the woman's name. I'd just put 'Best wishes' if I were you. It's simpler. Er, Rudi, maybe you'd better leave the letter writing to me in future.

16 SOLVING PROBLEMS

 3.01

The first suggestion the company got was a joke really, but it won the $100 bonus. The suggestion was that the bonus be reduced to $50.

3.02

1

After many expensive and unsuccessful attempts to promote the restaurant with posters and T-shirts, the owner, Martha Sanchez, finally came up with a winner. She offered free lunches for life to anyone who agreed to have the name and logo of the restaurant tattooed on a visible part of their bodies. To date, 50 people have become walking advertisements.

2

A lot of time was wasted on electronic devices that could authenticate signatures and on educating customers of the bank to look after their cheque books. Someone suggested using passwords, but people always forgot them. Finally, the bank manager had a different idea – why not simply put a photograph of the account holder on each cheque?

3

The company quickly realised that there is no way of making industrial cleaners exciting. Special offers and competitions had limited success. So they tried something silly instead. The company's name was changed to the New Pig Corporation. All products were labelled with the New Pig logo, the hotline was changed to 800-HOT-HOGS and its company address to 1 Pork Avenue. Did it work? Well, growing at a rate of 10% a year, New Pig currently employs more than 300 people and enjoys sales of over $80 million.

 3.03

Extract 1

A OK, we both know the problem. **Basically**, we can't get retail stores to stock our new product. They say it's too expensive. So the question is: how do we get access to the customer?

B **What if we offered it on a sale or return basis?**

A No, I don't think so. If we did that, we'd just create cashflow problems for ourselves.

B Hm. Well, **another option would be to sell it direct online**.

A It's a possibility, but I really don't think we know enough about e-commerce to take the chance. And if we start bringing in internet specialists, we could end up spending a fortune.

B Of course, we wouldn't have this problem if we'd priced the product more sensibly in the first place.

 3.04

Extract 2

A Right, our objective for this meeting is to think of ways we can get the supplies we need. As I'm sure you've all heard our sole supplier is about to go bankrupt!

B Hopefully, it won't come to that, but if it does, we'll certainly have to act fast. **Supposing we bought the company out?**

A What, and took on all their debts? I don't think so!

C **Alternatively, we could just manufacture our own components.** I've spoken to our technical department. They say they can do it.

A Yes, but do you have any idea how long it would take to get an in-house production facility operational?

C Well, what choice do we have? Unless we do something, we'll be out of business within six months!

B What I want to know is why our suppliers didn't tell us they were in trouble. If we'd known this was going to happen, we could have had our own production plant up and running by now.

 3.05

Extract 3

A **What I want to know is**: how do we maintain our profit margins with labour costs rising the way they are?

B Well, it seems obvious, but how about raising prices? I mean, even with a 2% price rise, we'd still be very competitive.

C No, I'm afraid that's not an option. This is an extremely price-sensitive market.

B I know that, but what else do you suggest? If we don't cover our costs, we'll soon be running at a loss.

A Now, let's not panic. **The answer could be to shift production** to somewhere like South-East Asia. We've talked about it before.

C And close down our plants here? Wouldn't it be easier if we just tried to renegotiate with the unions – get them to accept a lower pay offer?

A If we'd been able to get the unions to accept a lower pay offer, John, we wouldn't be considering outsourcing to Asia.

 3.06

Extract 4

A Now, what on earth are we going to do about all this unsold stock piling up in the warehouses? If we don't move it pretty soon, there'll be no space for new product. And we'll be left with a lot of old product nobody wants! So, ideas? Anybody?

B Well, in my opinion, our product development cycle is way too short. **Why don't we delay** the new product launch to give us time to sell existing stock?

A This is a technology-driven business, Robert. If we don't continually upgrade our product, the competition will.

B And if we didn't all keep upgrading every three months, we wouldn't have this problem!

C Wait a minute, wait a minute! This old stock, **couldn't we just sell it off** at a discount to create space for the new stuff? Say, 15%?

A I'd rather not start talking about a 15% discount at this stage, if you don't mind.

C Well, if we'd discounted it sooner, we wouldn't have had to be so generous.

 3.07

Extract 5

A Now, I've brought you all here to discuss a very serious matter. Someone in the company – we don't know who – is passing on information to the competition. I'm sure I don't need to tell you that in a business like ours it is essential we protect our competitive advantage. So, … what do we do?

B Are you telling us we have a spy amongst us?

A If I wasn't, Simon, we wouldn't be here now.

C Well, let's think. We already restrict access to important files, but what about encrypting our most confidential information as well? It's common practice in most companies these days. I'm surprised we don't do it already.

A I'm afraid it's more serious than just downloading data off the company server. This person seems to be recording meetings and private conversations as well.

B You're joking!

A (coughs)

B Erm, sorry, it's just that I can hardly believe this.

C Well, **maybe it's time we involved** the police. Clearly a crime is being committed here.

A It most certainly is. And I would have called the police in already if I'd thought it would do any good. But, I don't want our spy, whoever it is, to know we know. So, unless we have to, I'd rather see if we can deal with this ourselves first. And who knows? Perhaps we can even turn the situation to our advantage …

 3.08

1 Hennessy Cognac

It's close to midnight and you're relaxing after a long, hard day at the office. The barman's waiting to take your order. You don't know what to have. You look at a table in the corner where an attractive group in their early twenties seem to be having fun. 'What are they drinking?' you ask the barman. 'Hennessy martinis, madam. They're the latest thing. Would you like to try one?' You've never heard of it. 'Sure,' you reply. The barman pours the dark golden drink into a cocktail glass. 'Hey, this isn't at all bad!' you say. You order a couple more and can't wait to tell your friends about your new discovery.

What you don't know is that those rich kids in the corner are getting paid to drink this stuff. They're part of an ingenious campaign dreamt up by the Hennessy marketing department to influence people's choice of drinks in bars all over the States. 'Stealth marketing' they call it. Over the past six months Hennessy have been interviewing and recruiting young, good-looking people to go into bars in New York, Chicago, San Francisco, LA and Miami and order Hennessy cocktails, tell bar staff how to make them if they don't know and buy drinks for anyone they like. Hennessy pays for their drinks and they get $50 a night for the job.

Clever. But does it work? Yes, brilliantly! Hennessy sales have increased ever since the campaign. In 1997 Hennessy finally broke the one-million-case-a-year barrier in the US. And today Hennessy sponsors party nights all over the world from Paris to Kuala Lumpur. Of course, the secret is out now. But that hasn't stopped other companies copying the strategy to influence those customers who believe they cannot be influenced.

2 Harley-Davidson

Harley chief, Richard Teerlink, was quick to realise that the company's greatest asset was its customers. So the first thing he did was build up the Harley Owners' Club which now has nearly half a million members. He also recognised the trend towards higher-income customers, for whom a Harley was a status symbol. These yuppies, rich urban bikers or Rolex riders, as they were sometimes called, were clearly the key to the company's survival. By creating an extended family of Harley enthusiasts fighting to save a great American legend from Japanese attack, Teerlink was able to work effectively on the emotions of his target market.

But Teerlink was a practical businessman too. He knew that he couldn't ignore the technical side. So Harley executives were sent to Japan to learn some of the Japanese quality assurance techniques. More significantly, Harley-Davidson immediately got rid of all of its executive vice-presidents and replaced them with three self-directed teams: one to create demand; one to manufacture the products; and one to provide customer support. The next step was to set up the Harley Institute which offers every employee up to eighty hours of training a year.

In a final masterstroke, Teerlink persuaded the International Trade Commission to increase the tax on imported Japanese motorbikes over 700ccs from 4.4% to an enormous 49.4% for a fixed period of time to give American manufacturers time to recover.

And recover they did. By 1988 when Harley-Davidson threw its 85th birthday party in Milwaukee, 40,000 Harley lovers had come from all parts of the United States to attend with Harley executives riding at the head of each convoy. By 1989 Harley was again the number one heavyweight bike company in the US with 59% of the market. Today it's still growing by 8 to 10% a year and enjoying record sales of around $2 billion.

CASE STUDY: ADVERSE REACTIONS

 3.09

A Welcome to the Rosberg Business Podcast. I'm your host David Robinson and today we turn our attention to the pharmaceutical industry. My guest this morning is Yvonne Latimer, the newly appointed CEO of Zantis-Nilay, the result of the acquisition announced just a little earlier this morning of Istanbul-based Nilay Medical by Zantis Pharmaceuticals. Ms Latimer, thank you for joining us.

B Thank you for inviting me, David.

A Now, Zantis, of course, is a major player in the US and Latin America, but this is an unusual step for you, isn't it, venturing into Europe?

B Well, David, that's a good question, but, you know, no major company can afford not to operate globally these days. We've consolidated our position in the Americas. Now it's time to look to Europe and Asia.

A So Zantis is ready to move to the next level.

B Indeed, we are. Have you seen our stock price?

A I have. Going through the roof! So, OK, you're looking to expand, but why Turkey? I mean, the pharmaceutical industry is very well developed in France, Germany, Switzerland and the UK, but you've made what some see as a surprise acquisition with

Nilay Medical. What's the thinking behind it?

B Well, first of all, let me say that Turkey has enormous depth of experience in drug development. Nilay is a first-class company. As you know, in this business the quickest way to speed up research is often to acquire a company which already has the expertise you need. Nilay is extremely strong in antiviral research, an area we're very interested in.

A I see.

B Plus, Turkey has a lot of strategic value for us. It's obviously well positioned geographically for both European and Asian markets. Turkey's entry into the EU may be some years away, but we expect that to happen. When Turkey does become a member, it'll be the biggest country in the EU with the second highest population. Furthermore, Turkey has strong cultural connections with a trading bloc of Asian republics, formerly under the control of Russia, but now free markets.

A That's interesting.

B We did our homework on this deal, David, and we're very excited about it.

A And the markets certainly seem to be excited too. But not everyone is so positive, are they? Some people are saying that you plan to finance the takeover by selling off less profitable parts of the company.

B Yes, they are saying that. But what you have to remember, David, is that Nilay is a vertically integrated company – it not only does drug research, it also owns several raw materials suppliers and a domestic distributorship. This gives it almost complete control of the pharmaceutical supply chain in Turkey. But Zantis-Nilay will be a global operation. We're more interested in focusing on our core business – the development of life-saving drugs.

A So the non-research parts of the business could go?

B It's an option. There will also be the usual drive to increase efficiency in certain areas, to flatten the corporate hierarchy. We may want to de-layer – remove some of the middle levels of management and merge the two corporate cultures.

A Ah, now there you've raised the issue of culture, which is something I wanted to talk to you about. Turkey is a Euro-Asian and Islamic country. Zantis has little or no experience in this region. Don't you foresee problems there?

B Not at all. This was a very 'friendly' takeover. Let me talk you briefly through our change management program …

 3.10

Extract 1

I think the worst thing has been the redundancies. A lot of my closest friends have lost their jobs. I mean, OK, you expect some job losses, but really there was no kind of respect in the way this was done. It was just 'We're sorry, but there's no place for you now'. I think it would have been more professional to offer some kind of counselling or career coaching in the months after people left the company. But we never even heard from head office. They just left it to the

line managers to give the people the bad news – very badly handled, if you ask me.

Extract 2

Well there has certainly been a lot of checking up on the Turkish managers. And plenty of inspections of lab procedures too. We've had them filling out questionnaires and performance sheets for months! To be honest, I think this just creates bad feeling and mistrust. I'm not comfortable with it – people wandering around with a clipboard asking questions all the time. And I should know. I'm one of the guys they sent from the States to ask the questions!

Extract 3

It has been a nightmare. The other week we had some guy over from head office doing these random checks. Kept coming into the laboratory in the middle of our experiments. To be fair, he was a nice enough guy, apologised for what he was doing. But he didn't sound very convinced that what he was doing was useful. What I don't understand is, if the people at Zantis thought we were a successful enough company to buy, why are they checking up on us now? Don't they trust us?

Extract 4

I don't think we're getting enough information from the senior management. It's like they don't want to involve us in any of the decision-making. For example, it was never fully explained to us why certain parts of the Nilay business were sold off. It seems to me they've broken up a very successful Turkish company for global strategic reasons we are not informed about. Anyway, I just keep my thoughts to myself, do as I'm told. It's only six years till I retire, so what's the point in complaining? But I miss the old family atmosphere.

Extract 5

Let me put it this way, there's a lot more competitiveness between the research teams now. I mean, scientists are pretty competitive to begin with, but it's much worse now. This is what always happens when you merge two companies. You get job replication. Before this takeover I was coming up for promotion. I had a clear career path. But now I'm just wondering who's going to be fired – me or the American guy they've brought in to do the same job as me? When I first heard about the acquisition, I was quite excited and looking forward to sharing knowledge and expertise with the Americans. We're doing important work on antiviral drugs and this is a great opportunity for us to collaborate. But there's no real synergy. I blame the top management.

Extract 6

It's quite depressing to see so many good people leaving the company and a whole lot more are talking about it. The attitude is very much 'jump before you're pushed'! Of course, for the people who do stay on, the prospects are good, but this is not what we acquired the company for. Cynics may say we just wanted a way into Europe and Asia and some valuable assets to sell off, but that's not the way Zantis does business. At least, it didn't use to be. We are a people company. When they offered me a transfer to Istanbul, I thought, hey, this will be a great opportunity. But now I'm thinking maybe I'll stick it out a couple of years and then head back home.

Extract 7

Bring back Ahmet Barak, that's what I say. I don't want to sound disloyal, but this Latimer woman is not doing a good job as CEO. It was fine during the 'honeymoon' period just after the takeover. But now she seems to think she's back in North Carolina with all these efficiency studies. What we need is a shared vision, but to be allowed to manage things our way, the way we've managed them for seventy years. I have a lot of respect for the American researchers they've sent over, but they should let our Turkish managers run the business. They know what they are doing. They don't need a hundred questionnaires to tell them how to lead!

Extract 8

It's true there hasn't really been an opportunity to build the team. I mean, it's never easy bringing two corporate cultures together, but we need to allow some time to create a real team spirit. For example, it might be a good idea for some of the senior managers to go on some kind of retreat, you know, get away from the workplace and talk things through in a more relaxed environment. Also, I'd like to see the more junior staff mixing more outside work. Would a few company barbecues now and then be too American? I mean, there are some great beaches just outside the city.

Extract 9

I think the main problem is things have moved too fast. We're trying to integrate too quickly. I work in sales. I used to just sell to Turks. Now because my English is OK, they've put me in charge of Italy, Greece, the Baltic and Syria! I'm proud to be promoted, but I don't seem to be making any more money than I used to. But I get on quite well with my American colleagues. Some of them organised a barbecue at the beach the other day. It was fun, but not quite what they were expecting, I don't think. Nobody told them that the first sunny day we get, twelve million people head for the beach!

Extract 10

Frankly, I don't take too much notice of what happens here on the management side. I have my research. That's all I care about. Speaking English as the company language is, of course, a stupid idea. You lose a lot of good people that way. My own English is, er, quite basic, but they can't replace me so easily. Some intercultural training might be good. It seems to me that Americans talk a lot about teamwork, but, er, really it is everyone for themselves. We can learn a lot from each other. But first we must learn some respect.

17 GOING GREEN

 3.11

Well, OK, here you've got two well-known companies actually doing something constructive about the environment and, obviously, I welcome this kind of initiative. But you have to put it into perspective. I mean, aviation is responsible for – what? – about 3% of the world's total carbon emissions, so even though one major airline switching to alternative, renewable energy is a good thing, it's really not very significant when you think that the total number of flights is expected to double by 2030. If you ask me, it's governments who need to be setting limits on carbon emissions and taxing those who exceed them. The thing about companies suddenly deciding to do something about their environmental record is that it's usually too little too late. And they tend to address the symptoms,

not the cause, of the problem. I used to work for a computer hardware company. Did you know that up to 30% of a computer is toxic material? So, again, when one manufacturer says it's going to recycle its old PCs, so what? Sure, it's a step in the right direction, and it makes that particular firm look good, but it's simply not going to have much of an effect. Until companies stop just thinking about their shareholders and start taking their other stakeholders seriously – especially the communities their businesses affect – nothing's going to change.

 3.12

To be quite honest with you, I get sick and tired hearing people going on about big business destroying the planet. I read a recent MORI poll on globalisation and apparently 92% of people in Britain think the government should protect the environment, even if that conflicts with the interests of business. Give me a break! Big business is nothing more than a reflection of the consumerist society it serves. Consumers want cheap food, right? Healthy, sure, but above all, cheap. They want nice clothes – not the products of slave labour if they can help it, no, of course not, but, let's face it, why don't those clothes cost twice as much? Figure it out. You can't have it both ways! Whenever I hear about a clothes manufacturer saying it's working to improve conditions in its factories, I think 'greenwashing'! Greenwashing's when a company really just uses the 'green thing' to improve its image. 'Oh, we're looking after our workers interests in the developing world!' Why do you think those companies have got factories in the developing world in the first place? You can be sure it's not to help them develop. It's simply more profitable. Now, when I hear about climate change being a political priority, it's the same thing. Greenwashing politics. And, in some cases, failed politicians greenwashing themselves. Call me cynical, but I've no time for it!

 3.13

I think it's a slight exaggeration to say that companies rule the world, but that is certainly the way things are going. Fifty-one of the world's biggest economies are corporations, so if you can utilise that kind of power, you really will have a tremendous effect. Unfortunately, too many firms just seem to see green issues as another marketing strategy. You have to ask yourself what the motivation is when Coca-Cola, a company whose brand alone is worth an estimated 70 billion dollars, donates just 20 million dollars to the Worldwide Fund for Nature. And I'm always worried when I see a company selling something for which a small percentage of the profit is going to charity. You may say a small percentage is better than nothing, but I wonder if that's really true when it is businesses themselves which contributed to the problem in the first place. Maybe furniture companies will be able to stop raising money to save the Brazilian jaguar, when they stop cutting down its forests to make kitchen tables. But everywhere you look you see irresponsible management – Enron, MCI and, of course, here in France, Société Générale – companies who don't seem to be accountable even to their shareholders, much less their employees, customers and the general public. Until corporate governance is improved, until the directors of the world's multinationals can

keep their own house in order, what chance is there that they can have a positive effect on the world itself?

 3.14

Maybe I'm an incurable optimist, but I genuinely do see a change in the way businesses operate in terms of their social and environmental impact. Partly, of course, this is just companies giving in to public pressure, I know. But I also think the spread of the Internet and the fact that we all have more access than ever before to information that was previously confidential has had an effect. For companies who just pollute and exploit it's only a matter of time these days before they get found out. So, we're seeing a lot of companies who haven't found a way to significantly cut their carbon dioxide emissions, counteracting that by planting thousands of trees, sponsoring research into cleaner energy. For the time being, that's the best most companies can do – balance out the good and bad, reduce their carbon footprint to zero. Now, when you look at internet companies, look how efficient and carbon-neutral they can be. Most people probably use Google. I use Everyclick, because when I use Everyclick a sum of money goes to charity every time I do a search. And I can even choose which charity that money goes to. So simple. And the Internet makes it possible. Another thing I do is invest in small businesses in emerging economies through an online microcredit company called Giva.org. It's just great. I get to choose where my money goes and receive regular reports on how the businesses I've lent money to are doing. And these are just two examples of how I see the Internet and the young generation of people running it redefining business. Oh, yeah, I've got a lot of faith in the future.

18 EATING OUT

 3.15

A   So, here we are. Hm, it's a bit more crowded than usual.

B   Nice place. Do you come here often?

A   Mm, yes. It's very convenient and the food is excellent, but it looks like we may have to wait for a table today. This place is getting more and more popular.

A   Our table's going to be a couple of minutes, I'm afraid, but we can sit at the bar if you like.

B   Oh, OK. I see what you mean about this place being popular.

A   Well, we shouldn't have to wait too long. Now, what would you like to drink?

B   Oh, just a fruit juice or something for me.

A   OK … er, excuse me.

B   … So, I'm not really sure how I ended up in financial services.

A   Me neither. I studied law at university, but I never wanted to work for a bank. Right. **I'll just see if our table's ready**.

A   OK, this is their standard menu …

B   Mm. It all looks very good.

A   … and those are the specials. Let me know if you want me to explain anything.

B   Thanks. I may need some help. So, what do you recommend?

A Well, they do a great lasagne. But perhaps you'd like something more typically English.

B Mm, yes. And perhaps something a bit lighter.

A **Is there anything you don't eat?**

B No, not really. I'm allergic to mussels, that's all.

A Oh, that's a pity. The mussels are a speciality. But, erm, **you could try the lamb. That's very good here. It comes with potatoes and a salad.**

B Mm. That sounds nice. But isn't it a little too heavy?

A Well, you could have it without the potatoes. Or perhaps you'd prefer the cod …

A **Shall we order a bottle of the house red?**

B Well, maybe just a glass for me.

A Oh, let's get a bottle. We don't have to finish it

B Oh, well, I suppose not. **Could we order some mineral water too?**

A Sure. Sparkling or still?

B This is absolutely delicious. How's yours?

A Not bad at all. More wine?

B Not for me, thanks. So, how do you think the meeting went this morning?

A Quite well, I think. Of course, we still have a lot of things to discuss …

A Now, how about a dessert?

B Oh, better not. I'm on a diet.

A Me too. But it doesn't stop me. How about peaches in wine? That's not too fattening.

B More wine! James, we have another meeting this afternoon, remember.

B Right. **I'll get this.**

A Oh, no, you don't. I'm paying.

B But you paid yesterday, James. It's my turn.

A No, no, **I insist.** You're my guest.

 3.16

Conversation 1

A … So, Hiro. What's this fugu? It's a kind of fish, isn't it?

B Ah, yes. Er, it's rather unusual, er …

A Traditional Japanese dish, eh?

B Yes, but, er, **it's a little exotic. You may not like it.**

A No, no, I like trying new things. Fugu sounds good to me.

B **I think you'd prefer something else.** Fugu can be … a little dangerous.

A A bit spicy, you mean? Don't worry about that. I love spicy food.

B No, not spicy. It's, er … It's poisonous.

A It's what?

B Poisonous.

A Poisonous?

B If it isn't cooked the right way, yes.

A Well, I …

B Some people love it. And this is a very good restaurant, but thirty people die every year from bad fugu. **Really, I think you should try something else.**

A Yeah, well, sure. I think you're probably right. Maybe I'll have the tempura instead.

B Yes, tempura. Much better idea, David.

 3.17

Conversation 2

A Now, Hans, we thought you might like to try the local speciality.

B Ah, yes?

C Yes, it looks a little strange at first. But you'll love it. You like shellfish, don't you?

B Well, I like prawns. And the mussels we had the other day were excellent.

C Then you'll really enjoy this. It's squid.

B Squid?

C Yes, like octopus, you know?

B Yes, I know what squid is.

C Ah, but this is not just squid.

B No?

A No, this is something really special. It's served in its own ink – as a sauce.

B It's served in ink?

A Yes, you know, the black liquid that squid make.

B Erm, yes. It sounds a bit … Actually, I hope you don't mind, but could I just have something a bit simpler?

C Well, if you're sure you don't want to try it. It's really very good.

B Yes, I'm sure it is, but, erm …

 3.18

Conversation 3

A Now, is there anything you don't eat, Louise?

B Well, I am on a special diet at the moment, Jean-Claude. I hope that's not a problem.

A No, of course not. This is a very good menu. I am sure we can find something you'll like. What can't you eat?

B Well, I can't eat anything fried. In fact, no fat at all. Nothing made of pastry or cooked in oil. No red meat, of course. Not too much sugar. I can eat white fish but only boiled.

A What about the chicken here? That's very plain and simple.

B Is there a sauce on it?

A Yes, it's a delicious cream and wine sauce.

B No cream, I'm afraid.

A No cream?

B Or wine. I'm not allowed any alcohol at all. Not that I drink much anyway.

A I see. Well, I'm sure they'll serve it without the sauce.

B Hm. How's the chicken cooked?

A Er, it's roast chicken, I imagine.

B I can only have grilled.

A I'll ask them to grill it.

B Hm. I'd prefer fish really.

A Well, how about the trout?

B Is it boiled?

A No, baked in the oven.

B Hm. I may not like it. **What does it come with?**

A **It comes with potatoes and fresh vegetables.**

B Oh, I can't eat potatoes. All that carbohydrate! Vegetables are OK. But no beans and …

19 TELECOMMUNICATIONS

 3.19

Extract 1

Operator Excuse me, Mr Kessler. Mr Gorsky has joined you.

PK Ah, thank you. Hello, Jarek.

JG Hello, Peter. Sorry, I had a bit of a problem getting through.

PK That's OK. We're just waiting for Sulaiman. He's e-mailed to say he's gone down to Port Rashid to see what's happening with our deliveries and he'll phone in on his mobile from there. So, **let's go ahead and start. Welcome to the meeting,** everyone. **Did you all get a copy of the agenda?**

Good … OK, before we start, let me introduce Jarek Gorsky. Jarek is the new chief engineer at our sister company in Warsaw. I've asked him to join us today because I'd like his input on how we handle some of these changes to specifications the client is asking for.

JG Hello, gentlemen.

PK All right, then, **let's get started. As you can see, we have several objectives today.** The main one, of course, is to agree an action plan that will get us back on schedule within the next three months. I spoke to Mr Al-Fulani yesterday and explained the situation. He's prepared to give us another few weeks to sort out our present difficulties and I have assured him that that is what we will do. I'm sure I don't need to remind you what's at stake here. Now, **I'd like to be finished by 10.30 if that's OK,** so can we keep our inputs quite short? And **let's also try to keep interruptions to a minimum…**

EN Er, Peter. Sorry to interrupt, but I suggest we skip item one on our agenda until we hear from Sulaiman.

PK Yes, I think that would be best. **Let's move straight on to item two …**

 3.20

Extract 2

EN **So just to recap on what we've said.** There are some problems we did not foresee between our two main work teams. There's been a language barrier. Our German engineers and Polish workers are speaking mostly German. The Pakistanis are more comfortable in English and are also having some difficulty with our work patterns, which are different from what they are used to in Dubai.

PK Thanks, Ernst … OK, so, **are we are all agreed that we need** some onsite training to resolve this problem? Can I hear your views, please?

EN I agree.

KI Agreed.

FN Yes, I agree.

JG Yeah, I think so.

PK Fine.

Operator Excuse me, Mr Al-Fahim has joined you.

PK Ah, thank you. Hello, Sulaiman. How are things at the port?

SA Hello, Peter. Not good, I'm afraid. The bad weather here has completely closed the sea-ports at Jebel Ali and Port Rashid. Nothing is either going in or coming out at the moment. I have my Pakistani team standing doing nothing while we wait for eight hundred window units, and until those are fitted, we can't complete the wiring and plumbing in the hotel complexes.

PK Don't we have back-up supplies in place for a situation like this, Sulaiman?

SA I'm sorry, Peter. This weather is really most unseasonal and we simply could not be fully prepared for it.

PK **Sorry, Sulaiman, I can't hear you very well.**

SA Oh,… Is that better?

PK Much better, thanks.

KI Er, **could I just come in here**?

PK Karim?

KI Yes, it's just that I want to say this is not only a cultural and supply problem. We have had so many changes to specifications – changes almost every week now. The client just keeps changing his mind. And this is making life very difficult for us all.

FN Karim's right. We've had to keep revising our work schemes to cope with all the changes.

PK Yes, it's a good point. I'll certainly bring all these changes to the attention of Mr Al-Fulani when I next speak to him. They're not in our original contract … **Right, we're running short of time.** I think what's needed here with all these delays and changes of plan is a fresh look at this entire project on a logistical level. Ernst, Jarek, can I leave that with you?

JG OK, Peter.

EN Yes, sure.

PK And keep me posted. I'm beginning to think we may even need to renegotiate our contract with Mr Al-Fulani. OK, **I think we've covered everything for now.** Let's schedule another meeting for next week. I'll e-mail you the details. **We'll have to finish there. Thanks everybody.**

20 NEGOTIATING

 3.21

Spend as much time as possible at the outset getting to know exactly who you're dealing with. Inexperienced negotiators tend to go straight in there and start bargaining. That may be OK for a small, one-off deal, but it's no way to build a long-term business relationship. So create rapport first. This could take several hours or several months! When you're ready to start negotiations make sure you agree on a procedure before you begin. And while they're setting out their proposals, don't interrupt. Listen. And take notes. Then have lunch! Don't be tempted to make your counter-proposals and enter the bargaining phase until after a good long break. You'd be surprised how much you can find out over a decent meal. Bargaining, of course, is the critical phase, but it can be surprisingly quick. If it isn't, break off and fix another meeting. Don't try to run marathons. When you do finally get to the agreement stage, agree the general terms, but leave the details to the lawyers – that's what they're there for. Close on a high note and remember to celebrate!

 3.22

Prepare thoroughly. If you don't, you won't know whether to accept an offer and may end up actually arguing with your own side, which is suicide in a negotiation. So, make sure you establish all the points you're going to negotiate and have a clear idea of your opening, target and walk-away position on each. Your opening position or OP is your initial offer – on price or whatever. Your TP, your target position, is what you're realistically aiming for. And your WAP or walk-away position is the point at which you walk away from the negotiating table. Always be prepared to do that. Know what your fall-back position or FBP is – what you'll do if you don't reach an agreement. Some people call this your BATNA, your best alternative to a negotiated agreement. You nearly always have a BATNA, however undesirable. But if you really haven't got one, you'd better be good at bluffing or you going to lose big time!

 3.23

Ideally, a successful negotiation is a kind of joint problem-solving meeting, where we identify each other's interests, wants and needs and then explore the different ways we could satisfy those. I say 'ideally', because it hardly ever is like that. Win-win negotiation is a great idea, but most people have a simple 'I win – you lose' mentality. So what do you do with the person who simply won't listen, who keeps interrupting, who becomes aggressive, who makes last-minute demands, who won't make a decision? I must have read dozens of books on negotiation tactics. The problem is, so has everybody else. So they don't really work. My only advice is: don't get personal – ever; don't agree to anything until you've discussed everything; don't make any concessions without asking for something in return; ask lots and lots of questions; and don't give in to pressure. Remember, if the answer must be now, the answer must be 'No'.

 3.24

Extract 1

A Now, the next thing is: **we'd like to see some movement on price.** We had a rather lower figure in mind than the one you've quoted us.

B OK. What sort of figure are we talking about?

A Well, something nearer to seven million euros.

B Now, **let me just check I understand you correctly**. You're offering us seven million for the whole construction contract?

A That's right.

B And what sort of time-scale are we looking at?

A We would expect you to complete the project within 18 months.

B How flexible can you be on that?

A Not very. We were hoping to have the plant fully in operation by next September.

B I see … Can I make a suggestion?

A Go ahead.

B Well, would you be willing to accept a compromise?

A That depends on what kind of compromise you had in mind.

B Well, what if we offered you an alternative?

What if you paid us two million in advance, two million mid-contract, and another 3.2 million on completion.

A On schedule?

B On schedule. 18 months … Or thereabouts.

A Hm. So that's 7.2 million euros in all.

B Correct.

A And what if you run over schedule?

B Then there would be a penalty. Let's say 25 thousand euros for each week we ran over schedule.

A Hm. I'm afraid this doesn't really solve our problem. What we need from you is a guarantee that the project will be finished on time.

B And, as you know, I can only give you that guarantee by bringing in more outside contractors.

A Which ups the price to your original bid of 7.8 million euros?

B Yes.

A At the moment we do not see this as a viable option.

B 7.8 million really is my best price on that.

A Well, in that case, I think that's about as far as we can go at this stage.

B Now, wait a minute. We're not going to lose this deal for 600,000 euros, surely … How about this …?

 3.25

Extract 2

A Right. We seem to be nearing agreement. But, erm, before we finalise things, can we just run through the main points once more?

B Sure.

A Now, you'll provide a series of eight two-day in-company seminars for our telesales team over the next six months. You yourself will be conducting most of the sessions with two other trainers, using materials especially designed to meet our specific needs and approved by us four weeks prior to the first seminar?

B That's correct.

A And, er, let me get this quite clear, each seminar is to have no more than 16 participants, is that right?

B Yes. We find the seminars are much more effective with smaller groups.

A Hm, I suppose you're right. It does also mean running more courses, but OK. Now, since we are booking eight seminars, we'll obviously expect a reasonable discount on your usual fee.

B Erm, yes. Could you give us an idea of what you're looking for? Because with this particular course …

A I would have thought a 15% discount was fair. So that's eight times £3,000 is £24,000 minus 15%, which is, erm, £3,600. And that would come to a total fee of £20,400. And you'd invoice us on completion of the whole series of seminars. Are these terms broadly acceptable?

B Er, well, just a moment. We haven't actually agreed on the discount yet. As I was about to say, with this particular course there wouldn't normally be such a large discount.

We offer 10% on five or more of our standard seminars, but this is a specially designed course for your personnel only. Obviously, we have to cover our development costs.

A   I should think you could cover them quite easily on just over £20,000, Mr Smart. No, my mind's made up. 15% – take it or leave it.

B   Well, now, **I'm afraid we could only accept this on one condition**.

A   Which is?

B   Erm, we'd want a 25% non-refundable deposit in advance …

A   Done.

B   You see, … erm, sorry?

A   25% deposit – no problem. I'll get accounts to make you out a cheque for, let me see, £5,100 … Well, that's it. I think we've earned ourselves a drink!

B   Erm, well, yes. Nice doing business with you.

 3.26

Right, well, when a team wants to sell a player, they agree a transfer fee. That's the price other clubs have to pay them if they want to buy that player. These vary a lot. For a young, talented player with lots of potential the transfer fee could be around three or four million pounds. Obviously, for a real international star, it could be anything up to twenty million. For a team like Manchester United that equals the club's annual profit. So buying a player is a big decision.

That's what the player's club gets, but what about the player? Well, every professional player has a FIFA agent. FIFA's the governing body for world football. And the agent's job is to negotiate terms with teams who want to buy the player. The average weekly wage in the UK Premier League is about £5,000, or £250,000 a year. Internationals get more and so do foreign players sometimes – it encourages them to come and live in England. So, basically, the wage for all the players is the same, with the stars getting maybe 10 or 15% more.

But, of course, the players don't just get a wage, they also get an annual fee, which is usually much, much more than the basic wage. Superstars can get anything from a one to four million pound annual fee. The fee is really just to stop them going to another team and it's their main source of income.

OK, contracts. Players' contracts can be for two, three or five years, and if a player wants to leave before his contract expires, he has to pay a penalty – maybe five million pounds or something ridiculous like that. But they usually work something out. There's no point having players who don't want to play for you anymore.

So, those are the main points to negotiate in a transfer. Other things might include a percentage of merchandising profits – from sales of shirts, caps, boots with the player's name on – and foreign players will often want a house and car provided as well, since they may only stay a few years. Some ask for free flights home to visit family. Oh, by the way, all those figures I've mentioned are net, not gross. Footballers don't like to worry about how much tax they're going to have to pay!

CASE STUDY: GOING UNDER?

 3.27

A   Lazzaro! Lazzaro, we have to talk. Lazzaro!

B   Not now, Mark! Can't you see we're having problems here? If we don't get this boat finished by this afternoon, we're never going to meet this order.

A   That's what I want to talk to you about. I just got off the phone with Mr Al-Wahdi. He's cancelling his order.

B   Cancelling? But we're almost ready to deliver. He can't just do that. He'll lose his deposit!

A   He says his boat's thirteen months late and he doesn't have to pay a thing.

B   So it's thirteen months late! Who does he think he is? You can't rush these things. This is a Pantera we're talking about.

A   He's already been on a five-year waiting list … for six years!

B   Well, what do you suggest we do?

A   Lazzaro, it's not just Al-Wahdi. This is the eighth cancellation this month. It can't go on. I'm out there trying to sell our product and we're just not keeping up with demand. I know I could sell eight hundred boats a year if you and Fabio would just do something about modernising this boatyard! We should be doubling production.

B   Eight hundred boats a year! Look, Mark, we've talked about this before. We simply don't have the capacity. There's no way we could ever make more than 450. You know that. And Corelli boats, they are a work of art!

A   A work of art! Lazzaro, a boat's a boat, mate. I can sell them all right. But you're just not making them fast enough!

B   So, what's the problem? As my old papa used to say, 'as long as demand exceeds supply, you have a very good business'. And thanks to you, my boy, we have higher sales this year than any of our direct competitors.

A   And the lowest profit margins! We're making half what we should be. Strewth! If costs keep going up, we'll be making a loss. Listen, Lazzaro. We're losing market share to the Americans. And with the euro so strong and the dollar so weak, that's not helping our exports either.

B   Well, you know we can't put any more money into this boatyard. We're heavily in debt, as it is.

A   I know that. But we simply have to get our costs down. For one thing, we're paying our production team far too much. We could economise there.

B   You have to look after your people, Mark. Did they teach you nothing at Business School?

A   And we'll have to increase our prices.

B   What? With the market so competitive?

A   Yes. Our customers would pay it. Did you know that people are getting so tired of waiting for new Corelli, they're buying second-hand ones for 20% more than the list price?

B   Hm … I had heard that, yes … So you think we should raise prices?

A   It's an option. Or we could try taking the company public to raise capital, but our accounts don't look too healthy right now.

B   Hm.

A   Or we could always accept Cascadia's offer and sell the company altogether.

B   Sell out to those Americans, you mean?

A   It's not what any of us want, Lazzaro, but it's a generous offer. Cascadia's looking to break into the European market with a premium product. They are prepared to pay more than we're worth because they love the Pantera.

B   Mark, you haven't been in this family very long. If you had, you'd know that no Corelli will ever sell this business! It's in our blood. Oh, I don't expect you to understand.

A   Look, Lazzaro, I understand. But you'll be retiring soon. You know what the doctors told you. You need to slow down. And Cascadia has offered to keep me and Fabio on to help them run the business, at least in the early stages.

B   Well, how considerate of them! But you seem to be forgetting one thing. This is my business. Not yours and Fabio's. Not yet. And the way things are going, it never will be! …

 3.28

Lazzaro

I have to face facts. I'm not getting any younger. It's time to retire, I know. But I cannot leave the business in this state. And selling out to Cascadia would just be a tragedy. The business my father built with his two hands lost forever! It's unthinkable! But who will take over when I am gone? Mark has been such a help these last two years building up our export sales, but I know he is frustrated with our slow production methods. He wants to 'technologise' everything. Fabio is a good boy, but a hothead – like me when I was his age! He's a marvellous boat builder, but a dreamer. Chiara, bless her – she's very wise for her age. And I have to admit some of her boat designs are truly brilliant. But she wants to build these little fibreglass things. Toys! That's not what Corelli is about! We work in wood. We build real boats. I suppose as my only son, Fabio will want to take over in time, but god only knows when he'll be ready for the responsibility!

Claudia

I'm worried about Lazzaro. He pretends he's fine, but he looks so tired. I just wish the children could agree on what to do with the business. What worries me is that if we sell it off, it'll break up the family. And I'm not sure selling is what Fabio and Mark really want to do. As for Chiara – well, she's more like Lazzaro than Fabio will ever be. She has so many ideas she wants to try out. I'm sure she'd be a real asset to the business if only Lazzaro would give her a chance. Sofia is a different matter. I think she'd just like to go back to Australia with Mark and her children and forget about the whole thing.

Mark

Well, it's not been easy fitting in with the family way of doing things. My Italian is still terrible, I'm afraid, but fortunately most of the time I'm dealing with our foreign clients. And I get on pretty well with the old man. We had a bit of an argument the other day, but, you know, it's funny, since we've been here in Como, I've really grown to love this business. And I'm convinced we can turn it around. Demand is not a problem. People love our boats! The main problem is production. It's so damned inefficient! But I have to be careful what I say to Lazzaro about that because this boatyard is his life. I know we need to pay our people well, but I think, considering their work rate, we may be paying them just a little too well. I'd like to see cuts there or some kind of incentive scheme. One thing we desperately need right now is capital. We could never go public with the debt we have and profits so low, but with just a little extra cash we could make the necessary changes, adopt more modern production methods and really get things moving!

Sofia

I first met Mark when we were both students at Sydney University. I was studying communication and he was doing his MBA. It was love at first sight! Well, it was something at first sight! We got married two years later and lived in Sydney for about six years before moving back here so Mark could help Papa run the business. Fabio is so useless! I'm sorry, he's my brother and everything, but it's true. It's really time he grew up – he's still more interested in girls, cars and jet-skis than anything else. Oh, he's a good engineer, just lazy. Mark's been totally awesome. I know he's had some problems adjusting to life here, but I don't know what Papa would do without him now. Personally, I do miss Australia – all those wonderful open spaces! But I don't want to hold Mark back if he thinks he can really save the company.

Fabio

If you ask me, the real problem is, Papa is too old-fashioned. He just cannot see that times have changed. Or he doesn't want to. I hate to admit it, but Mark's right. If we can't double our output in the next couple of years, we're going to go out of business or some big company will buy us up for nothing. Being the only son, there's a lot of pressure on me to take over from Papa when he retires, but I just don't know if I want that kind of responsibility. I mean I like the job I have now – I can do things my way – and if we took the offer from Cascadia and they employed me and Mark, I don't think I would have the employee mentality, you know? On the other hand, maybe me and Chiara could start up our own small business instead with the money from the sale. At least I wouldn't have to listen to Papa saying how wonderful Mark is all day. Drives me crazy! I know he's supposed to be this business genius, but I'm the next Corelli, not him! … Er, look, would you excuse me, only I'm meeting up with some friends. Sorry. I think's that's about all I have to say, anyway. So, hey, good talking to you.

Chiara

In some ways Papa still thinks I'm his little girl. When I told him I was going to be a designer, I think he thought I was going to be designing dresses not powerboats! I know he likes my designs. He just doesn't want to take a chance. It would mean making some changes at the boatyard, but Mark says the demand for smaller fibreglass boats is enormous. Production time is much shorter and labour costs lower too. And Fabio – he pretends to be this wild crazy guy – but he's smart. You know, he was top of his engineering class at Bologna. And he says we could go into production really quickly with my designs and start making a good profit. Oh, well, maybe Papa will listen after you have made your final report. To be honest with you, I never thought he'd ask for advice from outsiders, but I'm looking forward to seeing what you come up with.

Macmillan Education
Between Towns Road, Oxford OX4 3PP
A division of Macmillan Publishers Limited
Companies and representatives throughout the world

ISBN 978-0-230-71712-1

Designed by eMC Design
Illustrated by Julian Mosedale p12; Liam O'Farrell p22; Kim Williams p72
Cover design by Keith Shaw, Threefold Design Ltd
Cover photographs by BANANASTOCK, BRAND X.

Authors' acknowledgements
It's both strange and exciting revisiting a book you wrote almost five years
ago. So much has happened since the last edition. David Riley, who had
such a profound influence on the whole In Company series, is very sadly
no longer with us. But I'd like to acknowledge once again the guidance,
humour and support he offered all those years ago. Thanks, David.
My thanks are also due to Anna Cowper, the publisher, and Darina Richter,
commissioning editor, on the second edition. They've certainly helped me
improve on the original and exercised not a little patience in waiting for me
to do so! I'm tremendously grateful to my editor, Anna Gunn, designer John
Park, picture researcher Sally Cole and recording director Ian Harker for
giving a fresh look and feel to the material. Above all, once again, I thank
my wife Begoña. Her love and support keep me going as I hurtle towards 50
and wonder if I've anything left to say. She convinces me that I have.

The publishers would like to thank the following schools and teachers for
their help in developing the first edition: Bob Ratto, Byron, Rome; Angela
Wright, British Council, Rome; Norman Cain, IH Rome; Fiona Campbell,
Teach-In, Rome; Sue Garton, Lois Clegg and Irene Frederick, University
of Parma; Simon Hopson and Gordon Doyle, Intensive Business English,
Milan; Dennis Marino, Bocconi University, Milan; Mike Cruikshank,
Advanced Language Services, Milan; Christine Zambon, Person to Person,
Milan; Fiona O'Connor, In-Company English, Milan; Peter Panton,
Panton School, Milan; Colin Irving Bell, Novara; Marta Rodriguez
Casal, Goal Rush Institute, Buenos Aires; Elizabeth Mangi and Silvia
Ventura, NET New English Training, Buenos Aires; Graciela Yohma and
Veronica Cenini, CABSI, Buenos Aires; Viviana Pisani, Asociación Ex
Alumnos, Buenos Aires; Claudia Siciliano, LEA Institute, Buenos Aires;
Cuca Martocq, AACI, Buenos Aires; Laura Lewin, ABS International,
Buenos Aires; Charlie Lopez, Instituto Big Ben, Buenos Aires; Alice Elvira
Machado; Patricia Blower; Valeria Siniscalchi; Carla Chaves; Virginia
Garcia; Cultura Inglesa, Rio de Janeiro; Susan Dianne Mace, Britannia, Rio
de Janeiro; John Paraskou, Diamond School, Sèvres; Dorothy Pollev and
Nadia Fairbrother, Executive Language Services, Paris; Claire MacMurray,
Formalangues, Paris; Claire Oldmeadow, Franco British Chamber of
Commerce, Paris; Ingrid Foussat and Anne James, IFG Langues, Paris; Karl
Willems, Quai d'Orsay Language Centre, Paris; Louis Brazier, Clare Davis,
Jacqueline Deubel, Siobhan Mlačak and Redge, Télélangue, Paris; John
Morrison Milne, Ian Stride, Gareth East and Richard Marrison, IH Madrid;
Gina Cuciniello; Helena Gomm; Paulette Dooler.

The publishers would like to thank the following schools and teachers for
their help in developing the second edition: Sylvia Renaudon, Hannah
Leloup, Sven Steph at Transfer, Paris; Nadia Fairbrother at Executive
Language Services, Paris; Fiona Delaney at Formalangues, Paris; Paul
Chambers, Ruth Maslen at BPL, Paris; Moira Jansen and teachers at Anglo
English School, Hamburg; Patrick Woulfe and John Ryde at International
House, Hamburg; Charles Reid Dick, Christine Dlugokencky, Petra
Mocklinghoff, Marie-Colette Dodd, Orla Mac Mahon at Eurospeak,
Hamburg; Bill Cope at English School of Hamburg; Slavomir Gibarti,
Slovakia; Sylvie Jeanloz, France.

Many thanks to all the teachers around the world who took the time to
complete our In Company online questionnaire.

The authors and publishers would like to thank the following for permission
to reproduce their photographs: Alamy/Amana Images Inc p46(b), Arco
Images p65(b), Alamy/Oote Boe p35(tr), Alamy/Ethel Davis p35(br),Alamy/
Kevin Foy p58(br), Alamy/Tony Gale p35(tl), Alamy/Chris Herring
p124(b), Alamy/Mike Hill p35(bl),Alamy/Tim Hill p105, Alamy/Oleksiy
Maksymenko p113(tr), Alamy/Stephen Robson p35(ml), Alamy/Alex Segre
p104, Alamy/David Soulsby p55(ml), Alamy/Marina Spironetti p103(br),
Alamy/Associated Sports Photography p121(l), Alamy/Ace Stock p10,
Alamy/Bill Varie p29, Alamy/Vario Images GmbH & Co KG p35(bm);
Altrendo p11(br); Bananastock pp 49(br), 49(br), 53, 125(tl), 125(tm),
125(tr), 125(bl); 125(bm); Brand X p77(tl); Comstock p77(bm); Corbis
pp 8(3), 33(tr), 59(b), 132, Corbis/Phil Banko p 32(bl), Corbis/Benelux
p97, Corbis/Ingo Boddenberg p19(bl), Corbis/Jose Fuste Raga/Comet

p8(1), Corbis/Hulton Deutsch p69(b), Corbis/Randy Faris/Flame p32(br),
Corbis/Lars Halbauer/EPA p23(br), Corbis/Rainer Holz p7(1), Corbis/
Christian Liewig p121(m), Corbis/Charles Mann p32(t), Corbis/Sonja
Mehner p49(tl), Corbis/Moodboard p111(br), Corbis/Andria Patino
p32(bmr), Corbis/Christine Schneider/Zefa p18(bl), Corbis/M.Thomsen
p15(mr); Digg Logo courtesy of http://digg.com p78; Getty Images
p30(tr),Getty/Mike Clarke p133(ml), Getty/Peter Dazeley p52(br), Getty/
Bepi Ghiotti p52(ml), Getty/Robert Harding p8(2), Getty/Matthew Peters
p121(r), Getty/Susanna Price p52(tr); Iconica p 93(b); Image Bank pp
55(mr), 89, 100, 103(bl), 118; ImageSource p77(tr); Imagestate pp 7(2),
7(4), 41(tr), 80, 96(bl), 130, 130; Impact Photos/J.Wishnetsky p7(5); The
Kobal Collection/Eon/UA p48; Masterfile p18(br), Masterfile/Artiga
Photo p63(tl), Masterfile/Michael Goldman p114, Masterfile/Michael
Mahovlich p107, Masterfile/Jerzyworks p49(tr), Masterfile/Forest
Johnson p124(t), Masterfile/Holly Wilmeth p49(bl); Panos Pictures/
Stuart Freedman p54(b), Panos Pictures/Mark Henley p55(tr), Panos
Pictures/Mikkel Ostergaard p76(l), Panos Pictures/David Rose p77(br),
Panos Pictures/Jacob Silberberg p52(t); Photoalto p77(bl); Photodisc pp
77(tm), 110(ml), 125(br); Photographer's Choice p 56(b); Photolibrary
p 34(t), Photolibrary/Sebastien Boisse p32(b), Photolibrary/Christopher
Cumming p33(b), Photolibrary/Chad Ehlers p58(bl), Photolibrary/Nigel
Franci p34(b), Photolibrary/Marc Gilsdorf p30(br), Photolibrary/Fresh
Food Images pp23(bl), Photolibrary/Robert Harding p113(bl), Photolibrary/
Rune Johansen pp35(tm), 35(m), 25(tl),Photolibrary/Jacques Loic
p31(m), Photolibrary/Mode Images p78(b), Photolibrary/Michael Prince/
Flirt Collection pp77(3),58(tl), Photolibrary/Radius Images p110(mr),
Photolibary/David Stoecklein p58(tr), Photolibrary/ LWA-D.Tardif/Flint
Collection p16(br), Photolibrary/Jon Arnold Travel p24(b); Photonica
pp 30(tl), 119(tr); Rex Features/Sipa Press p76(r); Riser pp19(tl), 83(b);
Science Photo Library/US Library of Congress p70(bl); Stone pp 7(6),
11(tr), 39, 82(b), 87(t), 117; Taxi pp 19(mr), 40(t), 94; Bruce Tulgan
p36(bm); YouTube logo courtesy of http://www.youtube.com p78.

Picture research: Sally Cole/Perseverance Works Ltd

The author and publishers are grateful for permission to reprint the
following copyright material: Extract from 'I Am Woman, Hear Me Shop'
by Pallavi Gogoi from Business Week 14.02.05. Extract from 'The NY-LON
Life' by Stryker Mcguire and Michelle Chan, with William Under Hill in
London and Malcolm Beith and Anna Kuchment in NY from Newsweek
magazine 13.11.00 copyright © Newsweek 2001, reprinted by permission
of PARS International Corp. Adapted extract from Financial Times Guide
to Business Travel edited by Stuart Crainer and Des Dearlove copyright ©
London: Financial Times/Prentice Hall 2001, reprinted by permission of
Pearson Education Inc. Extract from 'In China, to get Rich is Glorious' by
Dexter Roberts and Frederik Balfour from Business Week 06.02.06. Extract
from 'The Decline and Fall of Europe' by Zakaria Fareed copyright © The
Washington Post 2008, first published in The Washington Post 14.02.08,
reprinted by permission of PARS International Corp. Extract from Funky
Business Forever by Jonas Ridderstråle and Kjell Nordström (London:
Financial Times Prentice Hall 2007), copyright © Financial Times/Prentice
Hall 2007, reprinted by permission of the publisher. Extract from When
Cultures Collide by Richard Lewis (Nicholas Brealey Publishers, 2006),
copyright © Nicholas Brealey Publishers 2006, reprinted by permission
of the publisher. Extract from 'How text addicts cost offices billions of
dollars in lost profits' by Hazel Parry from http://tech.monsterandcritics.
com. Adapted extracts from E-Writing by Dianna Booher (Pocket Books,
2001), copyright © Pocket Books 2001, reprinted by permission of Simon &
Schuster Inc. Extract from The Century in Sound track 12 by Bernard Shaw,
reprinted by permission of Society of Authors on behalf of the Bernard
Shaw Estate. Extract from www.firstdirect.com, reprinted by permission of
First Direct. Extract from 'Viral' advertising spreads through marketing
plans' by Theresa Howard copyright © 2005, taken from USA Today
22.06.05, reprinted by permission of the publisher. Extract from Riding
the Waves by Fons Trompenaars and Charles Hampden-Turner (Nicholas
Brealey Publishers, 1993), copyright © Nicholas Brealey 1993, reprinted by
permission of the publisher. Extract from 'Being Good is Good for Business'
from www.latinfinance.com. Extract from 'Bono Seeing 'Red' Over AIDS'
by Davos, Switzerland copyright N I Syndication 2006, first published
in The Times 26.01.06, reprinted by permission of the publisher. Extract
from 'Three-quarters of business travelers enjoy spending time away from
home' taken from www.dancewithshadows.com, reprinted by permission
of the publisher Extract from www.ecogeek.org. Extract from Getting Past
No by William Ury (Random House, 1991), copyright © Random House
1991, reprinted by permission of The Random House Group. 'Joke' from
The Complete Idiot's Guide to Winning Through Negotiations by John Ilich
copyright © John Ilich 1996 (Alpha Books, 1996). Advert from www.foe.
co.uk copyright © Friends of the Earth, reprinted by permission of Friends
of the Earth. Extract from 'Change is Good' from http://domino-watson.
ibm.com. Extract from 'Kiss goodbye to so much business travel' from www.
epopIT.com. These materials may contain links for third party websites. We
have no control over, and are not responsible for, the contents of such third
party websites. Please use care when accessing them.
Although we have tried to trace and contact copyright holders before
publication, in some cases this has not been possible. If contacted we will
be pleased to rectify any errors or omissions at the earliest opportunity.

Printed and bound in Hong Kong

2013 2012 2011 2010 2009

10 9 8 7 6 5 4 3 2 1